LEAVING CERTIFICATE HIGHER AND ORDINARY LEVEL

ESSENTIAL CONSTRUCTION STUDIES

REVISION JOURNAL

Steven Colgan
Thomas Sheppard

Published by:
Educate.ie

Walsh Educational Books Ltd
Castleisland, Co. Kerry, Ireland

www.educate.ie

Editor:
Ciara McNee

Design and layout:
Kieran O'Donoghue

Printed and bound by:
Walsh Colour Print, Castleisland

ISBN: 978-1-909376-78-6

INTRODUCTION

Essential Construction Studies complements the teaching, learning and revision of Leaving Certificate Construction Studies. It is aimed at both Higher Level and Ordinary Level students. The student journal is used in conjunction with a fully animated multimedia presentation, which the teacher will display in class.

KEY FEATURES

JOURNAL

- The **structure** of the student journal will help pupils to take notes more quickly. This efficient method allows more time for classroom discussion.
- The journal also provides **homework** activities, which reinforce classroom learning.
- All **building details** are up to date with the most current building regulations and state examination trends.
- This exam-focused journal includes past **exam and exam-style questions** throughout to help the students to apply their knowledge to specific construction situations.
- Many activities require students to draw sketches, which will help them to develop **good exam techniques.**
- Partially complete illustrations, which students must finish, teach students **how to sketch in proportion.**
- Other **important exam skills,** such as correct labelling and annotation, are emphasised throughout.
- **Passive design concepts** are emphasised, as are the most modern sustainable building technologies and practices used in the construction industry today.
- Once completed, the journal will act as an exam **revision aid** for students.
- **Exemplars** are provided for many exam-style questions, specifically orientation of buildings and room layout questions.
- Calculations are solved step by step, providing pupils with authentically worked examples.

PRESENTATIONS

- The presentations include clear, **full-colour illustrations,** numerous **photographs** and hundreds of **animations** that bring pupils through the entire construction process.
- The presentations also explain **key building design concepts** in a manner which is engaging and accessible to all students.
- All **detailed drawings** in the presentations are animated step by step to assist classroom work and student revision.
- The stimulating and engaging animations help to assist in the understanding of complicated concepts.

Typical strip foundation sectional detail

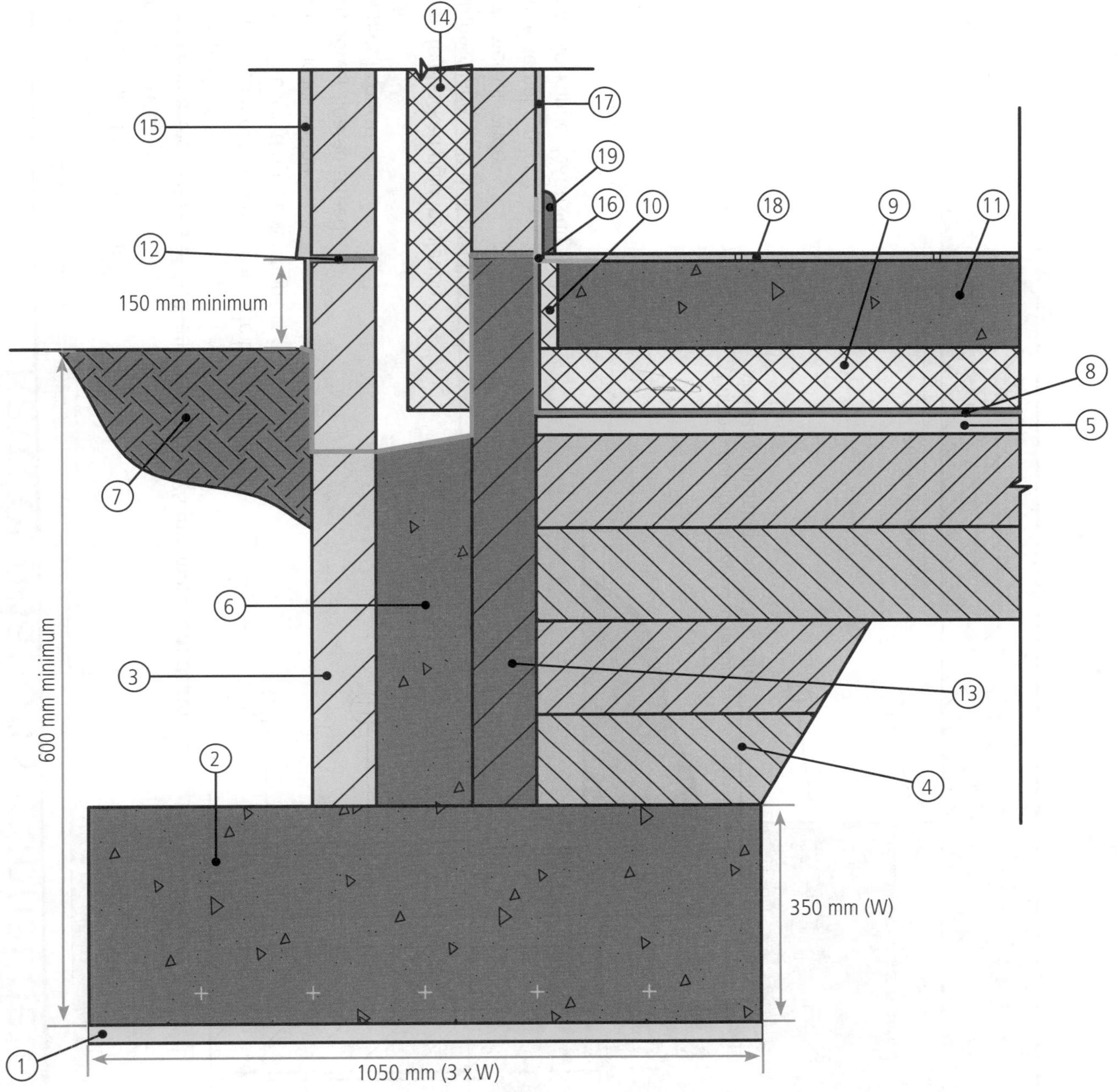

Scale 1:10

1. 30 mm sand blinding
2. Reinforced concrete foundation
3. 100 mm x 225 mm x 450 mm concrete block
4. Hardcore compacted in layers of 150 mm minimum, 225 mm maximum
5. 30 mm sand blinding
6. Weak concrete infill to base of cavity
7. Subsoil
8. Radon barrier
9. 100 mm foil-backed rigid insulation
10. 25 mm edge insulation
11. 150 mm concrete floor
12. Damp-proof course
13. Thermal block inner leaf rising wall
14. 100 mm foil-backed rigid insulation
15. 19 mm external render
16. Airtightness tape seals wall and floor
17. 12 mm internal render
18. 300 mm x 300 mm x 12 mm ceramic tiles
19. 100 mm x 18 mm skirting board

Raft foundation sectional detail

1. Reinforced concrete raft foundation
2. 75 mm sand blinding
3. Hardcore compacted in layers of 150 mm minimum, 225 mm maximum depth
4. Radon barrier
5. 100 mm x 225 mm x 450 mm concrete block inner leaf
6. 100 mm foil-backed rigid insulation
7. 25 mm edge insulation
8. 75 mm power floated screed
9. Damp-proof course
10. Subsoil
11. 100 mm foil-backed rigid insulation
12. Airtightness tape seals wall and floor
13. 12 mm internal render
14. 19 mm external render
15. Thermal block inner leaf rising wall

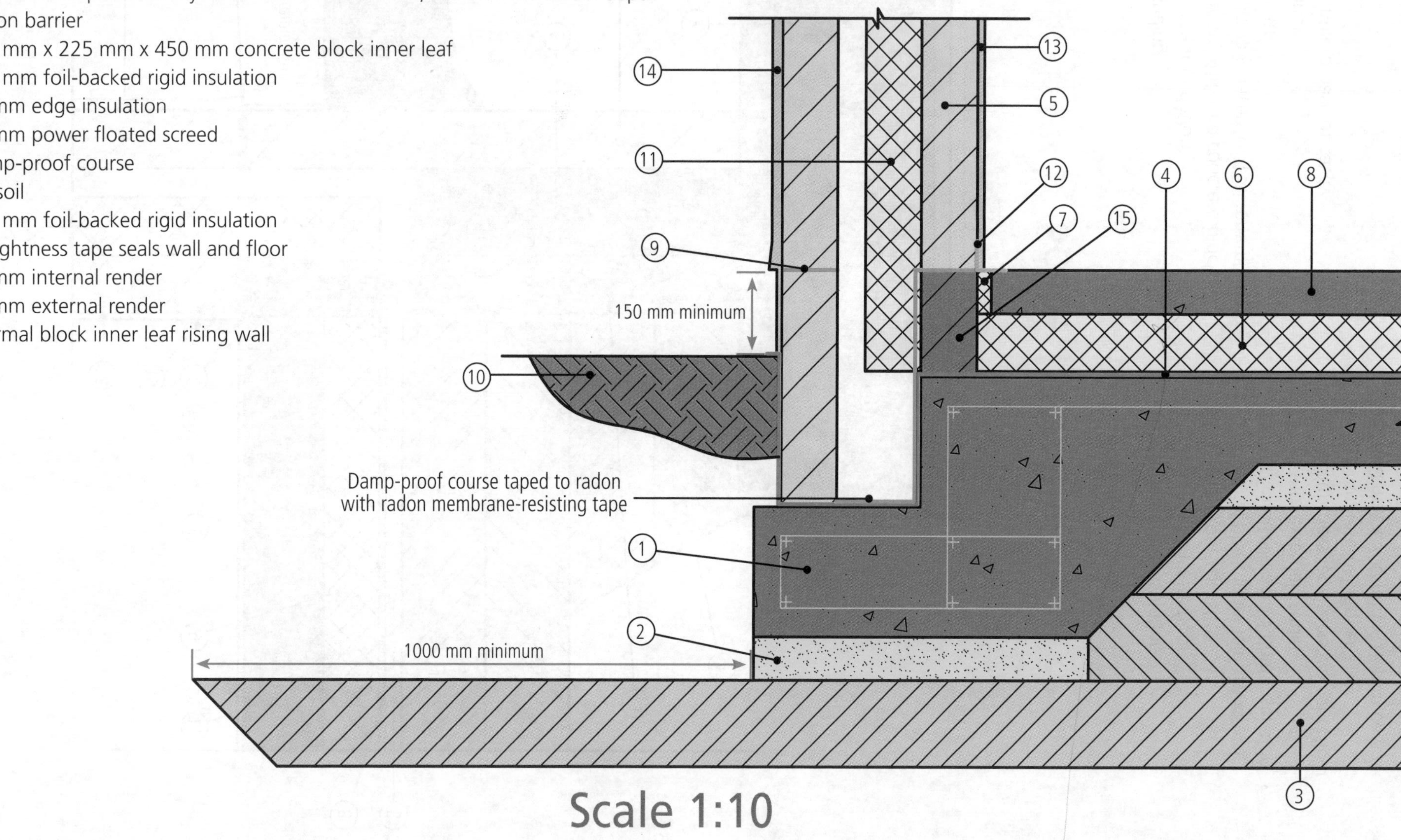

Scale 1:10

Pile foundation detail

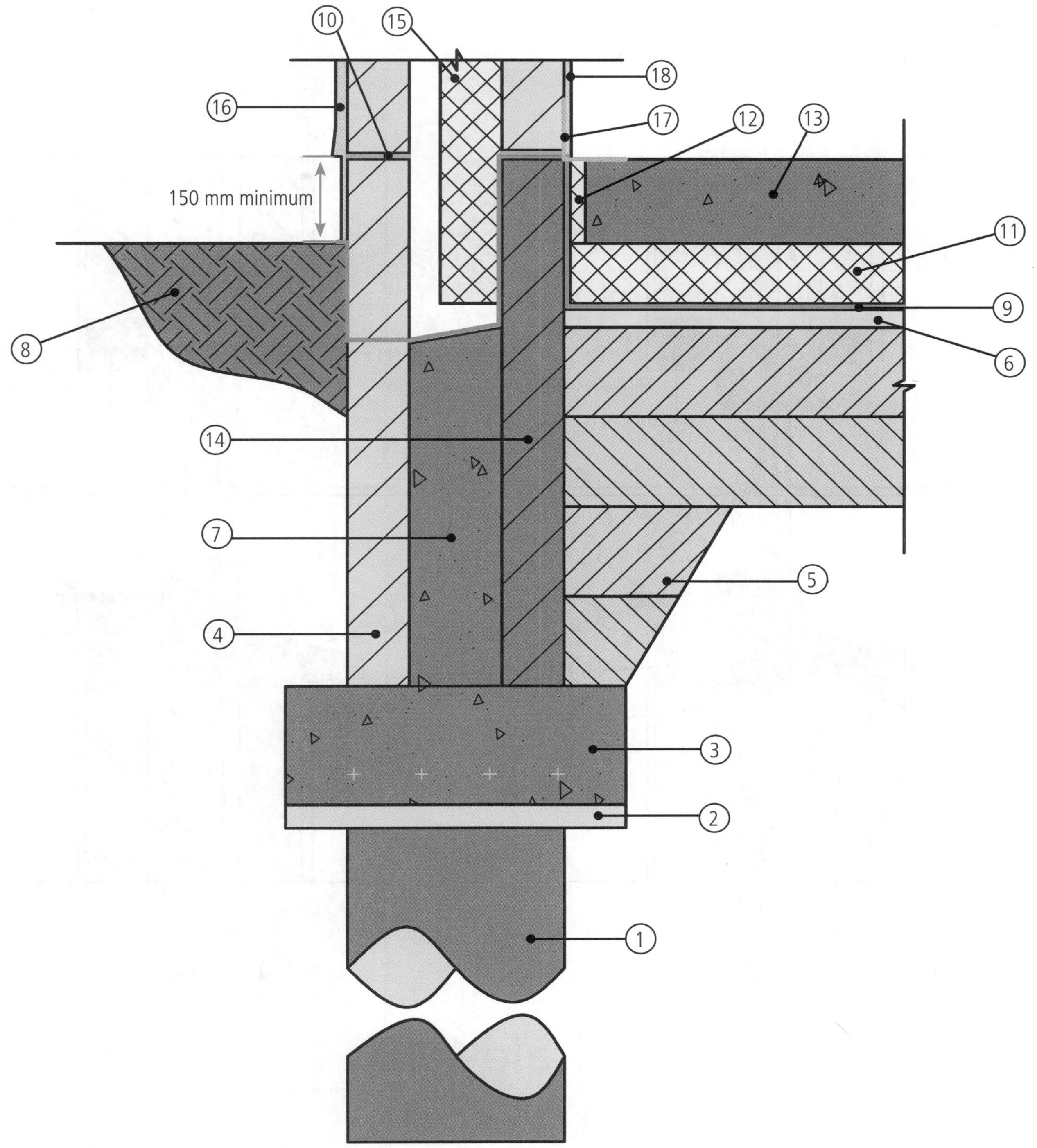

Scale 1:10

1. Ø350 mm short-bored pile
2. 40 mm lean concrete blinding
3. Reinforced concrete foundation
4. 100 mm x 225 mm x 450 mm concrete block
5. Hardcore compacted in layers of 150 mm minimum, 225 mm maximum depth
6. 30 mm sand blinding
7. Weak concrete infill to base of cavity
8. Subsoil
9. Radon barrier
10. Damp-proof course
11. 100 mm foil-backed rigid insulation
12. 25 mm edge insulation
13. 150 mm concrete floor
14. Thermal block inner leaf rising wall
15. 100 mm foil-backed rigid insulation
16. 19 mm external render
17. Airtightness tape seals wall and floor
18. 12 mm internal render

Window lintel, cill and jamb detail

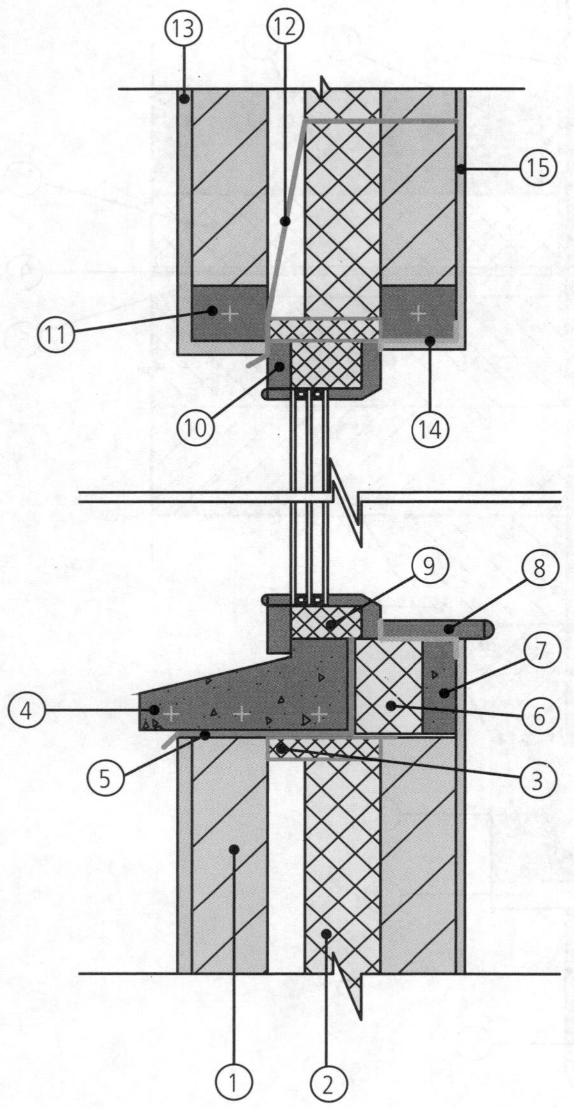

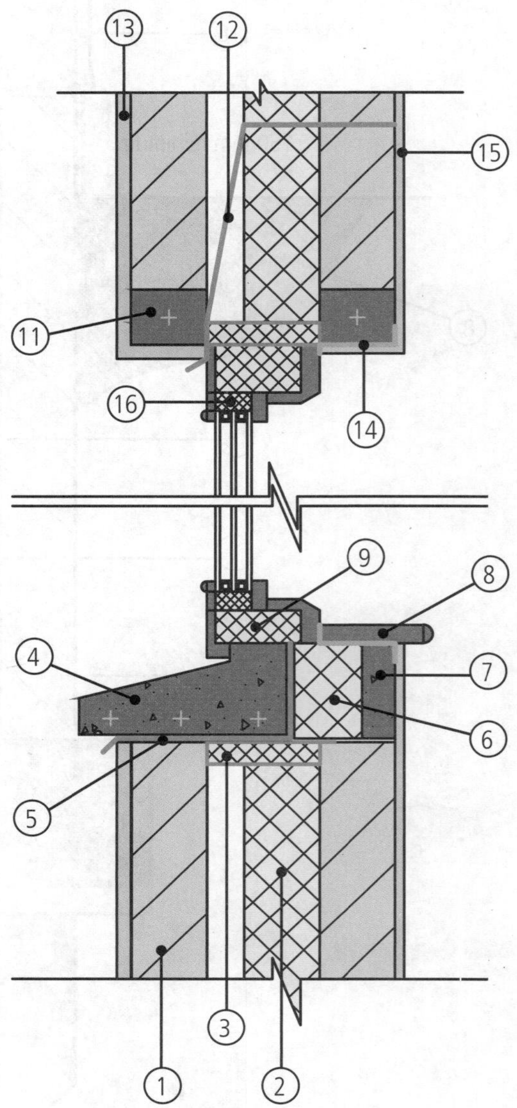

Scale 1:10

1. 100 mm x 225 mm x 450 mm concrete block
2. 100 mm foil-backed rigid insulation
3. Prefabricated cavity closer
4. Prefabricated concrete cill
5. Damp-proof course tray
6. 100 mm foil-backed rigid insulation
7. Weak concrete infill
8. 150 mm x 25 mm window board
9. 150 mm x 80 mm triple-glazed window-cilll with thermal break
10. 150 mm x 80 mm window head/jamb with thermal break
11. 100 mm x 75 mm precast concrete lintel
12. Stepped damp-proof course
13. 19 mm external render
14. Airtightness tape sealing inner leaf and frame
15. 12 mm internal render
16. 40 mm x 80 mm window casement

Door threshold and lintel detail

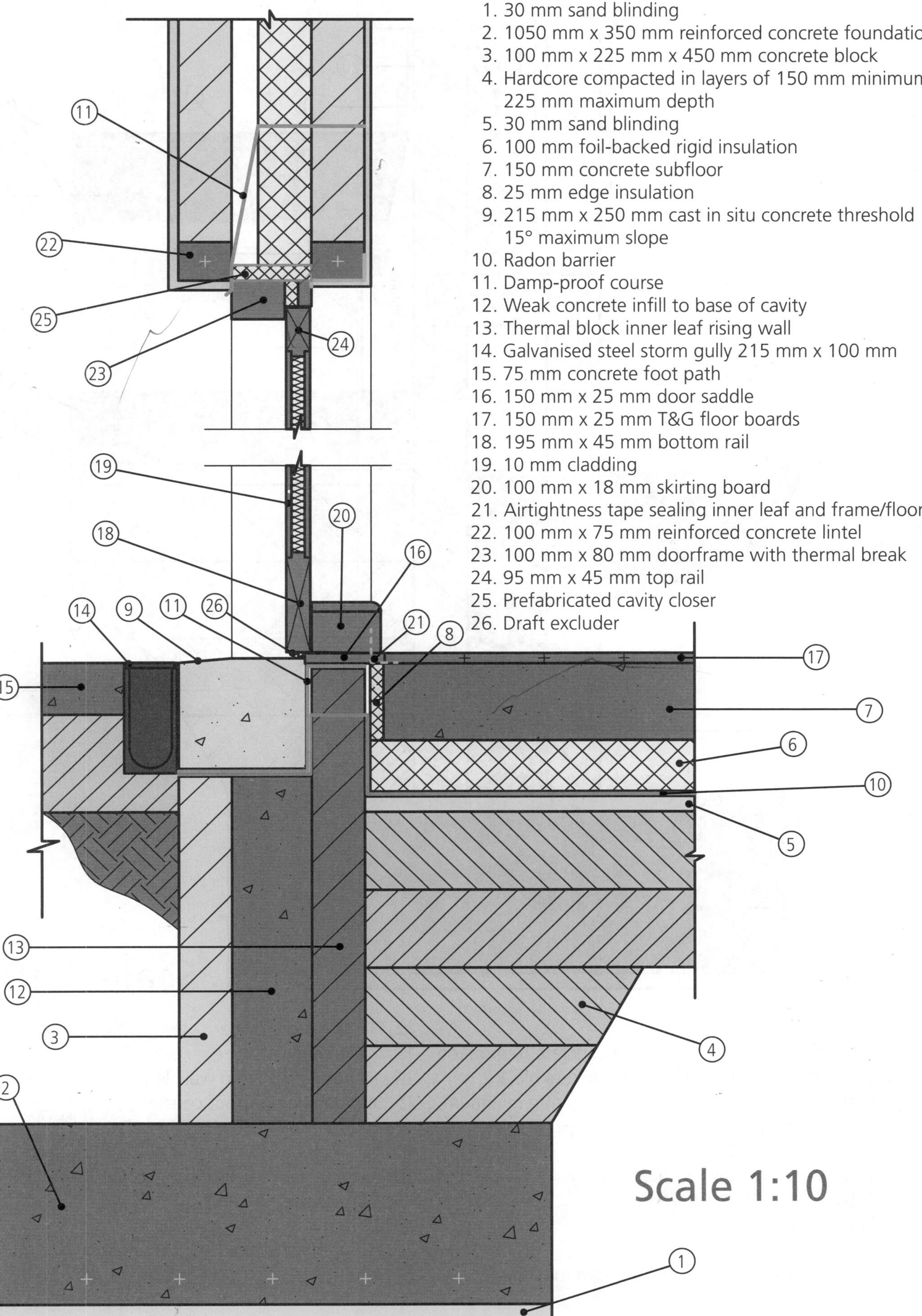

1. 30 mm sand blinding
2. 1050 mm x 350 mm reinforced concrete foundation
3. 100 mm x 225 mm x 450 mm concrete block
4. Hardcore compacted in layers of 150 mm minimum, 225 mm maximum depth
5. 30 mm sand blinding
6. 100 mm foil-backed rigid insulation
7. 150 mm concrete subfloor
8. 25 mm edge insulation
9. 215 mm x 250 mm cast in situ concrete threshold 15° maximum slope
10. Radon barrier
11. Damp-proof course
12. Weak concrete infill to base of cavity
13. Thermal block inner leaf rising wall
14. Galvanised steel storm gully 215 mm x 100 mm
15. 75 mm concrete foot path
16. 150 mm x 25 mm door saddle
17. 150 mm x 25 mm T&G floor boards
18. 195 mm x 45 mm bottom rail
19. 10 mm cladding
20. 100 mm x 18 mm skirting board
21. Airtightness tape sealing inner leaf and frame/floor
22. 100 mm x 75 mm reinforced concrete lintel
23. 100 mm x 80 mm doorframe with thermal break
24. 95 mm x 45 mm top rail
25. Prefabricated cavity closer
26. Draft excluder
Scale 1:10

Suspended timber floor

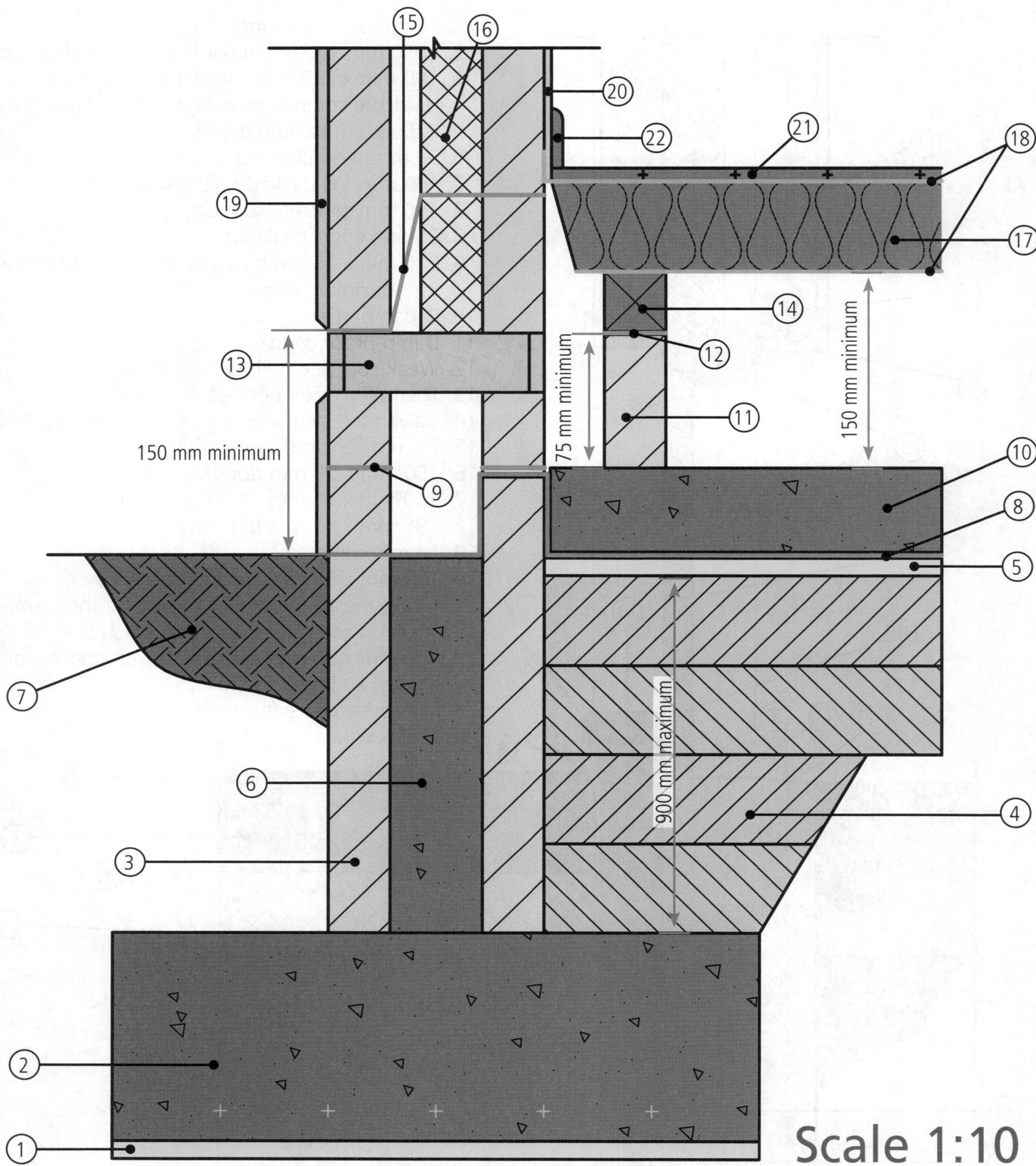

Scale 1:10

1. 30 mm sand blinding
2. 1050 mm x 350 mm reinforced concrete foundation
3. 100 mm x 225 mm x 450 mm concrete block
4. Hardcore compacted in layers of 150 mm minimum, 225 mm maximum depth
5. 30 mm sand blinding
6. Weak concrete infill to base of cavity
7. Subsoil
8. Radon barrier
9. Damp-proof course
10. 150 mm oversite concrete (100 mm minimum)
11. Tassel wall 2.13 m maximum span
12. Damp-proof course
13. Ø100 mm vent pipe
14. 100 mm x 100 mm wallplate
15. Stepped damp-proof course
16. 100 mm foil-backed rigid insulation
17. 150 mm x 50 mm joist at 400 mm centres
18. Airtightness membrane taped to wall
19. 19 mm external render
20. 12 mm internal render
21. 150 mm x 25 mm T&G floor boards
22. 100 mm x 18 mm skirting board

Eaves and ridge detail slate

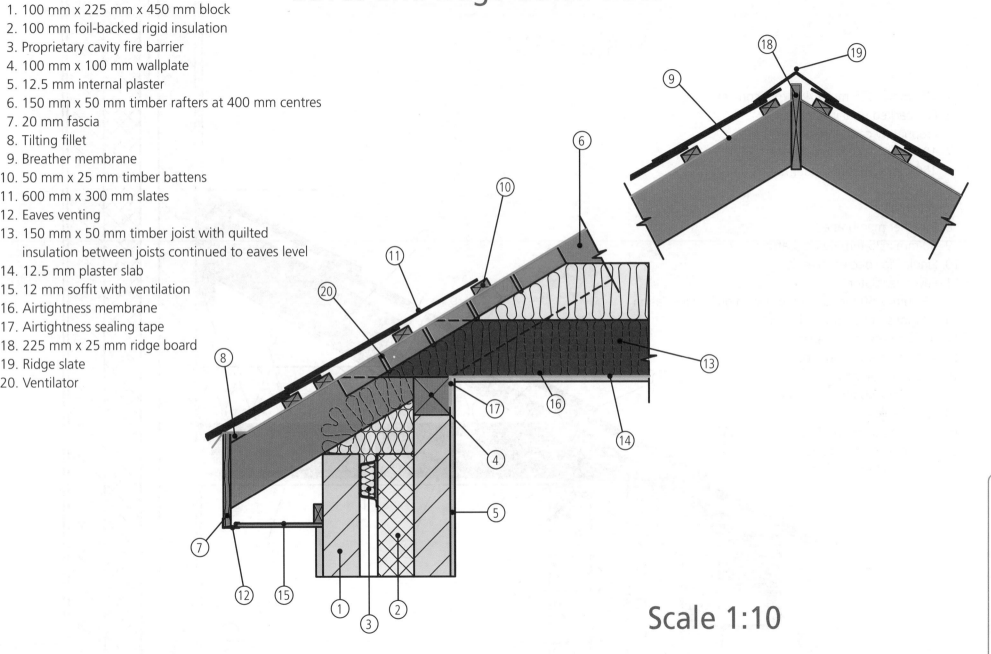

1. 100 mm x 225 mm x 450 mm block
2. 100 mm foil-backed rigid insulation
3. Proprietary cavity fire barrier
4. 100 mm x 100 mm wallplate
5. 12.5 mm internal plaster
6. 150 mm x 50 mm timber rafters at 400 mm centres
7. 20 mm fascia
8. Tilting fillet
9. Breather membrane
10. 50 mm x 25 mm timber battens
11. 600 mm x 300 mm slates
12. Eaves venting
13. 150 mm x 50 mm timber joist with quilted insulation between joists continued to eaves level
14. 12.5 mm plaster slab
15. 12 mm soffit with ventilation
16. Airtightness membrane
17. Airtightness sealing tape
18. 225 mm x 25 mm ridge board
19. Ridge slate
20. Ventilator

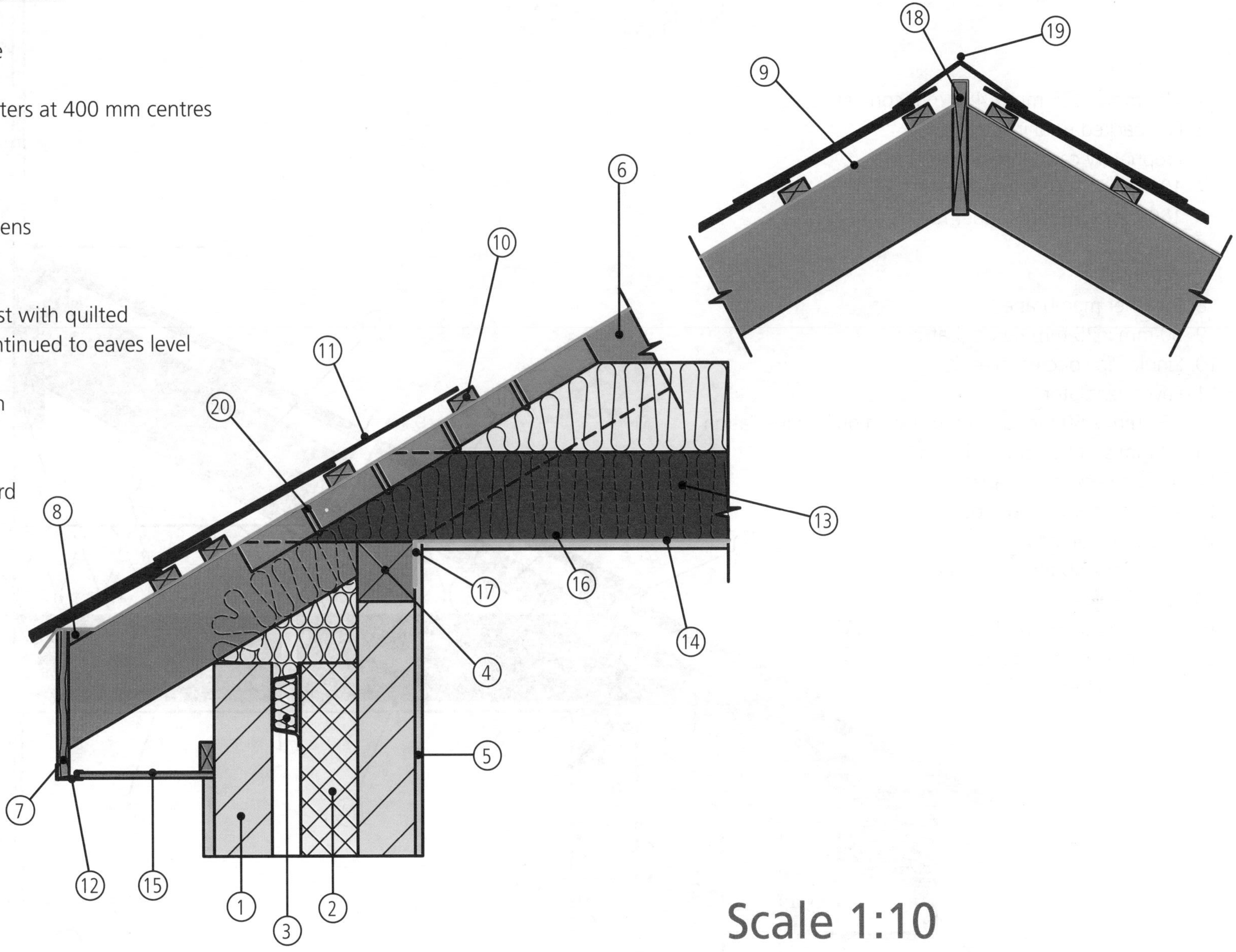

Scale 1:10

Tiled lean-to roof

Scale 1:10

1. 100 mm x 225 mm x 450 mm concrete block
2. Foil-backed rigid insulation
3. Proprietary cavity fire barrier
4. 100 mm x 100 mm wallplate
5. 150 mm x 50 mm timber rafters
6. 20 mm fascia
7. Tilting fillet
8. Breather membrane
9. 50 mm x 25 mm timber battens
10. Single lap concrete tiles
11. Eaves ventilator
12. 150 mm x 50 mm timber joist with quilted insulation
13. 12 mm soffit with ventilation
14. Airtightness membrane
15. Airtightness sealing tape
16. 150 mm quilted insulation
17. 200 mm x 50 mm wallplate
18. Lead flashing
19. Stepped damp-proof course
20. 12.5 mm internal render
21. 19 mm external render

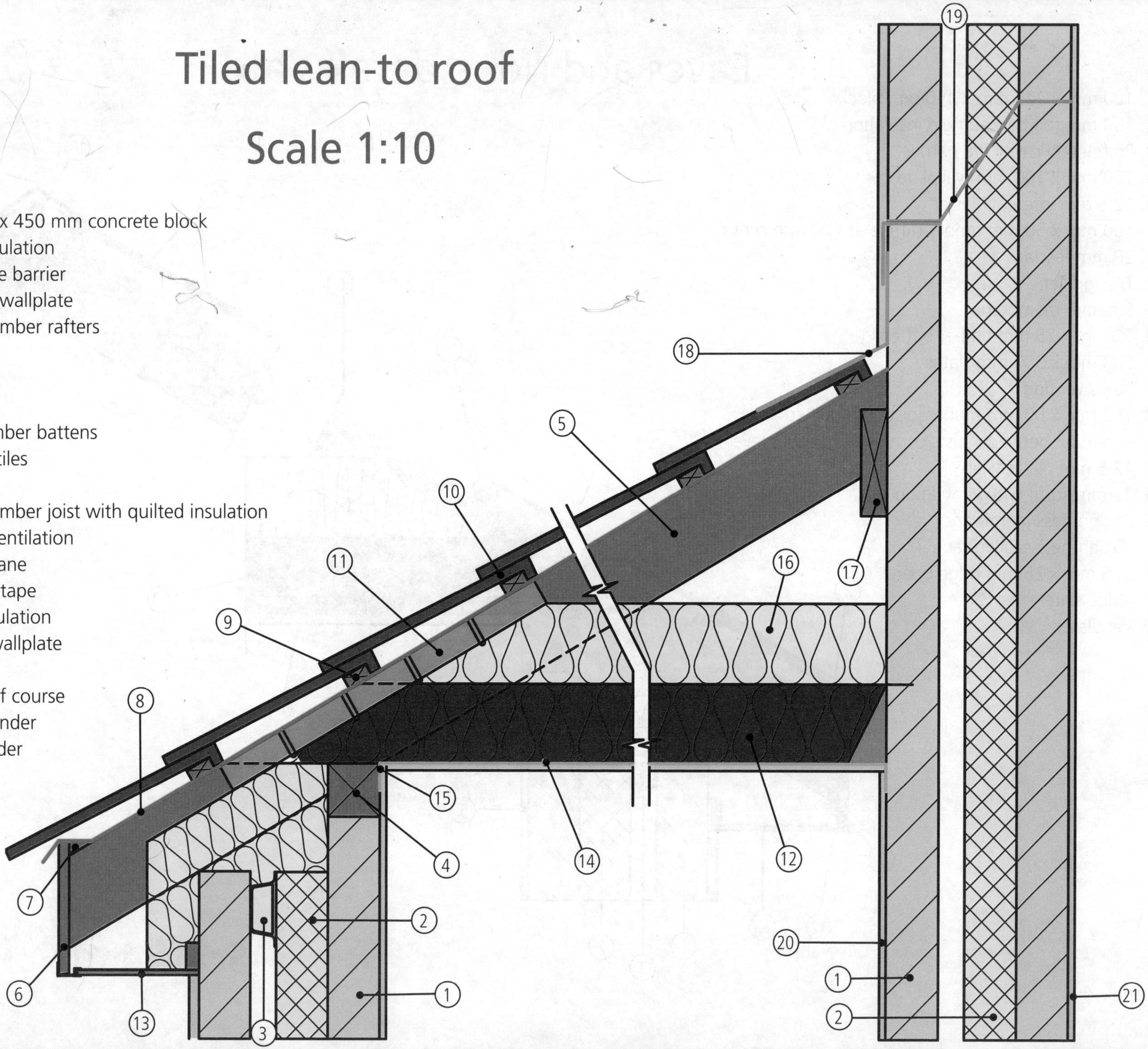

Warm deck flat roof

Scale 1:10

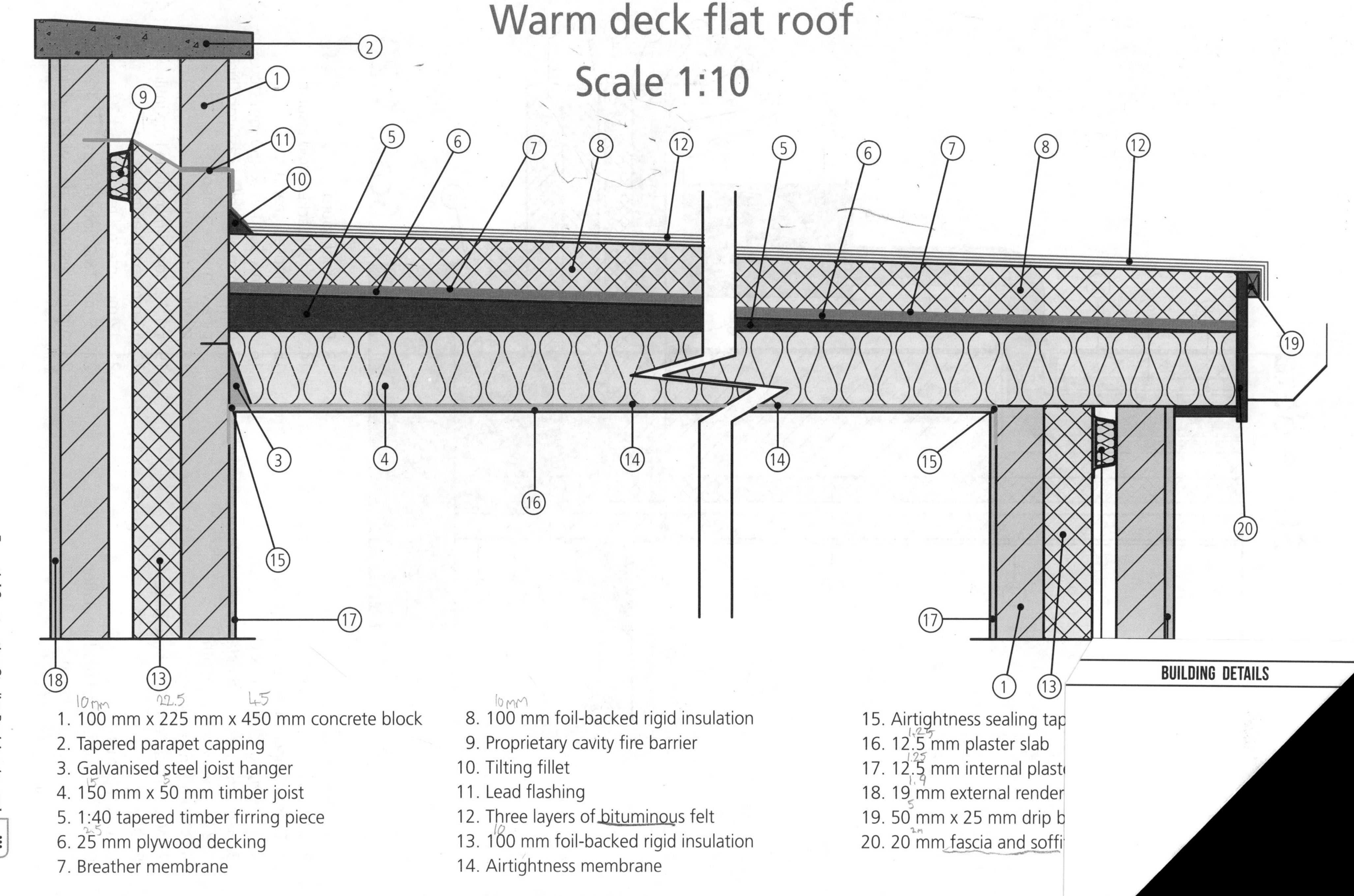

1. 100 mm x 225 mm x 450 mm concrete block
2. Tapered parapet capping
3. Galvanised steel joist hanger
4. 150 mm x 50 mm timber joist
5. 1:40 tapered timber firring piece
6. 25 mm plywood decking
7. Breather membrane
8. 100 mm foil-backed rigid insulation
9. Proprietary cavity fire barrier
10. Tilting fillet
11. Lead flashing
12. Three layers of bituminous felt
13. 100 mm foil-backed rigid insulation
14. Airtightness membrane
15. Airtightness sealing tap
16. 12.5 mm plaster slab
17. 12.5 mm internal plast
18. 19 mm external render
19. 50 mm x 25 mm drip b
20. 20 mm fascia and soffi

Stove detail

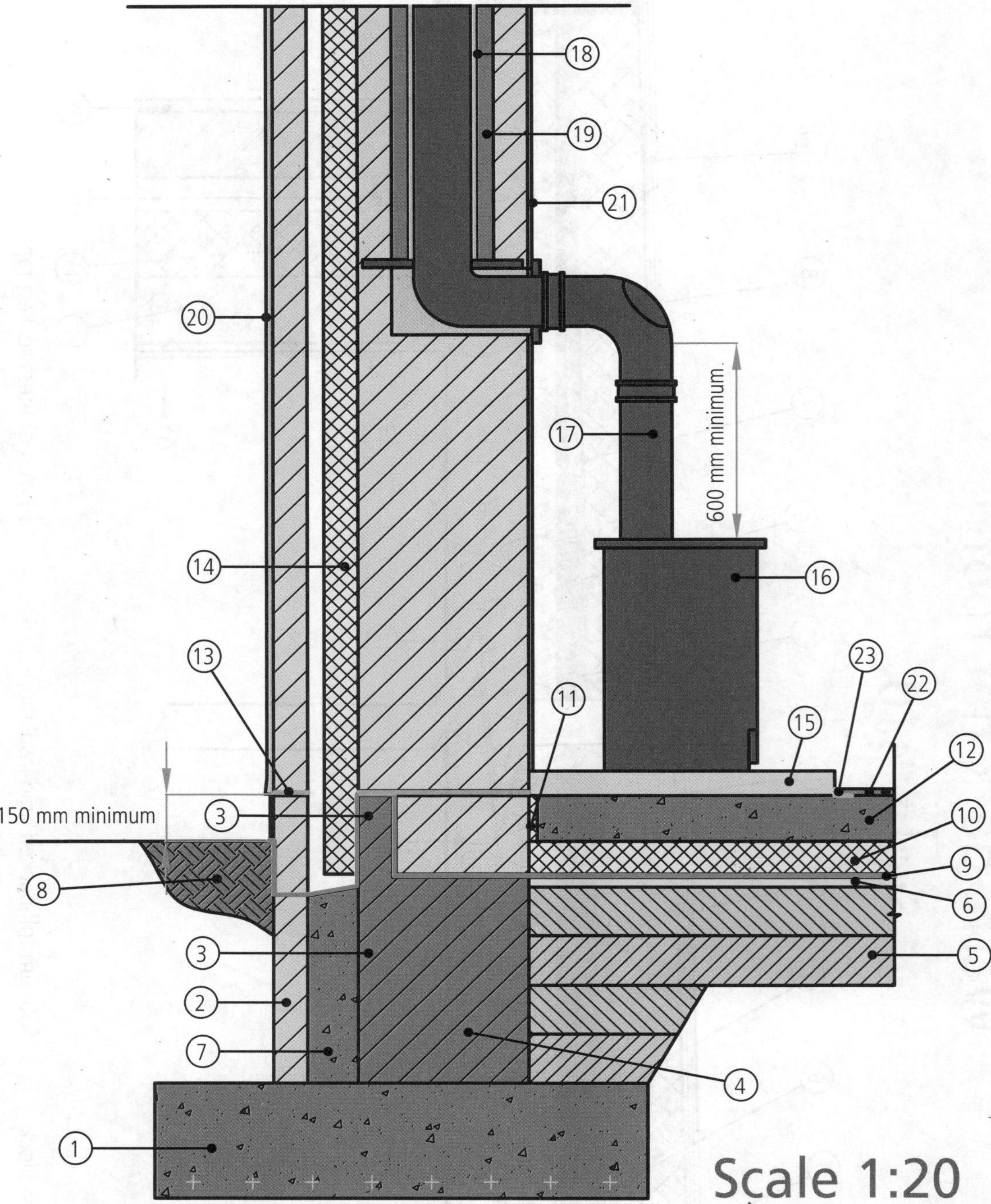

Scale 1:20

1. Reinforced concrete foundation
2. 100 mm x 225 mm x 450 mm concrete block
3. Thermal block inner leaf rising wall
4. 400 mm concrete block chimney jamb
5. Hardcore compacted in layers of 150 mm minimum, 225 mm maximum depth
6. 30 mm sand blinding
7. Weak concrete infill to base of cavity
8. Subsoil
9. Radon barrier
10. 100 mm foil-backed rigid insulation
11. 25 mm edge insulation
12. 150 mm concrete floor
13. Damp-proof course
14. 100 mm foil-backed rigid insulation
15. Superimposed hearth
16. 700 mm x 500 mm x 450 mm stove
17. Ø 150 mm enamelled cast-iron flue pipe with access door
18. Ø 200 mm flue liner
19. 1:1:12 non-combustible lime infill
20. 19 mm external render
21. 12 mm internal render
22. 25 mm T&G floor boards
23. Airtightness tape seals wall and floor

2 2 4 8 16 32 64 128

Timber frame rising wall de

BUILDING DETAILS

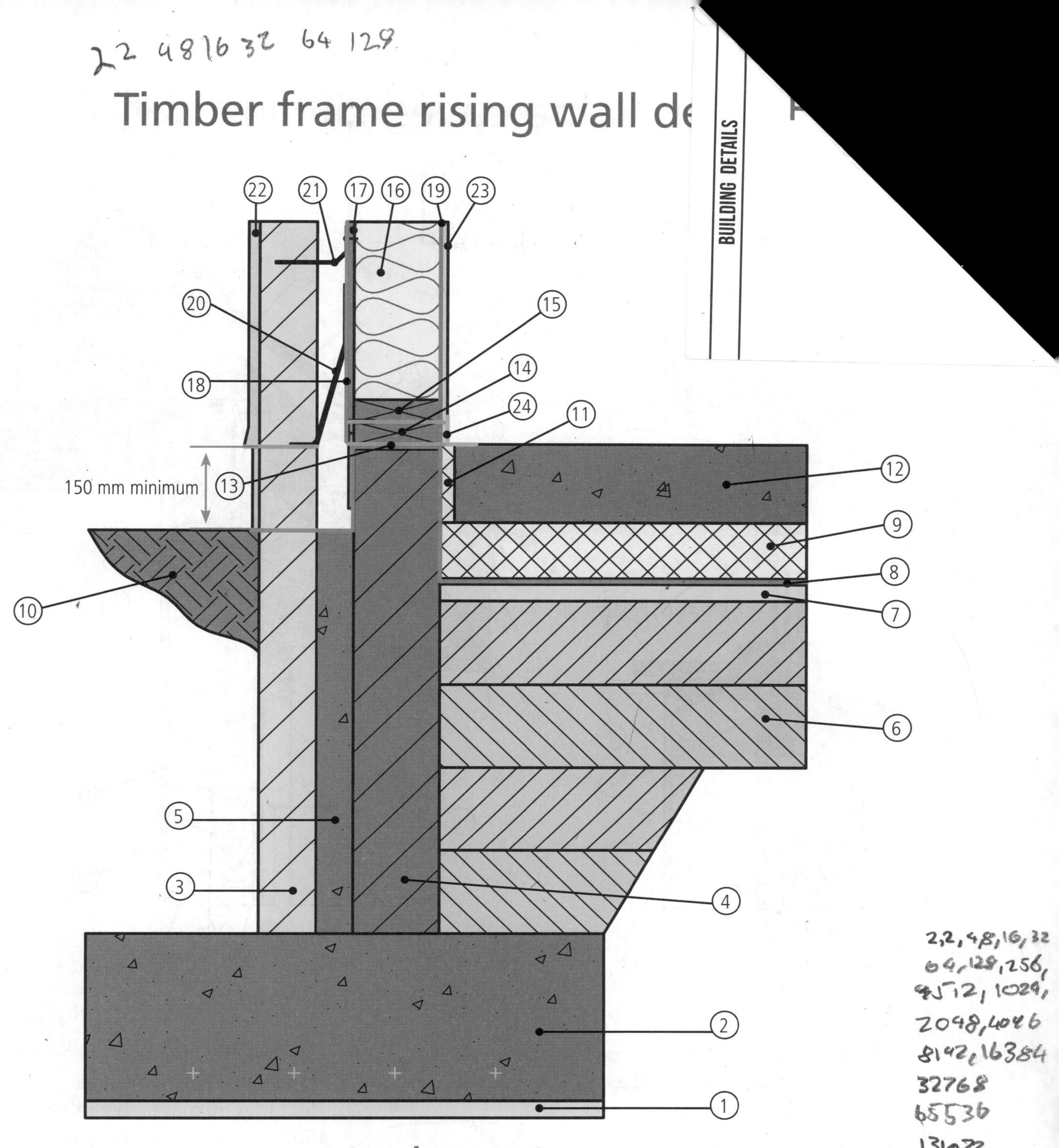

2,2,4,8,16,32
64,128,256,
512, 1024,
2048,4096
8192,16384
32768
65536
131072

Scale 1:10

1. 30 mm sand blinding
2. Reinforced concrete foundation
3. 100 mm x 225 mm x 450 mm concrete block
4. 150 mm x 225 mm x 450 mm concrete block inner leaf
5. Weak concrete infill to base of cavity
6. Hardcore compacted in layers of 150 mm minimum, 225 mm maximum depth
7. 30 mm sand blinding
8. Radon barrier
9. 100 mm foil-backed rigid insulation
10. Topsoil
11. 25 mm edge insulation
12. 150 mm concrete floor
13. Damp-proof course
14. 150 mm x 50 mm soleplate
15. 150 mm x 50 mm bottom rail
16. 150 mm x 50 mm timber stud with 150 mm insulation
17. 12 mm plywood sheeting
18. Breather membrane
19. Vapour check
20. Anchor strap
21. Wall tie
22. 19 mm external render
23. 12.5 mm plasterboard slab
24. Airtightness tape

Timber frame eaves, cill and detail

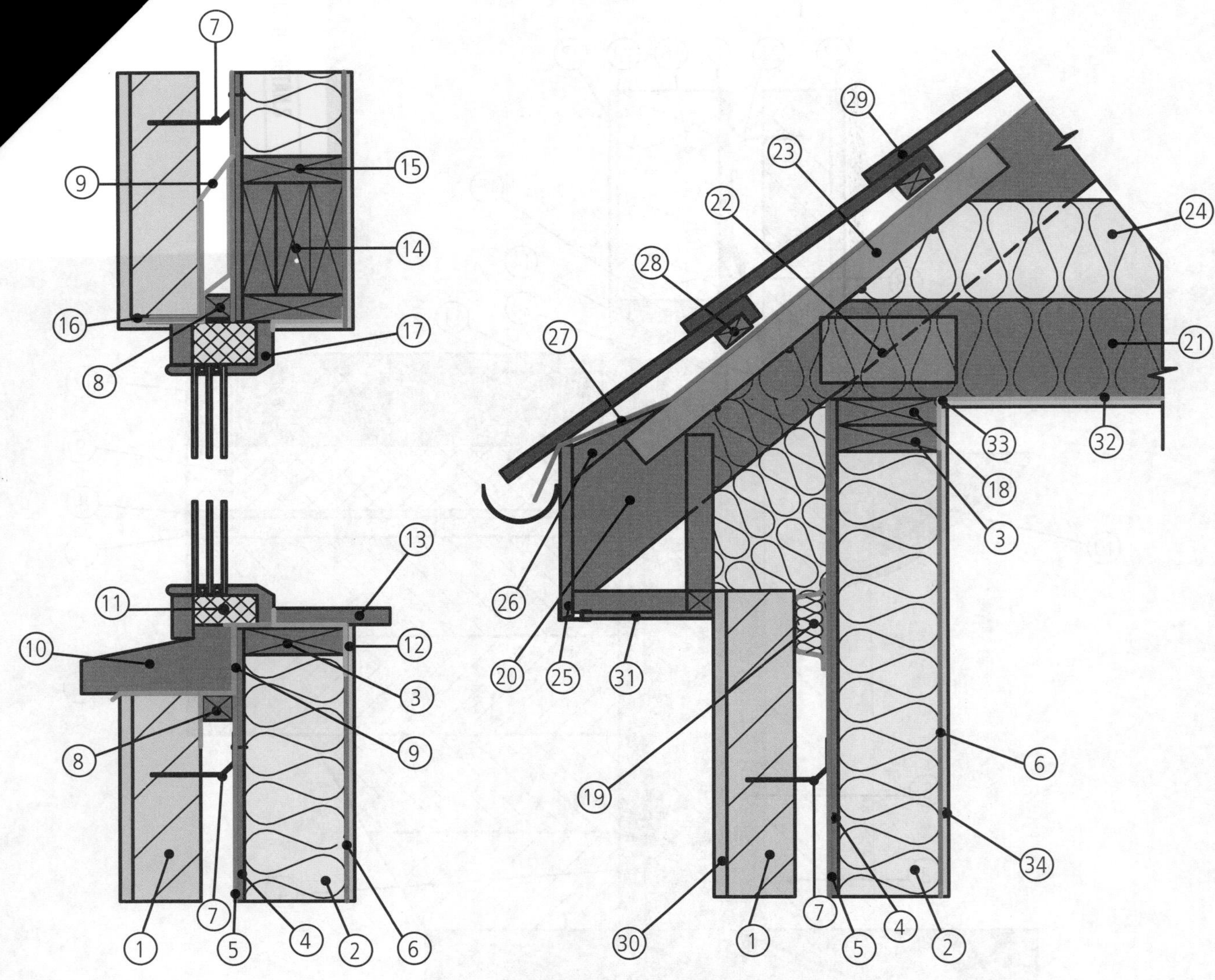

Scale 1:10

1. 100 mm x 225 mm x 450 mm concrete block
2. 150 mm x 50 mm timber stud with 150 mm insulation
3. 150 mm x 50 mm top rail
4. 12 mm plywood sheeting
5. Breather membrane
6. Vapour check
7. Wall tie
8. Proprietary cavity barrier
9. Damp-proof course
10. Concrete cill
11. 150 mm x 80 mm triple-glazed window-cill with thermal break
12. Airtightness tape
13. Window board
14. Timber lintel
15. Sole plate
16. Steel lintel
17. 150 mm x 80 mm triple-glazed window head with thermal break
18. 150 mm x 50 mm head plate
19. Proprietary cavity fire barrier
20. 150 mm x 50 mm timber rafter
21. 150 mm x 50 mm timber joist
22. Nail plate
23. Eaves ventilator
24. 150 mm quilted insulation
25. 20 mm fascia
26. Tilting fillet
27. Breather membrane
28. 50 mm x 25 mm timber battens
29. Single lap concrete tiles
30. 19 mm external render
31. 12 mm soffit with ventilation
32. Airtightness membrane
33. Airtightness tape
34. 12.5 mm plasterboard slab

Passive foundation

Scale 1:10

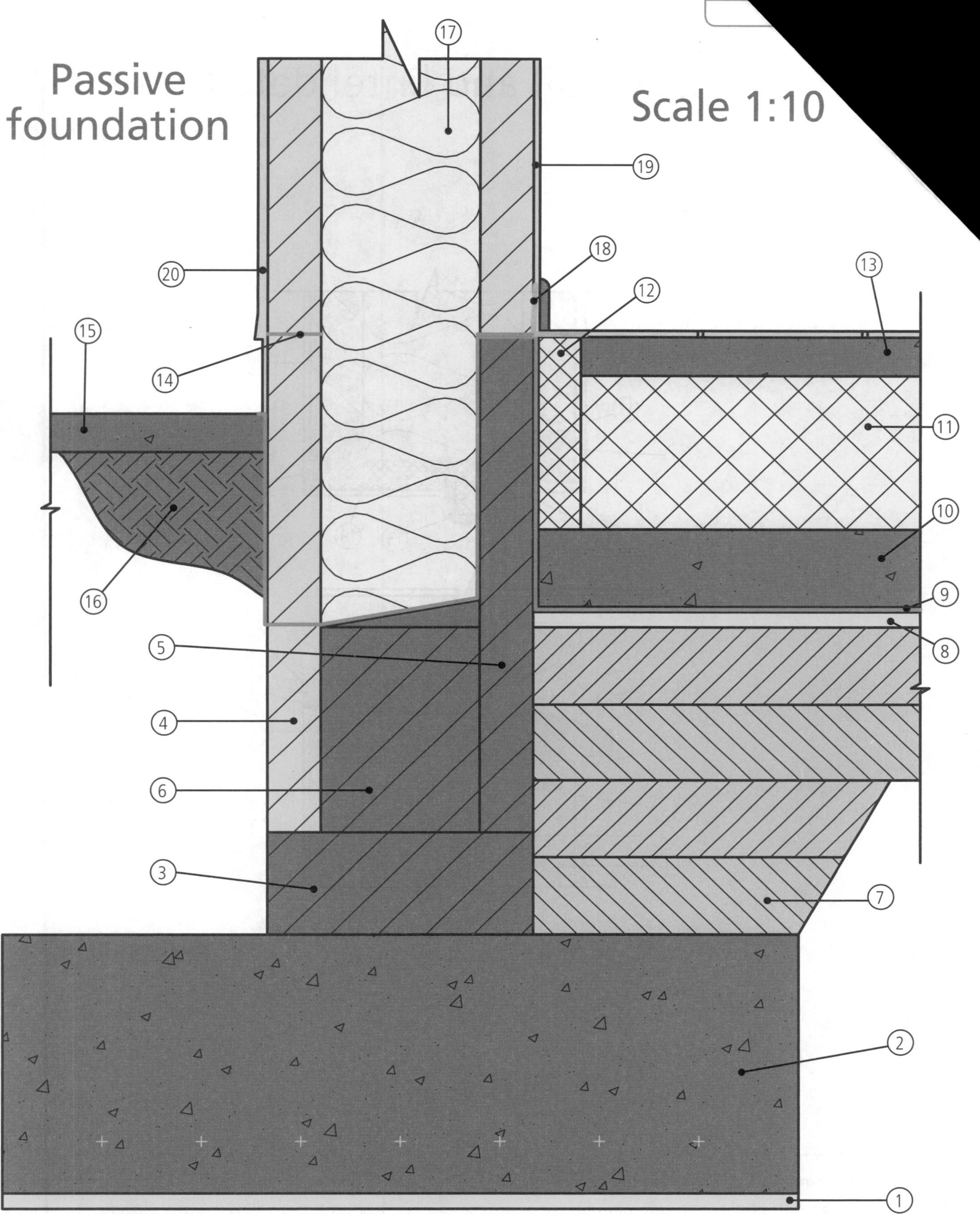

1. 30 mm sand blinding
2. Reinforced concrete foundation
3. Concrete block footing
4. 100 mm x 225 mm x 450 mm concrete block
5. Thermal block rising wall
6. Thermal block cavity infill to base of cavity
7. Hardcore compacted in layers of 150 mm minimum, 225 mm maximum depth
8. 30 mm sand blinding
9. Radon barrier
10. 150 mm concrete subfloor
11. 300 mm foil-backed rigid insulation
12. 80 mm edge insulation
13. 75 mm concrete screed
14. Damp-proof course
15. 75 mm concrete footpath
16. Subsoil
17. 300 mm quilted insulation to base of cavity
18. Airtightness tape
19. 12 mm internal render
20. 19 mm external render

Passive cill and lintel detail

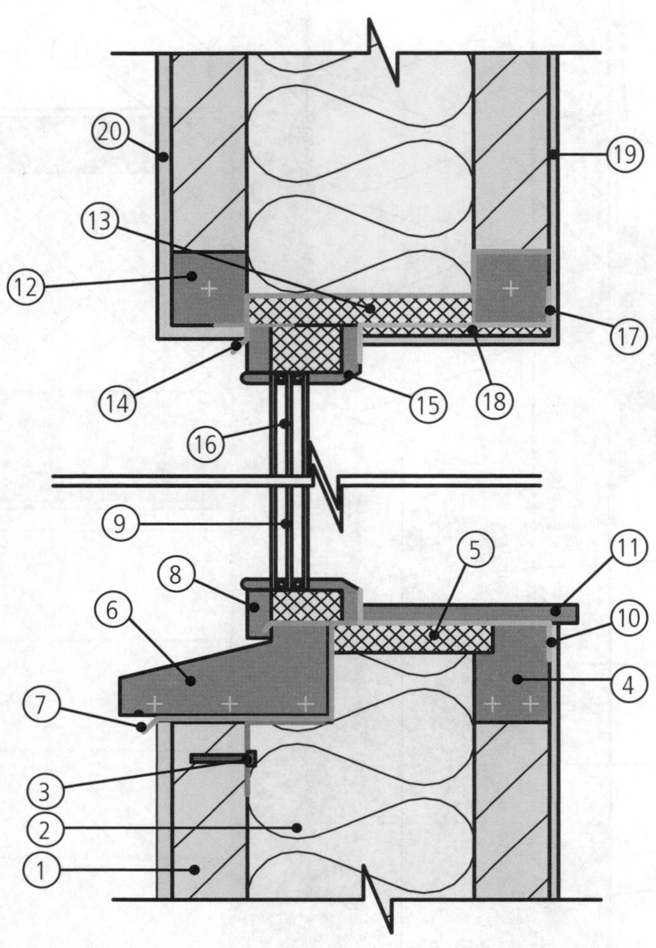

Scale 1:10

1. 100 mm x 225 mm x 450 mm concrete block
2. 300 mm quilted insulation to base of cavity
3. Steel fixing angle
4. 100 mm x 125 mm concrete block
5. 40 mm prefabricated cavity closer
6. 125 mm x 225 mm precast concrete cill
7. Damp-proof course tray
8. 150 mm x 80 mm window frame with thermal break
9. Triple-glazing
10. Airtightness barrier
11. 300 mm x 25 mm window board
12. 100 mm x 75 mm precast concrete lintel
13. 40 mm prefabricated cavity closer
14. Stepped damp-proof course
15. 150 mm x 80 mm window frame with thermal break
16. Triple glazing
17. Airtightness barrier
18. 15 mm rigid insulation
19. 12 mm internal render
20. 19 mm external render

Passive eaves detail

Scale 1:10

1. 100 mm x 225 mm x 450 mm concrete block
2. 300 mm quilted insulation
3. 40 mm prefabricated cavity closer
4. Lightweight thermal block
5. 100 mm x 75 mm wallplate
6. 225 mm x 40 mm common rafters at 600 mm centres
7. 225 mm x 40 mm ceiling joist at 600 mm centres
8. 10 mm soffit
9. 20 mm fascia
10. Breather membrane
11. 50 mm x 25 mm timber battens
12. 600 mm x 300 mm slates
13. Gutter
14. 60 mm rigid insulation, with 50 mm ventilation
15. Airtightness membrane
16. Dropped ceiling
17. Airtightness tape
18. Layers of 200 mm quilted insulation (Note the continuity of insulation at the eaves)
19. 12 mm internal render
20. 19 mm external render (acrylic)

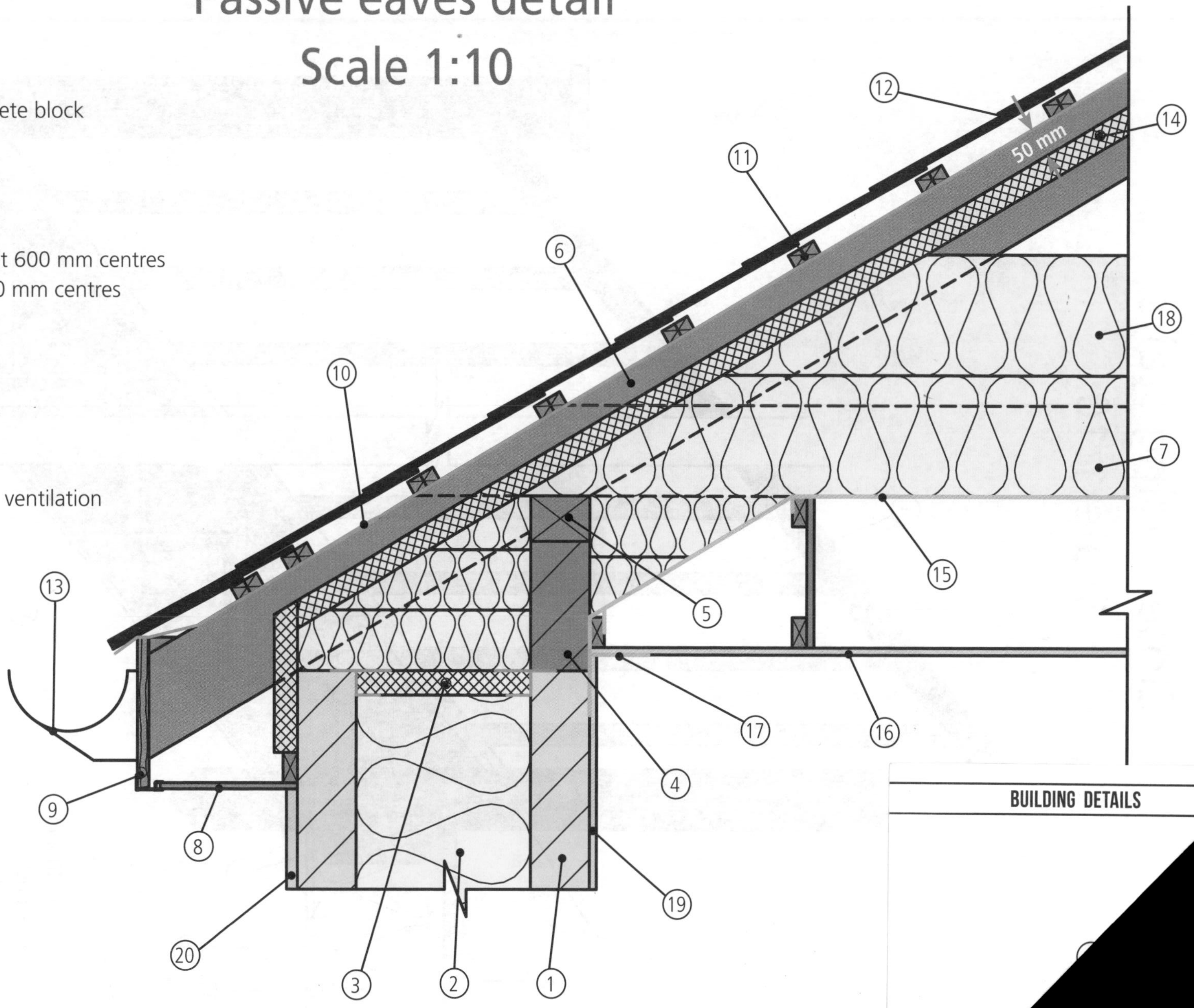

50 mm

BUILDING DETAILS

Closed string stairs
Scale 1:10

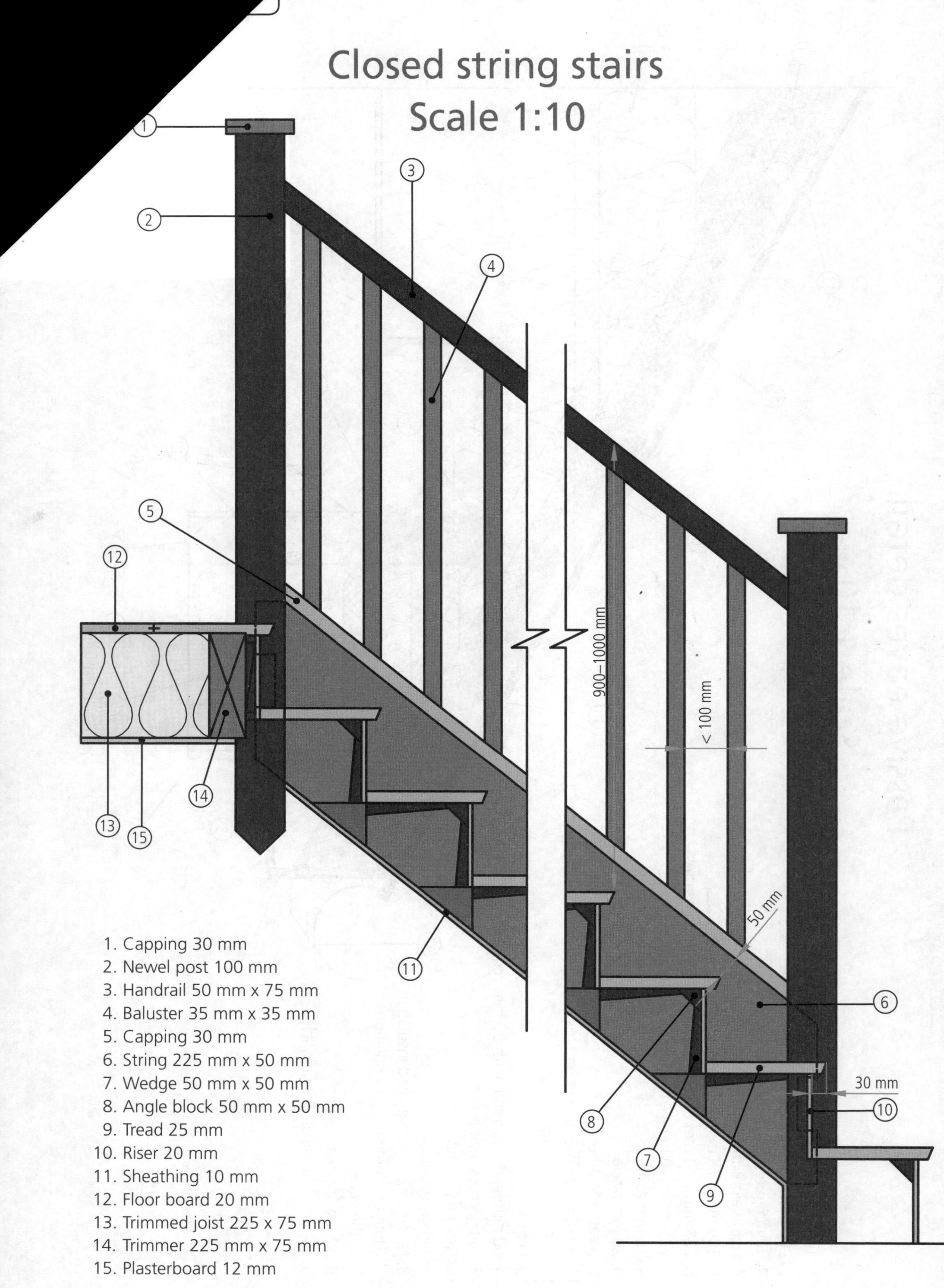

1. Capping 30 mm
2. Newel post 100 mm
3. Handrail 50 mm x 75 mm
4. Baluster 35 mm x 35 mm
5. Capping 30 mm
6. String 225 mm x 50 mm
7. Wedge 50 mm x 50 mm
8. Angle block 50 mm x 50 mm
9. Tread 25 mm
10. Riser 20 mm
11. Sheathing 10 mm
12. Floor board 20 mm
13. Trimmed joist 225 x 75 mm
14. Trimmer 225 mm x 75 mm
15. Plasterboard 12 mm

☐ PLANNING PERMISSION

1. (a) Planning permission is required whenever a person wishes to __________ any site or land.

(b) Development is considered as ______________________________

____

(c) Typical examples of development include:

- erecting any ________________ on the land.
- ____________________ of any land or structure.
- __________ any ___________________ structure.
- ____________ any ___________________ of any land or structure.

2. List the four types of planning permission that can be granted.

____

____

____

____

☐ REQUIREMENTS FOR PLANNING PERMISSION

3. To apply for planning permission, you need:

(a) a planning _____________________.

(b) the full ______________________ in which ______________________ for permission has been published (within two weeks of submitting the form).

(c) one copy of the ____________________.

(d) the appropriate _________.

(e) ______________________ the landowner/landlord.

(f) a letter from ______________________.

(g) six copies of the ____________________. The scale of map should not be less than 1:1000 in built-up areas and 1:2500 in all other areas.

NEWSPAPER NOTICE

4. (a) The ______________________ must be submitted.

(b) The local authorities have a list of _____________ newspapers on their websites.

(c) The notice must be ____________________ in red on the page.

SITE LOCATION MAP

5. (a) A site location map shows the ______________________ in the surrounding area.

(b) It must be of an appropriate scale:

- ______________ for urban areas.
- ______________ or ______________ for rural areas.

(c) The site must be ______________ in ______.

(d) The Ordnance Survey ________________ must be visible.

(e) ________ must be clearly indicated on the map.

SITE NOTICE

6. The site notice must be:

(a) in position on the site for ______________ before the planning application is submitted.

(b) ______________ from the road.

(c) located in a ___________ position.

(d) clear and ________________.

SITE LAYOUT MAP

7. (a) _______ copies of the site layout map must be submitted to the planning authorities.

(b) The scale must not be less than ______________.

(c) The _______________ must be marked in red.

(d) ____________ must be clearly indicated on the map.

(e) It must show ____ and other features.

(f) The position of the _____________ should be shown on the site layout map.

ARCHITECTURAL DRAWINGS

8. (a) _____ copies of all detailed drawings must be submitted.

(b) Detailed drawings include drawings of _____________, _________ and _________ and must be drawn to a scale of not less than ________.

(c) Six copies of ______________ must be submitted. These are to include details of external __________, __________ and __________.

(d) _________ of documents must be included. This must list all plans, drawings and maps.

PLANNING APPROVAL

9. (a) The planning authority gives a decision on the application. This can take between _________ and _________.

(b) If planning permission is refused, the applicant may ________________________________ the decision to ______________.

(c) Should the planning authority fail to ___________ the applicant of a decision within two months, then the planning permission is ___________________________________.

(d) Planning permission, once granted, is valid for _________________.

☐ DESIGN GUIDELINES

SELECTING A SITE

10. The following steps are involved in selecting a site:

(a) Check the ___________________________________.

(b) _______________ the surrounding landscape.

(c) Decide on the _____________ of the building.

(d) _________ with the landscape.

LOCAL AREA DEVELOPMENT PLAN

11. Describe what a local area development plan is. Explain why it is an important reference document for anyone looking to develop land in an area.

____

____

____

____

____

____

____

____

READING THE LANDSCAPE

12. People are often advised to 'read' the landscape in which they wish to build a house. Explain why this is important and outline some of the ways in which a landscape might influence the design of the house being built.

____

____

____

____

____

____

____

____

CHOOSING WHERE ON THE SITE TO BUILD

13. The ______________ and ______________ of your house relative to the site can have a dramatic effect on:

(a) the amount of ____________________ available.

(b) the amount of ___________ the house can obtain from its surroundings.

(c) the ______________ of the house, in relation to the surrounding landscape.

DESIGNING FOR NATURAL LIGHT

14. (a) Ireland's light quality is influenced by its location in the ______________________, and its position relative to the ___________.

(b) There are three constants in terms of light when designing houses:

- The sun rises in the ___________ and sets in the ___________.
- The sun is ______________________ at noon.
- The sun is ___________ in the sky in the summer than in winter.

APPLYING THE GUIDELINES

15. On the given plans, indicate an appropriate layout for the following rooms:

- two bedrooms.
- the kitchen.
- the sitting room.
- the dining room.
- the utility room.
- the toilet.

Indicate the reasons for your choices in the space provided.

____

____

____

____

____

____

____

N
W
E
S

Appropriate room layout to make the best use of a site's natural light

ADDITIONAL GUIDELINES

16. (a) Orientation to the sun: ________° off south will reduce energy consumption by ________%.

(b) Fenestration

- The window area of ________-facing aspects should equal ________% of the total ______________.
- The window area of ________-facing aspects should equal ________% of the total ______________.
- Clean windows __________.

17. Draw a sketch showing the best orientation of a house to capture natural light. Make sure to indicate north and south in your answer.

SHELTER

18. Building an appropriately sheltered house can have a number of positive effects on the house, such as reducing draughts and heating costs and preserving the building. List four ways a building can use its surroundings to maximise its shelter.

____

____

____

____

LINKING WITH THE LAND

19. Everyone should be free to enjoy the rural landscape. Buildings should be designed to link with the land, and not appear as if they are 'dropped into' the site. Outline four ways in which buildings can be linked with the land.

____

____

____

____

____

Avoid 'dropping' the building into the landscape

DEALING WITH SLOPED GROUND

20. (a) Avoid ______________________ up and ______________________ of a site on sloped land.

(b) Instead, try to follow the natural slope of the land.

- Mimic the slope of the land using a ____________ roof.
- Design the house as a ______________________ ____________.
- Use a traditional ____________ house approach.

Houses improperly designed for sloped ground

21. Sketch three methods for building on sloped ground.

POSITIONING THE BUILDING

22. (a) When a person looks from a height to a ___________ slope, their eye is drawn to the ______________________________.

(b) Houses on ____________ slopes should be built ____________ to the road to ____________ their effect on the landscape.

(c) When a person looks from a height to a ___________ slope, their eye is drawn to the ___________.

(d) For the same reason, houses on ___________ slopes should be built ___________ from the road.

23. Indicate the correct position of
(a) a house build uphill and
(b) a house build downhill.

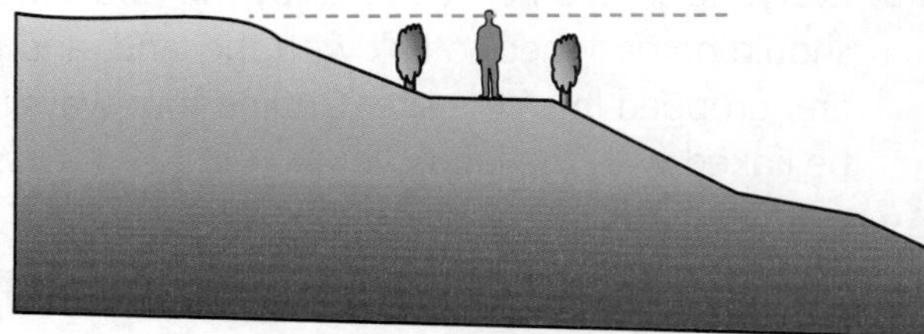

RIBBON AND CLUSTERED DEVELOPMENT

24. (a) Ribbon development occurs when a number of houses are built ______________________________.

(b) This has a high __________________ on the rural landscape.

(c) More traditional ____________ development, located off the main road, is recommended.

25. On the diagram, indicate
(a) ribbon development and
(b) clustered development.

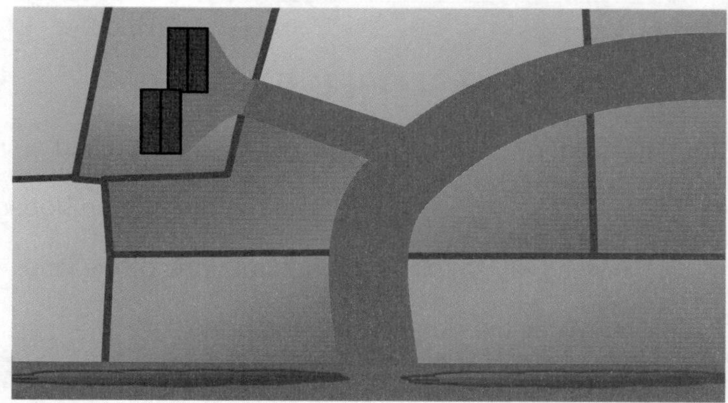

26. Given the sample sites on the next page, indicate the following on the site layout plans:

- the most appropriate position for a building on the site.
- the most appropriate orientation of the building.
- the most appropriate position of a septic tank system.
- the most appropriate design of a driveway and car parking area.
- any additional screening or planting required.

Continued

In each case, explain your choices. You must refer to the guidelines outlined in this chapter.

(a) ______________________________

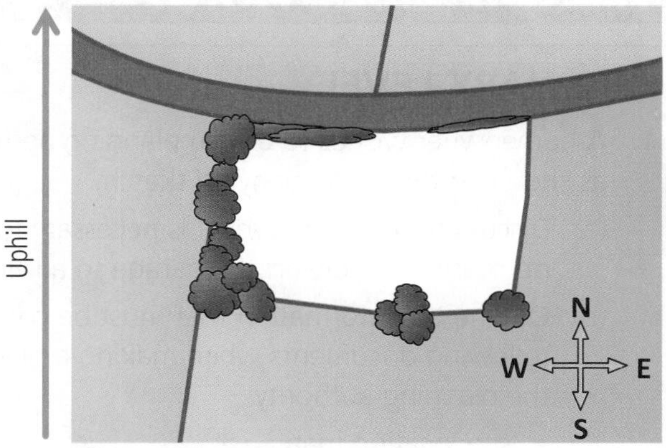

(b) ______________________________

(c) ______________________________

(d) ______________________________

Uphill

N W E S

Sample site layout 1

Uphill

N W E S

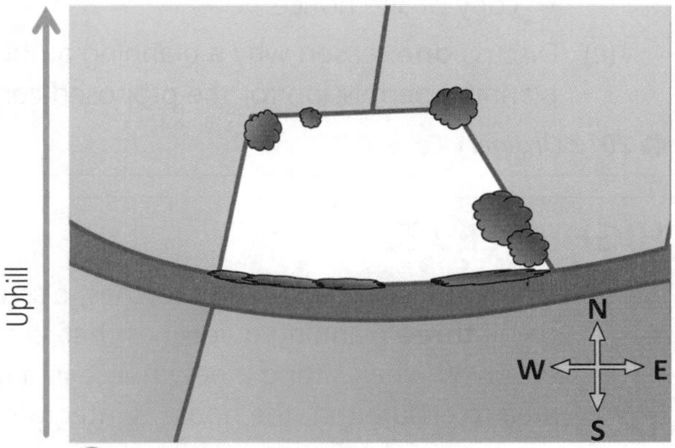

Sample site layout 2

N W E S

Uphill

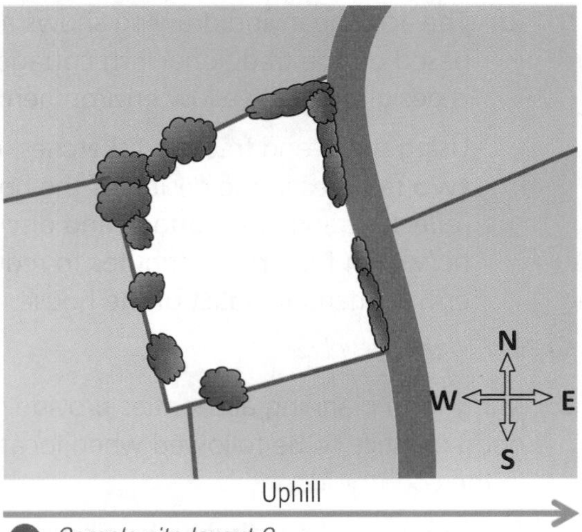

Sample site layout 3

N W E S

Uphill

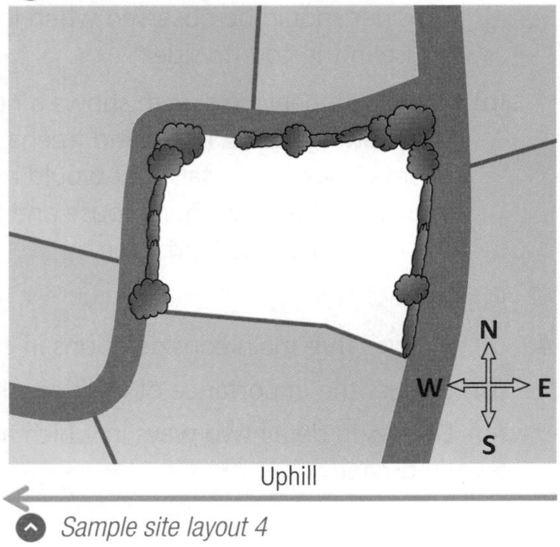

Sample site layout 4

THEORY QUESTIONS

ORDINARY LEVEL

1. A homeowner wishes to obtain planning permission to convert an existing garage to a living room, as shown in the accompanying sketch.

(a) Discuss two reasons why it is necessary to apply for planning permission to convert the garage to a living room.

(b) Outline the information that must be contained in **each** of the following documents when making a planning application to the planning authority:

- site location map
- copy of site notice.

(c) Discuss **one** reason why a planning authority might refuse planning permission for the proposed conversion.

2012 Ordinary Level Q7

HIGHER LEVEL

2. (a) Using notes and freehand sketches, discuss in detail **three** planning guidelines that should be observed when sitting a new house in a rural area to ensure that the house is integrated sensitively into the landscape.

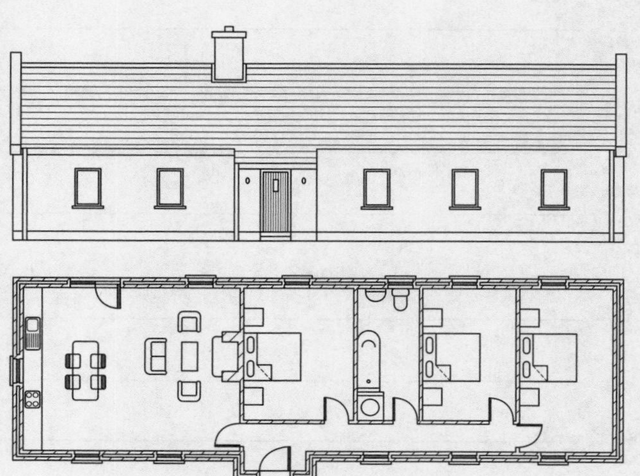

(b) The accompanying drawing shows a house based on the traditional Irish cottage. The house is designed to have low environmental impact.

Using notes and freehand sketches, outline **two** features in the design of the house that reflect a traditional cottage and discuss in detail how each feature contributes to reducing the environmental impact of the house.

2007 Higher Level Q6

3. Many local planning authorities provide guidelines outlining good practice to be followed when locating a dwelling house in the countryside.

(a) Discuss in detail **three** planning guidelines that you consider should be observed when locating a dwelling house in the countryside.

(b) The accompanying sketch shows a newly built house in a rural setting. Using notes and freehand sketches, outline in detail **two** proposals that would minimise the visual impact of the newly built house and thus help integrate the house into the landscape.

2006 Higher Level Q6

4. (a) Outline **five** main considerations in choosing a site for a dwelling house.

(b) Discuss the importance of each consideration you have listed at (a).

(c) Discuss in detail two ways in which a new house can be made to harmonise with the surrounding landscape.

2000 Higher Level Q5

2

SITE SAFETY

☐ SAFE PASS COURSE

1. (a) The ____________________ has one of the highest rates for workplace accidents in Ireland each year.

(b) The ____ programme was initiated to combat this.

(c) Before working on a site, ____________ must have _______ the ____________.

(d) ____________, ____________ and other ____________________ who visit the site regularly must also have completed the Safe Pass course.

(e) The course must be retaken ____________________ to keep workers up to date with any changes that may have occurred in ____________________.

☐ HAZARDS AND RISKS

2. Explain the terms (a) *hazard* and (b) *risk*, giving an appropriate example in each case.

(a) ____

____

____

____

(b) ____

____

____

____

ASSESSING RISK

3. (a) A risk assessment of each site should be carried out by the ____________________.

(b) This is a written record identifying:

- ____________________________________
- ____________________________________
- ____________________________________

(c) When assessing risk, we must consider:

- the ________ of the risk.
- the ________ of occurrence.

(d) Once the ________ and ________ have been determined, they can be placed on a __________ to establish the ____________________ of the ______.

4. Give an example of a typical hazard encountered on a building site. Determine both the severity and likelihood of the hazard, giving reasons for your answer. Using the risk assessment matrix, determine the overall risk for the hazard.

Risk assessment matrix

		Severity				
		Slightly harmful	**Moderately harmful**	**Quite harmful**	**Very harmful**	**Extremely harmful**
Likelihood	**Highly unlikely**	Trivial	Tolerable	Tolerable	Moderate	Moderate
	Quite unlikely	Tolerable	Tolerable	Moderate	Moderate	Substantial
	Likely	Tolerable	Moderate	Moderate	Substantial	Substantial
	Quite likely	Moderate	Moderate	Substantial	Substantial	Intolerable
	Highly likely	Moderate	Substantial	Substantial	Intolerable	Intolerable

____

____

____

____

☐ PERSONAL PROTECTIVE EQUIPMENT (PPE)

5. (a) The most basic safety precaution is to wear ______________________.

(b) PPE does not __________ the hazard; it merely ____________________ caused in the event of an incident.

(c) Essential PPE includes:

- ____________________
- ____________________
- ____________________
- ____________________
- ____________________

(d) Every worker should have their ______ set of equipment.

(e) The __________, __________ and _______ should be worn at all times.

(f) When necessary, specialist PPE is supplied, such as:

- ____________________
- ____________________

☐ SAFETY SIGNAGE

6. (a) The __________ and __________ of signs are standardised to indicate different instructions.

(b) Workers and visitors are notified as to the risks present on the site by a large sign at the __________, indicating the ____________________ on that particular site.

7. Fill in the meaning of each sign type.

1. ____________________
2. ____________________
3. ____________________
4. ____________________

① ② ③ ④

☐ WORKING WITH UNDERGROUND SERVICES

8. (a) List three risks associated with working near underground services.

(b) Clearly outline how these risks can be avoided or reduced.

Locating services using a radar detector

☐ EXCAVATIONS

9. (a) Each year, many accidents occur during excavations on construction sites. Outline the hazards associated with excavating sites.

(b) Using notes and neat freehand sketches, outline preventive measures that can be put in place to reduce these risks.

☐ WORKING AT A HEIGHT

10. (a) On a building site, workers are often required to work at a height. Outline three potential hazards of working at heights.

____

____

____

(b) Outline preventive measures to reduce the risk of working at a height.

____

____

____

____

____

☐ SCAFFOLDING

11. (a) Scaffolding is used to provide ____________ when working at a height.

(b) There are risks associated with using scaffolding, which include:

- the scaffold ________ due to ____________ being placed on it.
- the scaffold ____________.
- a person ____________ the scaffold.
- ____________ from the scaffold ____________.

(c) These associated risks can be reduced by correct design and the scaffold being installed by a ____________.

(d) Methods for the safe transfer of loads from the scaffold to the ground include:

- ____________ resting on ____________.
- ____________, which stiffens the scaffolding and stops it swaying.
- ____________ for concrete blocks or roof tiles.
- ____________ to structures.

12. Label the illustration of a typical scaffolding set-up.

1. ____________
2. ____________
3. ____________
4. ____________
5. ____________
6. ____________
7. ____________

800 mm min.
950–1200 mm
400 mm min.
1
2
3
4
5
6
7

13. Methods for preventing workers and objects from falling off the scaffold include:

(a) when working above a height of __________, a ______________________________ must be fitted ____________________ above the platform.

(b) the installation of a _________________.

(c) the installation of an ________________________________ at least ___________________ above the _______________.

(d) the use of __________ to contain waste and ________________ falling.

(e) properly installed ____________________.

(f) attachments such as ____________________ and ____________________.

(g) scaffolding must be wide enough to allow workers to ________________________________. If it is going to be used for both workers and materials, it must be a ____________________________ wide.

ACCESS TO SCAFFOLDS

14. (a) When accessing scaffold, it is best practice to use ________________________.

(b) If a ____________________________________ is not used, follow these guidelines:

- Ladder stiles should project __________ above the platform.
- The top of the ladder stiles should be __________ to the scaffold to prevent __________.
- The base of the ladder should be ___________________ to prevent __________________________ ____________.
- The slope of the ladder should not exceed ____ to _____________________.
- The stiles should be __________ on _________________.

15. Sketch the correct angle position for a ladder.

16. Sketch the correct way to secure a ladder at the base of scaffolding.

☐ MACHINERY ON SITE

17. (a) Outline the risks associated with using machinery on a construction site.

(b) Outline preventive measures to reduce these risks.

18. Draw a sketch showing the correct use of bunting on a site.

☐ ELECTRICITY (CORDED POWER TOOLS)

19. (a) Outline the risks associated with using corded power tools on a site.

(b) Outline preventive measures that reduce these risks.

☐ YOUNGER WORKERS

20. Records show that younger workers are more at risk of having an accident than experienced workers. List the factors that contribute to this.

21. The following strategies can be adopted to create a safety culture for young workers:

(a) ______________________ with more experienced workers.

(b) ensuring they are fully ______________ to carry out the required tasks.

(c) regular ______________________.

(d) regular ______________________.

(e) undertaking the ______________________.

THEORY QUESTIONS

ORDINARY LEVEL

1. (a) List **two** specific safety precautions that should be observed in **each** of the following situations and give **one** reason for each safety precaution listed:

- manually lifting a load from a floor.
- placing concrete in a foundation trench from a ready-mix truck.

(b) Using notes and neat freehand sketches, describe **two** items of personal protective equipment that must be worn on a building site and discuss the importance of **each** item to ensure the personal safety of workers on a building site.

2012 Ordinary Level Q6

HIGHER LEVEL

2. (a) Identify **two** possible risks to personal safety associated with **each** of the following:

(i) fitting a concrete window-cill on the second storey of a dwelling house.

(ii) laying pipes in a deep trench.

(iii) excavating in an area where there are underground electrical cables.

(b) Using notes and freehand sketches as appropriate, outline **two** safety procedures that should be observed to eliminate **each** risk identified at **(a)** above.

(c) Discuss in detail **two** reasons why younger workers are more vulnerable to accidents on construction sites and suggest **three** strategies to encourage a safety culture in younger workers.

2008 Higher Level Q2

3. (a) Identify **two** possible risks to personal safety associated with **each** of the following:

(i) slating a steeply pitched roof of a two-storey house.

(ii) working around a stairwell prior to having the stairs fitted.

(iii) placing a ladder against a scaffold.

(b) Using notes and freehand sketches, discuss in detail **two** safety precautions that should be observed to eliminate **each** risk outlined at **(a)** above.

(c) Discuss in detail **three** reasons that make a construction site a high-risk area for accidents at work.

2007 Higher Level Q2

4. (a) Identify **two** possible risks to personal safety associated with each of the following:

(i) scaffolding.

(ii) deep excavation.

(iii) use of electrical tools out-of-doors.

(b) Using notes and freehand sketches as appropriate, outline **two** specific safety precautions that demonstrate best practice in order to eliminate **each** risk identified at **(a)** above.

(c) Under the Safety, Health and Welfare at Work Regulations, it is compulsory for employers to have a safety statement. Discuss in detail **two** benefits of such a safety statement for employees in the construction industry.

2006 Higher Level Q2

SITE LAYOUT AND EXCAVATIONS

☐ PRELIMINARY WORKS

1. Topsoil is the top __________ of soil.

2. Why is the topsoil removed before foundations are laid?

____

____

____

____

☐ SETTING OUT THE SITE

3. (a) A baseline/datum point is a ________________ with a ________________.

(b) A baseline/datum point is important in construction because the outline of the building is __________ and ________________ from this line.

4. Using notes and neat freehand sketches, describe how the main lines of a building are set out.

____

____

____

____

____

____

____

____

5. Label the diagram showing the typical layout of a site.

1. ______________________________
2. ______________________________
3. ______________________________
4. ______________________________
5. ______________________________
6. ______________________________

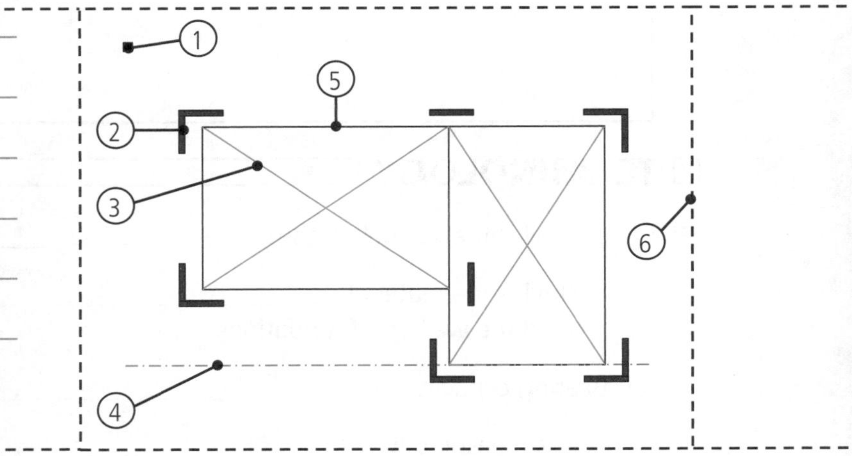

6. On the diagram provided, show how the profile boards should be checked for square. Use notes to explain your answer.

____

____

____

____

Check the profile boards for square

7. A builder is excavating a trench for building the foundations of a detached house. Using notes and neat freehand sketches, describe the stages of excavating this trench.

____

____

____

____

____

☐ TERMINOLOGY

8. (a) Subsoil is the soil below the __________. The __________ is about __________ deep.

(b) Backfill is the material ____________________ from the site. If it is suitable, it is used to fill in around the wall and foundations.

(c) Bearing capacity is the ______________________________ which the ground can carry.

This is measured in ______________________________ (N/m^2).

THEORY QUESTIONS

1. (a) With the aid of neat sketches, explain the procedure and method you would use when setting out a foundation for a garden wall to be built at right angles to the back wall of a dwelling.

(b) Write a short note on the following structural design terms:

(i) site datum

(ii) boning rods

(iii) site profiles

(iv) imposed loads

(v) dead loads

2. To prevent blockages in drainage pipes, it is vital that the pipes are laid at an appropriate fall in the direction of flow. Describe how a laser level can be used to check the pipe is being laid at the correct fall. Illustrate your answer using appropriate sketches.

3. In your own words, describe the process of preparing a green field site from initial preparation to marking out the site layout. Explain your answer by giving reasons for each key stage of the process.

☐ FOUNDATIONS

1. List the functions of a foundation.

____

____

____

____

2. (a) Settlement is the tendency of a building to ________ into the ground.
This is natural in all new buildings and will occur slowly over a period of years.

(b) As long as the building settles __________ (________________________),
there are generally no issues.

(c) Differential settlement occurs when one area of the foundation settles at

______________________________. This can lead to ________________ and

________________.

3 . In the spaces provided, draw sketches to explain each of the five most common causes of differential settlement.

Difference in bearing capacity

Frost heave

Soil contraction

Soil expansion

Foundation overloading

4. On the diagram provided, indicate how far away a tree should be planted from a building.

How far away a tree should be planted

5. List the design features of a foundation.

____

____

____

☐ DESIGN FEATURES OF FOUNDATIONS

1 WIDTH/PROPORTIONS

6. (a) Foundations work ______________ of the walls across ______________ to ______________ on the subsoil. This spreads the load over a greater area.

(b) Pressure = force per unit area. This means an increase in ________ results in a decrease in the ______________ to the soil.

7. Traditional strip foundations are always three times wider than the overall width of the wall, and the depth of the foundation is the same thickness as the wall. On the diagram provided, show these proportions.

Proportions of a foundation

2 RIGIDITY

8. Rigidity is a key design principle. Concrete beams and foundations are reinforced with steel bars to achieve rigidity. Using notes and neat freehand sketches, explain how the addition of steel bars achieves rigidity.

____

____

____

____

____

____

____

Foundation without steel reinforcement

Foundation with steel reinforcement

9. On the diagram provided, indicate the height at which reinforcing bars are located above the base of a foundation.

Height of reinforcing bars

3 MATERIALS

10. Foundations are made from concrete. Typically a ________ mix of concrete is used:

- ________ cement.
- ________ fine aggregate (sand).
- ________ coarse aggregate (gravel).

11. When using concrete in a foundation, air voids in the mix will ________________________________

____.

12. A builder must remove air voids from a freshly poured concrete mix. Using notes and neat freehand sketches, describe two methods the builder could use to remove air voids.

____

____

____

____

____

____

____

____

____

____

____

____

____

____

Method 1

Method 2

13. The following factors affect the strength of concrete in a foundation:

(a) incorrect placement and/or sizing of ____________.

(b) foundation placed at an ____________, which can lead to further settlement.

(c) pouring the foundation in inappropriate weather conditions, such as ____________________

____

____.

(d) placing the block work on a fresh slab ____________________.

(e) using an incorrect ____________ ratio.

(f) having too much ____ in the mix, caused by insufficient vibration/compaction of the concrete.

14. There are many types of foundation design used in modern buildings. Each foundation must be designed for the particular building. List the factors that must be taken into account.

____

____

____

____

15. Name four categories of foundation.

____

____

____

____

16. Complete the following table, listing the criteria for selecting a type of foundation.

Foundation type	Soil type	Bearing capacity of the soil
Typical strip foundation		Good bearing capacity
Raft foundation	Firm clay, soft clay, silt, loose gravel	
	Very soft clay, peat, loose gravel	Very poor bearing capacity Very poor bearing capacity on top but firmer soil deeper down

☐ STRIP FOUNDATIONS

17. Strip foundations are the most common type of foundation used for domestic dwellings. A strip foundation is a foundation that runs along the full length of each load-bearing wall. In the box provided, draw a sketch to show how a strip foundation runs along the perimeter of a house.

18. Strip foundations are best suited for situations where:

(a) the weight of the building is ______________________________.

(b) the weight of the building is ______________.

(c) the structural design of the building is ______________.

19. Draw arrows on the diagram to indicate the direction in which the weight exerted by the wall will spread out.

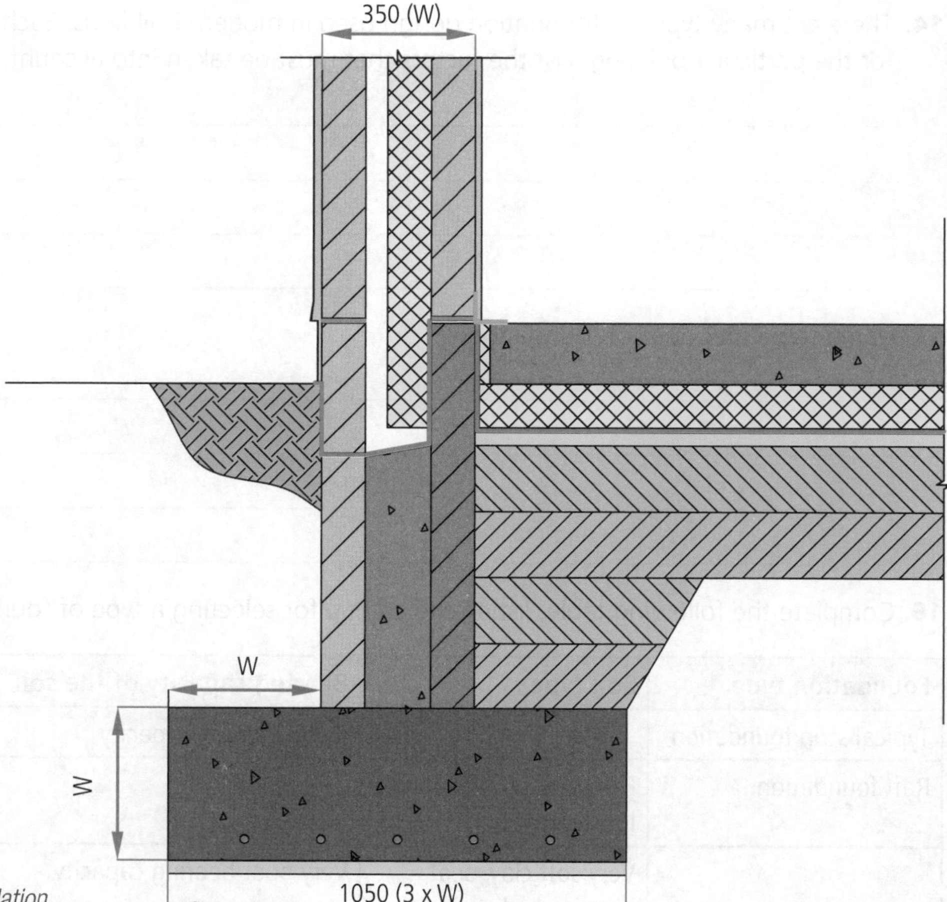

Weight distribution by a foundation

20. Weight exerted by the wall spreads out at ____° from the base of the wall to the soil. Due to this, the __________ of the foundation from the wall is equal to the _______ of the foundation.

21. Label the pictorial view of a strip foundation.

1. ______________________
2. ______________________
3. ______________________
4. ______________________
5. ______________________
6. ______________________
7. ______________________

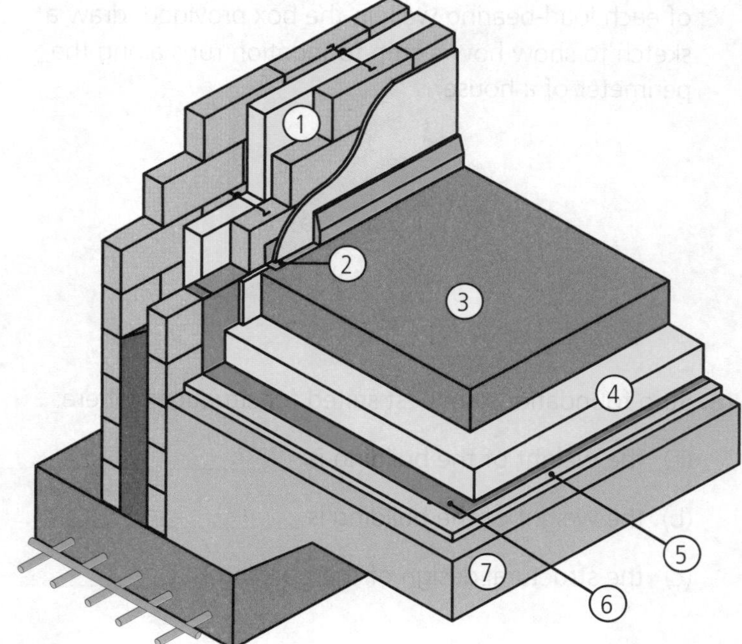

Pictorial view of a strip foundation

22. Label the sectional view of a strip foundation. Insert appropriate dimensions.

1. ______________________
2. ______________________
3. ______________________
4. ______________________
5. ______________________
6. ______________________
7. ______________________
8. ______________________
9. ______________________
10. ______________________
11. ______________________
12. ______________________
13. ______________________
14. ______________________
15. ______________________
16. ______________________
17. ______________________

Sectional view of a strip foundation

23. As an engineer, you have decided that a wide strip foundation is the most appropriate foundation to be used. Explain to your clients how a wide strip foundation functions, and why it is an economical choice of foundation. Use notes and neat freehand sketches to explain your answer.

____

24. A ______________________ is used if there is good bearing capacity rock near the foundation level. A trench is dug to reach the rock and concrete is poured in to fill the trench. This is an ______________________ foundation if the conditions are right.

25. Draw a sketch of a deep strip foundation.

26. In relation to construction, explain the term *hardcore*.

____

____

27. The building regulations state that hardcore should be compacted in layers with a minimum depth of __________ and a maximum depth of __________.

28. Hardcore can be sharp and jagged. How do builders on site prevent the hardcore from puncturing the radon membrane?

____

____

29. (a) On sloping sites, it may be necessary to use a __________ foundation.

(b) This reduces the amount of __________, __________ and __________ needed.

(c) To improve __________, steps are arranged to suit the height of the block work (__________).

(d) The diagram shows a typical foundation detail. Label the diagram and insert key measurements.

☐ RAFT FOUNDATIONS

30. A couple have decided to build a house. An investigation of the site has determined that the soil is of poor bearing capacity. As their engineer, you have recommended a raft foundation. Using notes and a neat freehand sketch, briefly describe the concept of a raft foundation.

____

____

____

____

31. (a) Rafts are used in areas where the soil is of __________ capacity.

(b) Spreading the weight of the building across the entire floor area considerably reduces the chance of __________ as the building 'floats' on the subsoil.

(c) Raft foundations are thickened at the edges and under load-bearing walls to __________ where needed.

32. Using notes and neat freehand sketches, describe the stages of raft construction.

33. Label the sectional view of a raft foundation. Insert appropriate measurements.

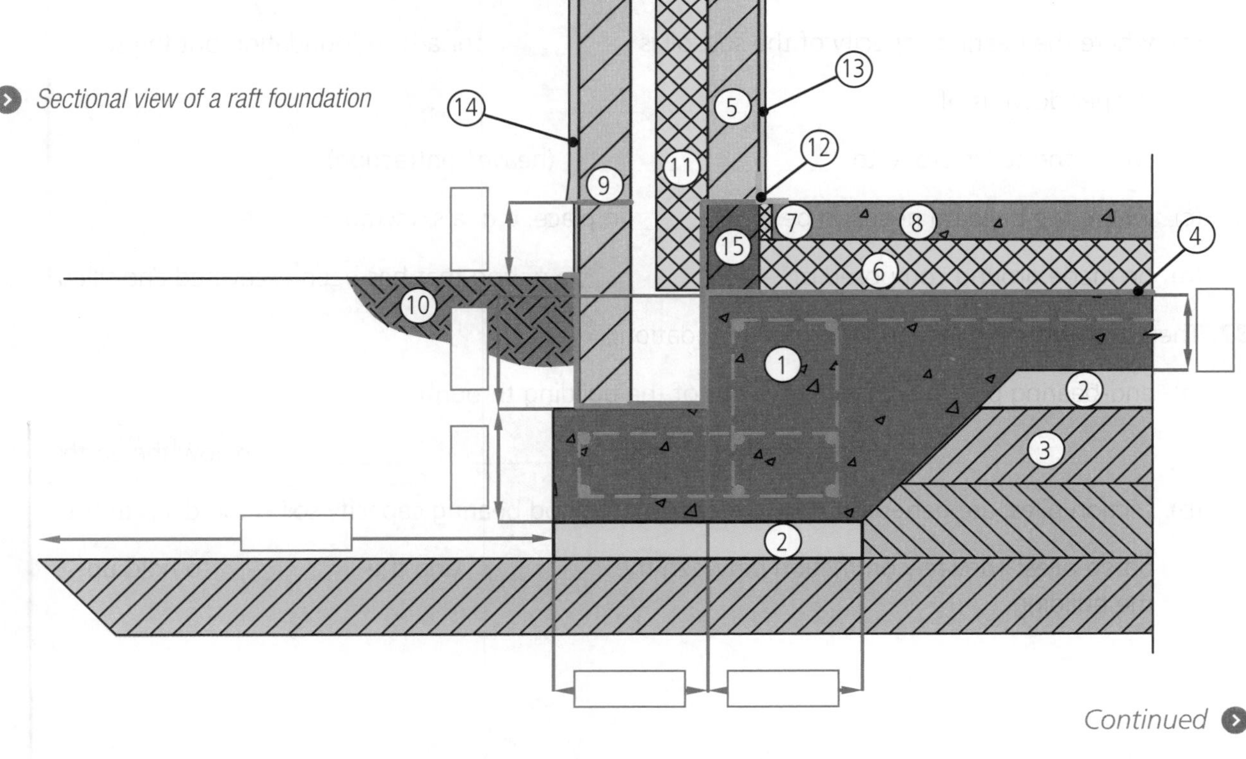

Sectional view of a raft foundation

Continued

1. ____________________

2. ____________________

3. ____________________

4. ____________________

5. ____________________

6. ____________________

7. ____________________

8. ____________________

9. ____________________

10. ____________________

11. ____________________

12. ____________________

13. ____________________

14. ____________________

15. ____________________

☐ PILE FOUNDATIONS

34. Using notes and a neat freehand sketch, briefly explain the concept a pile foundation.

35. A building's load is transferred to the piles through a reinforced concrete ring beam. Is the ring beam itself considered a foundation? Give a reason for your answer.

36. Piles are used:

(a) where the bearing capacity of the subsoil is __________ for a strip foundation but the soil deeper down is of ____________________.

(b) where the soil is prone to _______________ (heave/contraction).

(c) where the building needs to be __________ in place, e.g. a skyscraper.

(d) on made ground composed of __________, e.g. bog that has been excavated and filled.

37. There are two main categories of pile foundation:

(a) end-bearing piles: transfer the weight of the building through ____________________ to ____________________ below the earth.

(b) friction piles: are generally used in areas where good bearing capacity soil is too deep to use bored piles. They rely on friction between the __________ and the __________ to hold up the building.

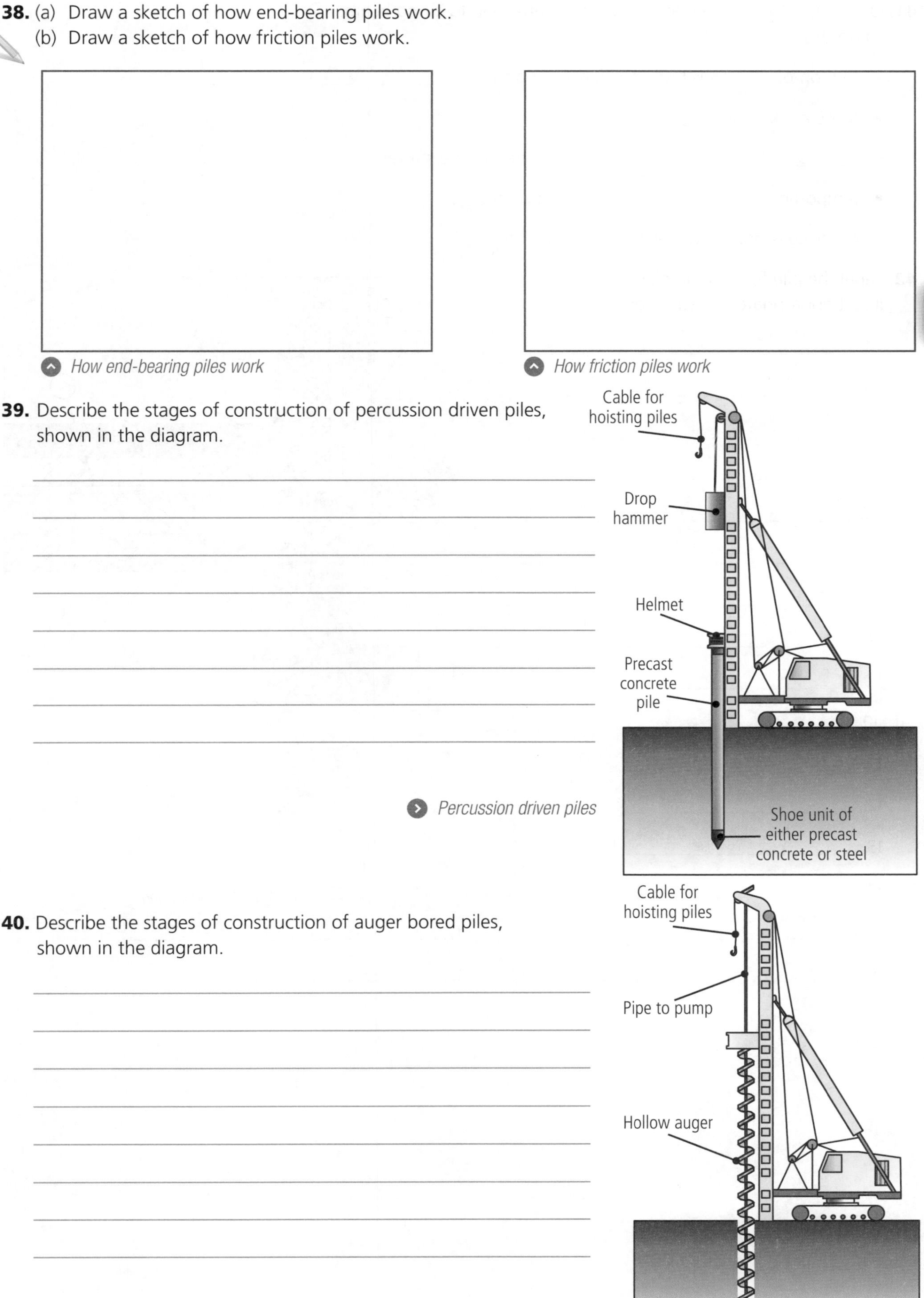

38. (a) Draw a sketch of how end-bearing piles work.
(b) Draw a sketch of how friction piles work.

How end-bearing piles work

How friction piles work

39. Describe the stages of construction of percussion driven piles, shown in the diagram.

Percussion driven piles

40. Describe the stages of construction of auger bored piles, shown in the diagram.

Auger bored piles

41. Once a pile has been created, it must be attached to a ring beam.
To do this:

- the top of the pile is broken off, exposing the ______________________________.
- these are known as ______________.
- a ______________________________ is tied to the starter bars.
- temporary ____________ is built around the cage.
- concrete is poured to create the ring beam.

42. Label the pile foundation diagram.
Insert appropriate measurements.

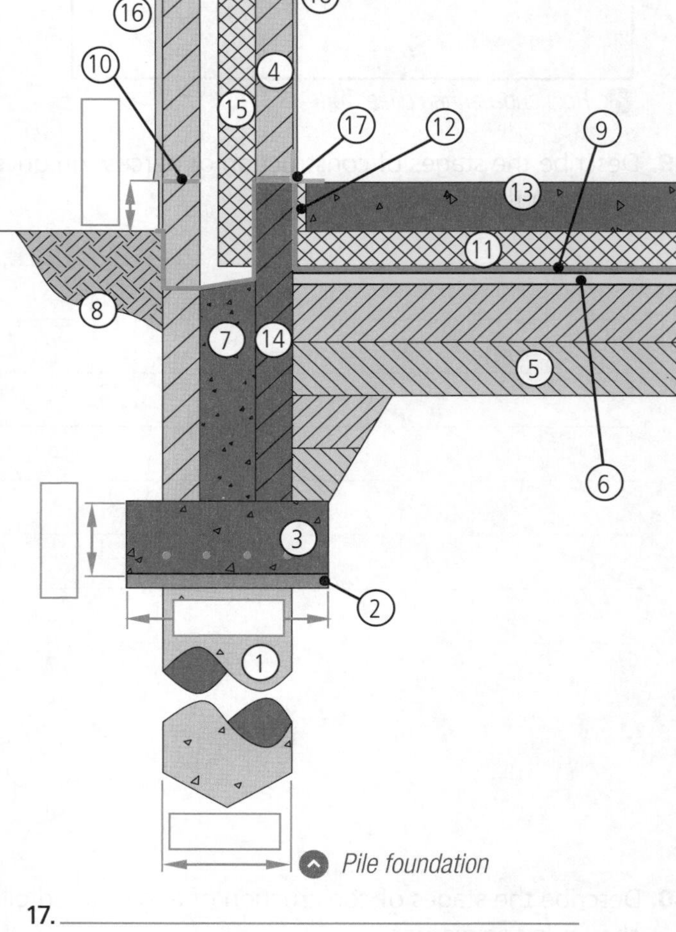

Pile foundation

1. ______________________________
2. ______________________________
3. ______________________________
4. ______________________________
5. ______________________________
6. ______________________________
7. ______________________________
8. ______________________________
9. ______________________________
10. ______________________________
11. ______________________________
12. ______________________________
13. ______________________________
14. ______________________________
15. ______________________________
16. ______________________________
17. ______________________________
18. ______________________________

THEORY QUESTIONS

ORDINARY LEVEL

1. A strip foundation is designed to support a 350 mm external wall of a dwelling house. The wall is of concrete block construction with an insulated cavity, as shown in the sketch.

(a) Describe, using notes and neat freehand sketches, the design of a typical strip foundation for the above external wall under the following headings:

- width and depth of trench
- finished level of concrete in foundation
- reinforcement of foundation
- position of wall on strip foundation

(b) Discuss **two** environmental reasons why a strip foundation is the preferred foundation type for the external wall of the house.

2012 Ordinary Level Q4

HIGHER LEVEL

2. Investigations indicate that a site on which a house is to be built has a moderately firm clay subsoil. Consideration is being given to using either a traditional strip foundation or a raft foundation.

(a) Show, with the aid of notes and freehand sketches, the design detailing for **each** type of foundation listed above. Indicate typical dimensions for each foundation.

(b) Recommend **one** of the above foundation types for the house and give **two** reasons in support of your recommendation.

(c) Identify **two** factors that could adversely affect the strength of concrete in a foundation.

2006 Higher Level Q4

3. (a) Discuss the importance of the use of steel in the manufacture of reinforced concrete, with reference to the:

(i) strength properties of both materials.

(ii) design considerations to avoid deterioration over time.

(b) Describe in detail, using sketches and notes, three methods of combining concrete and steel in the manufacture of concrete lintels.

(c) List **one** advantage of each method described in (b).

2002 Higher Level Q3

4. Trial holes indicate that the site on which a house is to be built has a loose gravel subsoil.

(a) Discuss in detail the considerations governing the choice of foundation for this house.

(b) Describe, with the aid of notes and detailed sketches, **two** types of foundation that would be suitable for the house.

(c) In the case of each type of foundation selected, state clearly **two** reasons why it is considered suitable.

2002 Higher Level Q5

GROUND FLOORS

☐ FUNCTIONS AND FEATURES

1. What are the functions of a ground floor?

2. Complete the list of design features of a ground floor.

(a) Strength and stability: Floors must be able to safely carry the ____________ ____________. This includes a range of ________ and ________ loads.

(b) Material selection: Material selection can have a large effect on the ________ and ________ qualities of the floor. For example, a tiled floor is easier to clean than a carpeted floor, but a carpeted floor creates a cosier environment.

(c) Durability: Floors must be made to last the ________ of the building without ________ or ________.

(d) Moisture and gas resistance: Ground floors must prevent any ________ or ________ from entering the building.

(e) Thermal insulation: Floors must be properly ________ to prevent ________ escaping through the floor. The floor should not act as a ________.

☐ STRENGTH AND STABILITY

3. By using notes and completing this diagram, explain what a dead load is.

Indicate how dead loads are transferred through the building

4. By using notes and completing this diagram, explain what a live load is.

Indicate how live loads are transferred through the building

☐ MATERIAL SELECTION

5. Using notes and neat freehand sketches, explain why hardcore filling is placed underneath a floor.

____

____

____

____

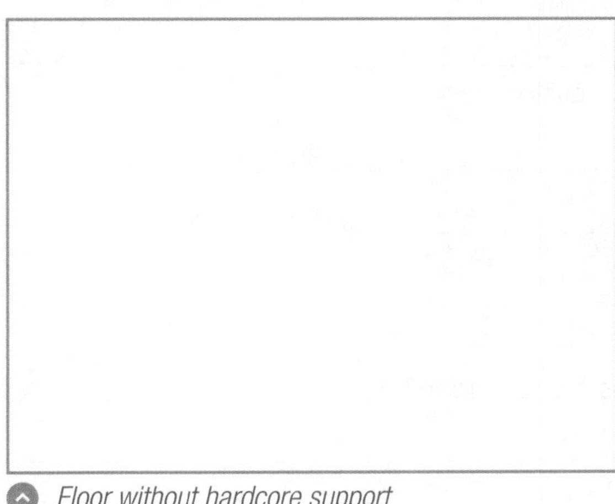

Floor without hardcore support

Floor with hardcore support

6. (a) To prevent any ____________ of the hardcore, it should be laid in layers not exceeding ________.

(b) Each layer is compacted with a ______________________________ to prevent __________ once the floor is constructed.

☐ MOISTURE AND GAS RESISTANCE

7. What is damp-proof course, shown in the diagram?

____

____

____

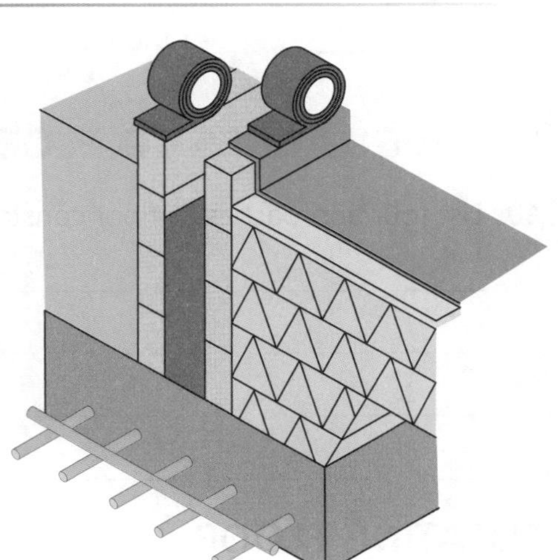

Damp-proof course

8. Indicate on the diagram the minimum height damp-proof course should be located above ground level.

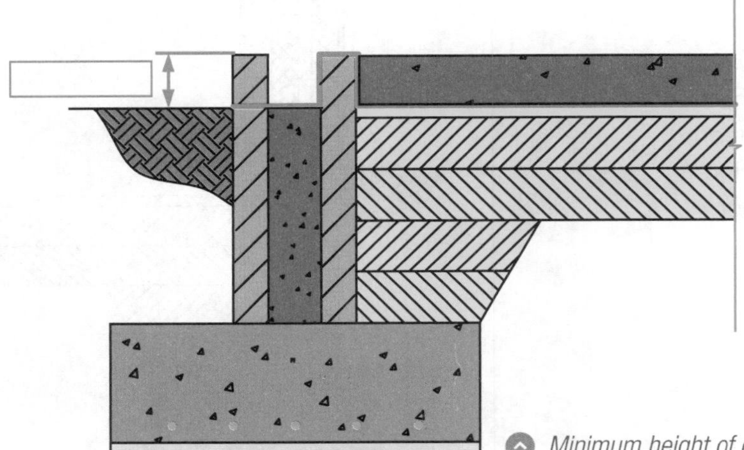

Minimum height of damp-proof course above ground level

9. On the diagram, draw a line to represent the correct position of damp-proof course. Using arrows, explain how a damp-proof course prevents moisture rising.

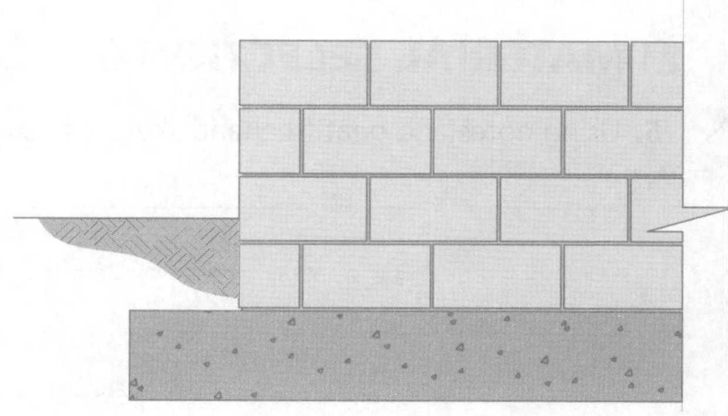

Position of damp-proof course and how it works

10. (a) In addition to damp-proof course, a ______________________________ is used to prevent moisture and gas from entering a building at floor level.

(b) To prevent the sharp hardcore from tearing the ____________________, 30 mm ____________________ is laid between the ____________________ and the hardcore.

☐ THERMAL INSULATION

11. What measures can be taken to prevent a floor acting as a cold bridge?

____

____

☐ DURABILITY

12. (a) The durability of a floor is determined by the durability of the ____________________.

(b) Different floor finishes can be used depending on the ______________ or ______________ of the floor.

☐ APPROACHES TO FLOOR CONSTRUCTION

13. List four approaches to floor construction.

____

____

____

____

FLOATING FLOOR

14. The diagram shows an incomplete drawing of a floating floor. For a floating floor, the main floor slab is poured over the insulation. Complete the diagram. Label the following parts on it: underfloor insulation, subfloor and edge insulation.

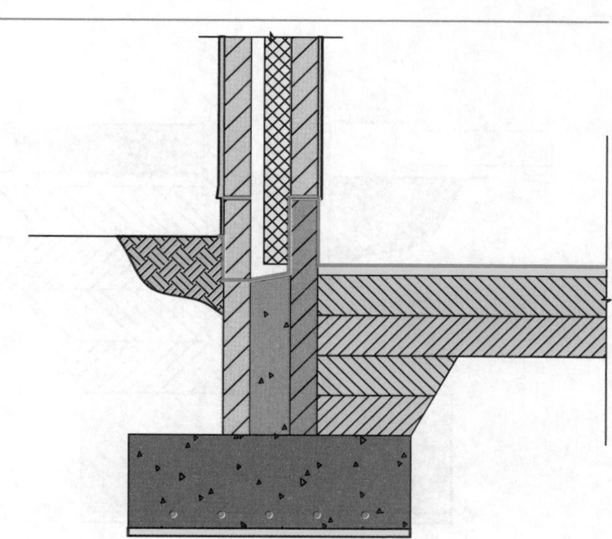

A partial drawing of a floating floor

SLAB AND SCREED FLOOR

15. The diagram shows an incomplete drawing of a slab and screed floor. In this type of floor, the main floor slab is placed under the insulation and a finishing layer of sand cement screed is laid on top of the insulation. Complete the diagram. Label the following parts on it: underfloor insulation, subfloor, edge insulation and screed.

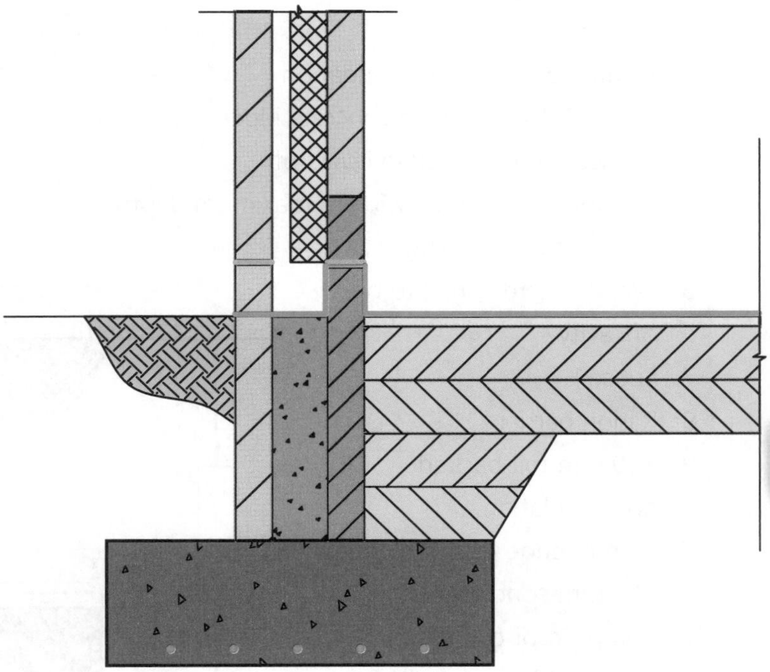

A partial drawing of a slab and screed floor

16. A couple building a home want to make an informed decision about the type of ground floor to install in their house. In the following table, compare the advantages and disadvantages of a floating floor and a slab and screed floor.

	Floating floor	Slab and screed floor
Advantages		
Disadvantages		

17. Complete the sectional view diagram of a solid timber floor. Insert the labels in the correct places. Add suitable measurements.

1. 30 mm sand blinding
2. Reinforced concrete foundation
3. 100 × 225 × 450 mm concrete block
4. Hardcore compacted in layers of 150 mm minimum, 225 mm maximum depth
5. 30 mm sand blinding
6. Weak concrete infill to base of cavity
7. Subsoil
8. Radon barrier
9. 100 mm foil-backed rigid insulation
10. 25 mm edge insulation
11. 150 mm concrete floor
12. Damp-proof course
13. Thermal block inner leaf rising wall
14. 100 mm foil-backed rigid insulation
15. 19 mm external render
16. Airtightness tape seals wall and floor
17. 12 mm internal render
18. Foam underlay
19. 150 x 25 mm engineered floor boards
20. 100 x 18 mm skirting board

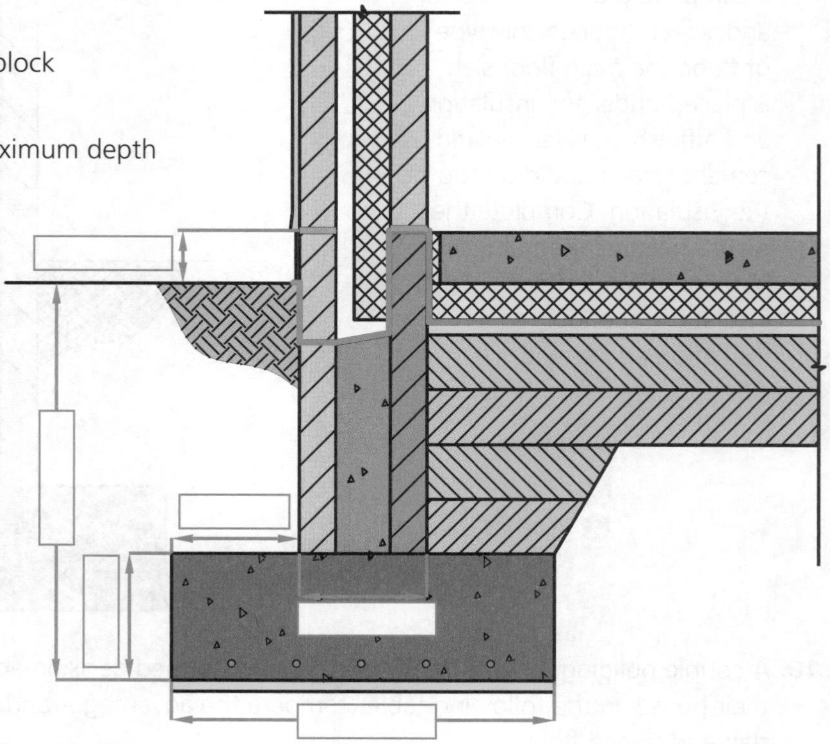

A sectional view of a timber floor

SUSPENDED TIMBER FLOOR

18. (a) What is a suspended timber floor?

____

(b) When might a suspended timber floor be chosen over a concrete floor?

____

____

19. (a) There are two types of suspended timber floor.

- The first uses ____________ wall. This is used when the depth of hardcore does ____________ 900 mm.
- The second uses ______________________________. This is used when the depth of hardcore ________ 900 mm.

(b) ______ are placed in the external wall for both types and spaces are left in the tassel wall to allow air to ________.

(c) This prevents the floor joist ______________ as ________ requires stale air to form.

20. On the diagram, label the tassel wall, the vent, the damp-proof course, the radon membrane, the wallplate and the joists.

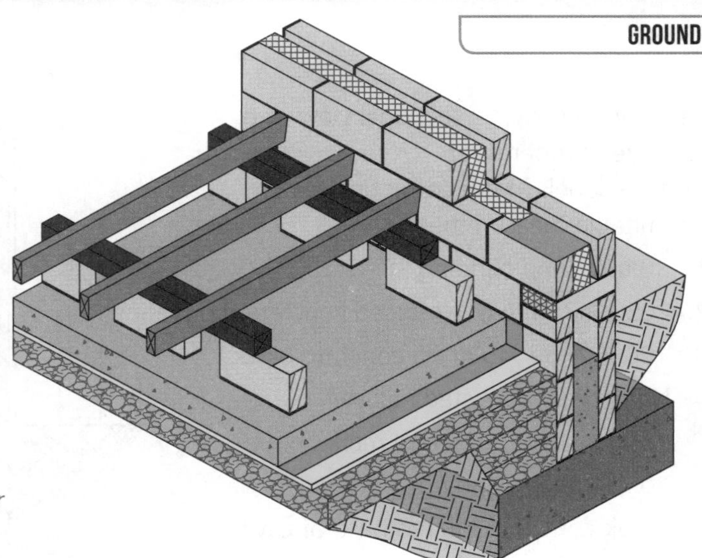

Suspended timber floor

21. In the following table, list the advantages and disadvantages of a suspended timber floor.

Advantages	Disadvantages

22. The diagram shows an airtightness membrane. What is the function of an airtightness membrane?

____

____

____

____

____

Airtightness membrane

Airtightness membrane

23. (a) Suspended timber floors are often used where the

________________________ exceeds 900 mm.

(b) At 900 mm, it is difficult to get the hardcore to ______________________

so a concrete floor can ____________________________.

(c) To prevent this, a __________ suspended timber floor is used. A hung floor consists of floor joists that are attached to the wall using

____________________________.

(d) For long spans, additional support can be supplied by

____________________________.

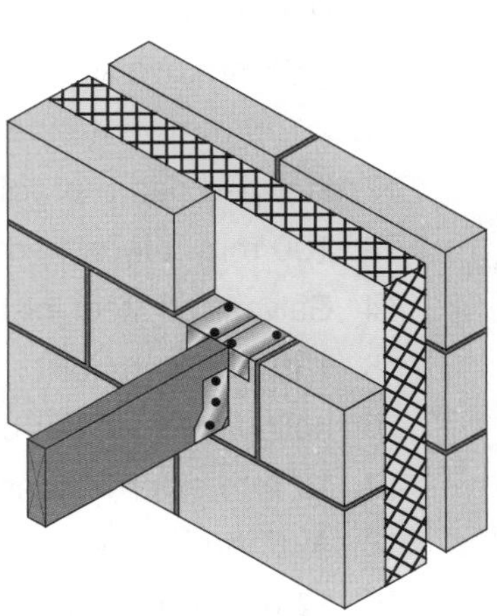

Galvanised steel hanger

24. The diagram shows a sectional view of a suspended timber floor.
Insert the labels in the correct places.
Add suitable measurements.

1. 30 mm sand blinding
2. 1050 × 350 mm reinforced concrete foundation
3. 100 × 225 × 450 mm concrete block
4. Hardcore compacted in layers of 150 mm min., 225 mm max. depth
5. 30 mm sand blinding
6. Weak concrete infill to base of cavity
7. Subsoil
8. Radon barrier
9. Damp-proof course
10. 150 mm oversite concrete (100 mm min.)
11. Tassel wall 2.13 m max. span
12. Damp-proof course
13. Ø100 mm vent pipe
14. 100 × 100 mm wallplate
15. Stepped damp-proof course
16. 100 mm foil-backed rigid insulation
17. 150 × 50 mm joist

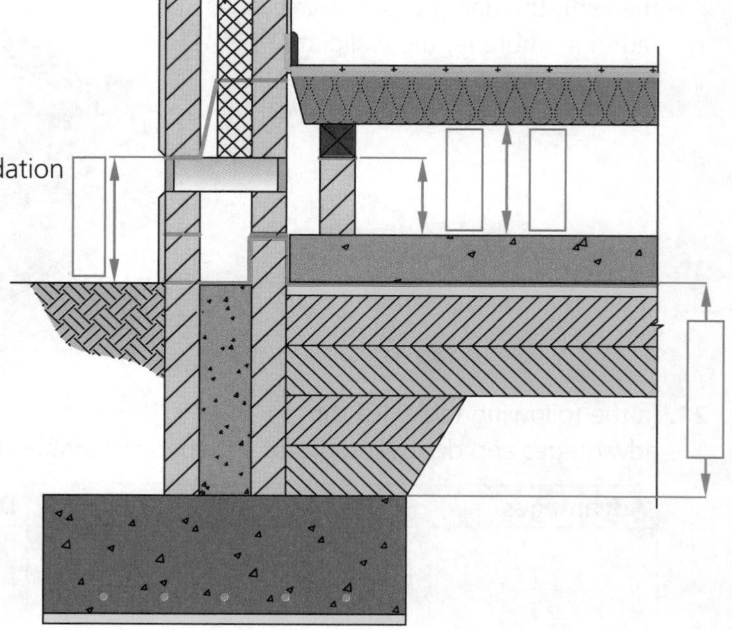

Sectional view of a suspended timber floor

18. Airtightness membrane taped to wall
19. 19 mm external render
20. 12 mm internal render
21. 150 × 25 mm T&G floor boards
22. 100 × 18 mm skirting board

25. The incomplete diagram shows a sectional view of a wall-hung, suspended timber floor.
Complete the diagram and insert the labels and suitable measurements.

1. 30 mm sand blinding
2. 1050 × 350 mm reinforced concrete foundation
3. 100 × 225 × 450 mm concrete block
4. Hardcore compacted in layers of 150 mm min., 225 mm max. depth
5. 30 mm sand blinding
6. Weak concrete infill to base of cavity
7. Subsoil
8. Radon barrier
9. Damp-proof course
10. 150 mm oversite concrete (100 mm min.)
11. Ø100 mm vent pipe
12. Stepped damp-proof course
13. 100 mm foil-backed rigid insulation
14. Galvanised steel joist hanger
15. 150 × 50 mm joist
16. Rolled steel joist (RSJ)
17. 19 mm external render
18. Airtightness membrane taped to wall
19. 12 mm internal render

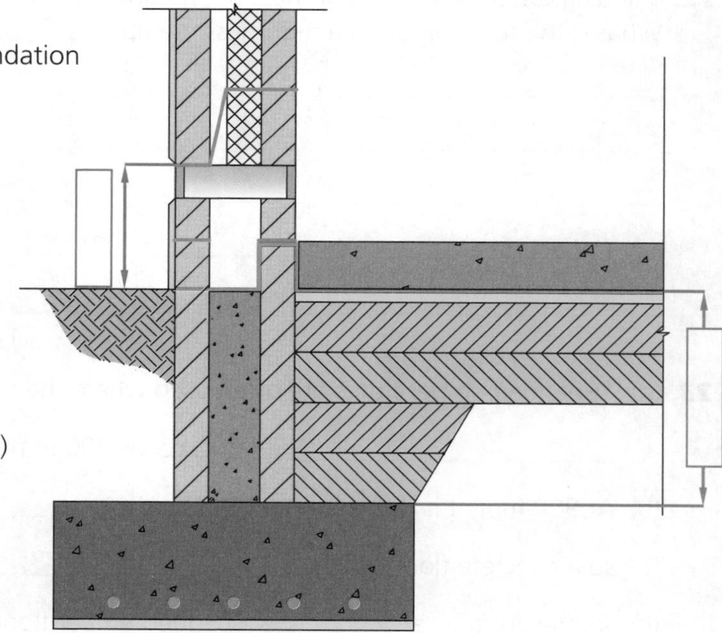

Sectional view of a wall-hung, suspended timber floor

20. 150 × 25 mm T&G floor boards
21. 100 × 18 mm skirting board

SUSPENDED CONCRETE FLOOR

26. (a) Suspended concrete floors are used as an alternative to ______________________________.

(b) They must be designed by a ______________________.

(c) There are two main types of suspended concrete floor:

- ____________________________
- ____________________________

27. A couple are building a home that requires a suspended floor. The couple want to make an informed choice on the type of floor to use. Their architect has informed them that they have the option to build a suspended concrete floor. In the following table, list the advantages and disadvantages of this type of floor.

Advantages	Disadvantages

28. (a) How does a cast on-site, suspended concrete floor differ to a cast on-site concrete floor?

____

____

(b) Why would a suspended concrete floor be used instead of a regular concrete floor?

____

____

29. Block and beam suspended concrete floors consist of pre-stressed concrete T-beams spanning the length of the building. Infill blocks are placed between the beams to make up the floor surface. Complete and label the sectional view of a block and beam floor.

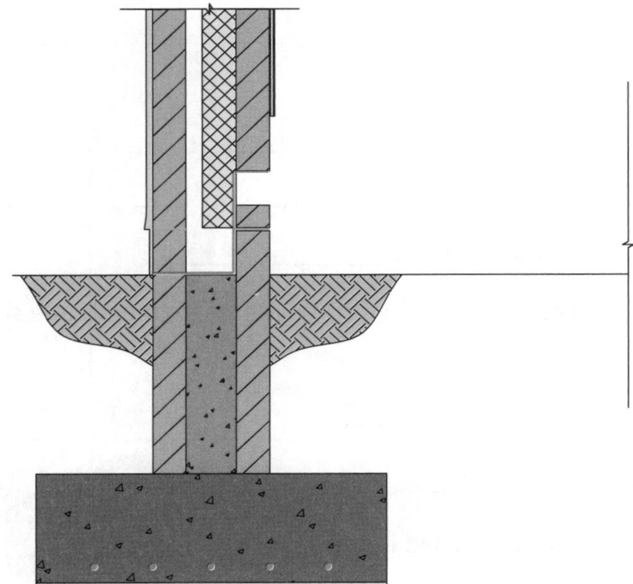

T-beams and infill blocks

☐ RADON

30. (a) Radon is a naturally occurring ______________________.

(b) It has no __________, __________ or __________ and it is virtually ____________ in a house without specialist equipment.

(c) If it gathers in an enclosed space, it can build up to __________________.

(d) ____________ exposure to radon gas has been proven to be a major cause of __________ in Ireland today.

(e) Radon is measured in ___________________________ per metre cubed (Bq/m³).

(f) ____________ is the recommended safe level of radon in domestic dwellings.

(g) ________ houses in Ireland are estimated to have a concentration of radon that exceeds __________.

31. On the diagram, show possible entry points for radon.

Radon entry points

32. What causes radon to enter a house?

____

____

____

33. Name two methods of preventing radon entering a house. Explain the principle behind each approach.

____

____

____

____

____

____

34. (a) Radon membrane also prevents ________________.

(b) It is usually installed by a ___________. The entire membrane should be __________, particularly around __________ and __________.

(c) The radon membrane must cover the _________________________ and across the ______________. This prevents radon entering the house through the ________________.

(d) Damp-proof course is still used in the __________ and ______________.

35. On the diagram, draw the radon membrane.

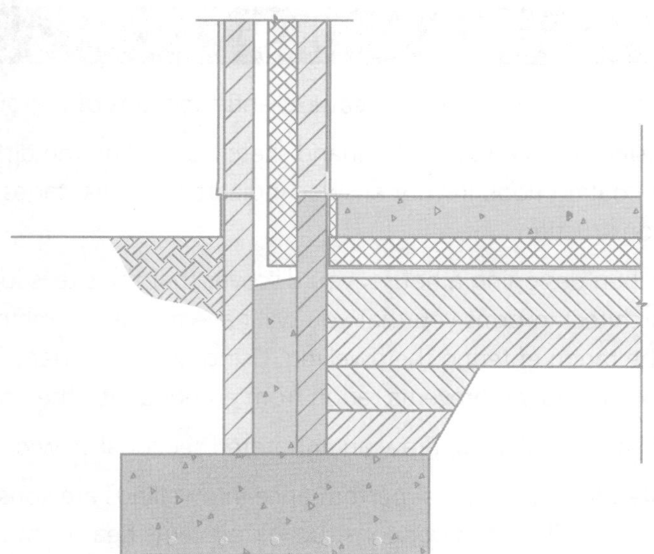

Insert the radon membrane

36. (a) Radon sumps are an ____________________ of preventing radon.

(b) A prefabricated plastic or homemade concrete box is placed in the ____________________.

Radon sump

37. After consulting the Radiological Protection Institute of Ireland's radon map, it was discovered that a house was being built in an area with a high concentration of radon gas. It was decided to use a radon sump in conjunction with a radon membrane.

How does a radon sump remove radon from a building? Use notes and neat freehand sketches to explain your answer.

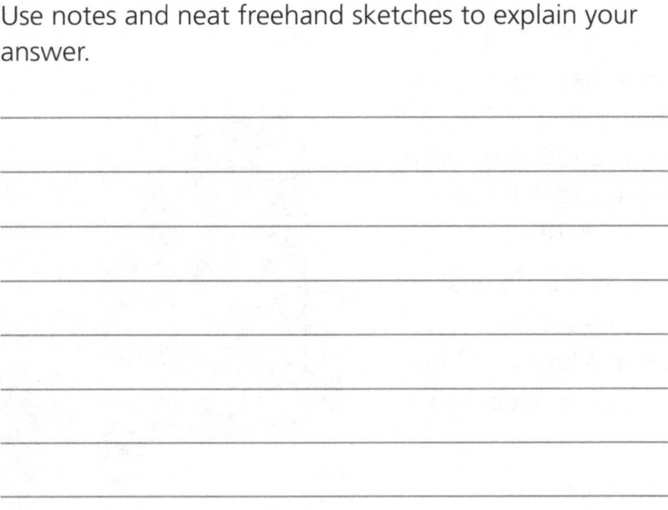

THEORY QUESTIONS

1. Describe the key design features and functions of a ground floor.
2. Using notes and neat freehand sketches, outline the differences between a slab and screed floor and a floating floor. In your answer, indicate the advantages and disadvantages of each method of floor construction.
3. When designing a house, you discover that the site is located in an area of high radon content. The architect informs you that you will have to use a combination of passive and active approaches to prevent the radon entering the dwelling. Using notes and neat freehand sketches, describe each approach and explain how it prevents radon from entering into the house.
4. To a scale of 1:10, draw an annotated sectional view of a suspended concrete floor.
5. Standards of thermal performance in dwellings are constantly improving. Describe three ways that a modern floating floor construction prevents heat from escaping out of a structure. Illustrate your answer with a neat annotated sketch.
6. In your own words, explain how dry rot can be prevented in a suspended timber floor. Illustrate your answer using neat annotated sketches.

ORDINARY LEVEL

7. A living room has a solid concrete ground floor with a 20 mm quarry tile finish as shown. The external wall of the living room is a 350 mm concrete block wall with an insulated cavity. The wall is plastered on both sides. The foundation is a traditional strip foundation.
   (a) To a scale of 1:5, draw a vertical section through the external wall and ground floor. The section should show all the construction details from the bottom of the foundation to 400 mm above finished floor level. Indicate the typical sizes of **four** main components.
   (b) Show on your drawing the typical design detailing to prevent a thermal/cold bridge at the junction of the concrete floor and the external wall.

2010 Ordinary Level Q1

HIGHER LEVEL

8. An insulated suspended timber ground floor abuts the external wall of a dwelling house, as shown in the accompanying sketch. The external wall is a 350 mm concrete block wall with a 150 mm cavity. Rigid insulation board is fixed in the cavity. The suspended timber floor has a 25 mm tongued and grooved hardwood finish.
   (a) To a scale of 1:5, draw a vertical section through the external wall and the suspended timber ground floor. The section should show all the construction details from the bottom of the foundation to 400 mm above finished floor level. Include **four** typical dimensions on your drawing.
   (b) Indicate clearly the position of a barrier that would prevent radon gas entering the dwelling.

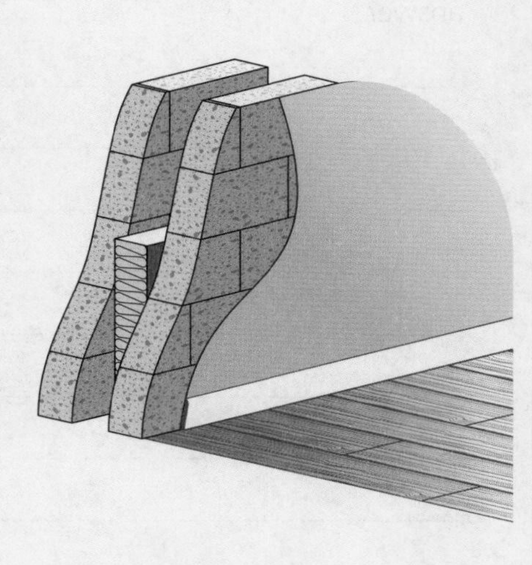

2009 Higher Level Q1

EXTERNAL WALLS

☐ FUNCTIONS AND FEATURES

1. What are the functions of an external wall?

2. List the design features of an external wall.

☐ DESIGN FEATURES

1 STRENGTH AND STABILITY

3. The strength and stability of a wall depends on three factors. Explain each factor.

(a) The components used:

(b) Its slenderness ratio:

(c) The distribution of the applied load:

4. Indicate on the diagram how the bonding of blocks disperses the applied load.

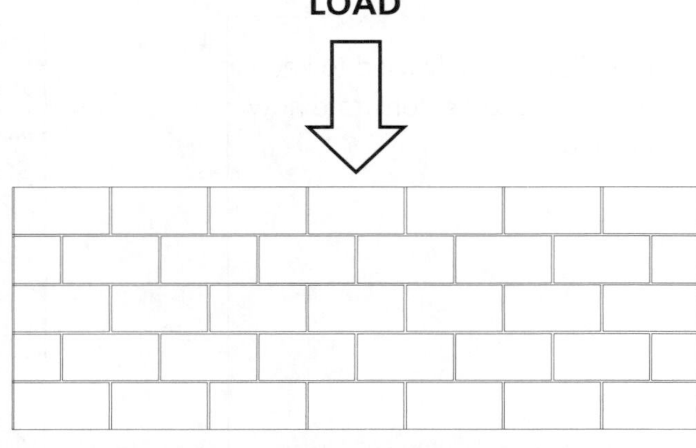

How the bonding of blocks disperses the applied load

2 WEATHER RESISTANCE

5. As Ireland's climate is so wet, preventing moisture penetration poses a significant challenge to any builder. Using notes and neat freehand sketches, describe three methods to prevent moisture penetration at an external wall.

Method 1: __________

Method 2: __________

Method 3: __________

3 FIRE RESISTANCE

6. In the event of a fire, walls should be built so that they remain stable for a minimum of __________ to allow enough time for a person to __________.

7. What does the fire resistance of a building depend on?

4 THERMAL INSULATION

8. Properly designed buildings should ensure that heat generated in the __________. Failing to do this results in __________, and an increase __________.

9. Rigid insulation between the walls is typically used to keep in the heat. On the diagram, use arrows to demonstrate how insulation keeps heat in a building.

How insulation keeps heat in a building

10. Use notes and neat freehand sketches to explain the thermal mass effect.

5 AIRTIGHTNESS

11. In relation to airtightness, explain the term *permeable*.

12. (a) What effect does the movement of air through a cavity wall have?

(b) Describe a method of preventing this.

13. Draw a sketch showing how to ensure airtightness.

6 ACOUSTIC INSULATION

14. Name and explain the factors that make a cavity wall a good insulator. Use notes and neat freehand sketches to elaborate your answer.

____

____

____

____

____

____

____

____

Factor 1

Factor 2

15. Indicate on the diagram the sizes of a standard brick and block.

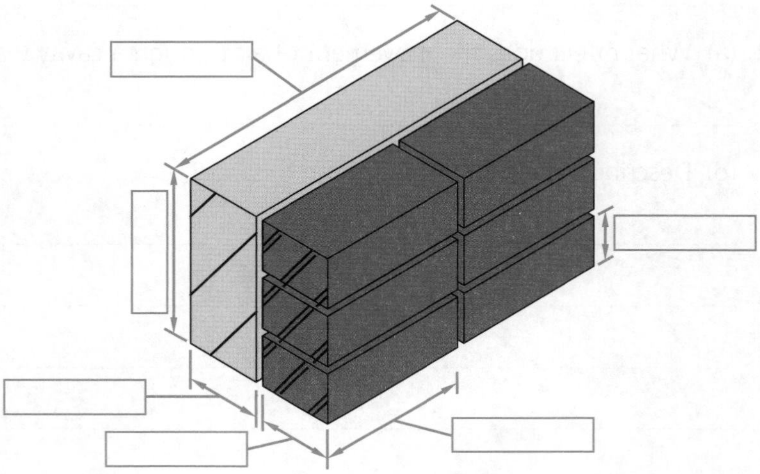

The sizes of a standard brick and block

7 AESTHETICS

16. (a) As most of the ______________________ of a house is made up of walls, the wall finish is hugely important for the ______________ of the overall building.

(b) The most common type of finishes include:

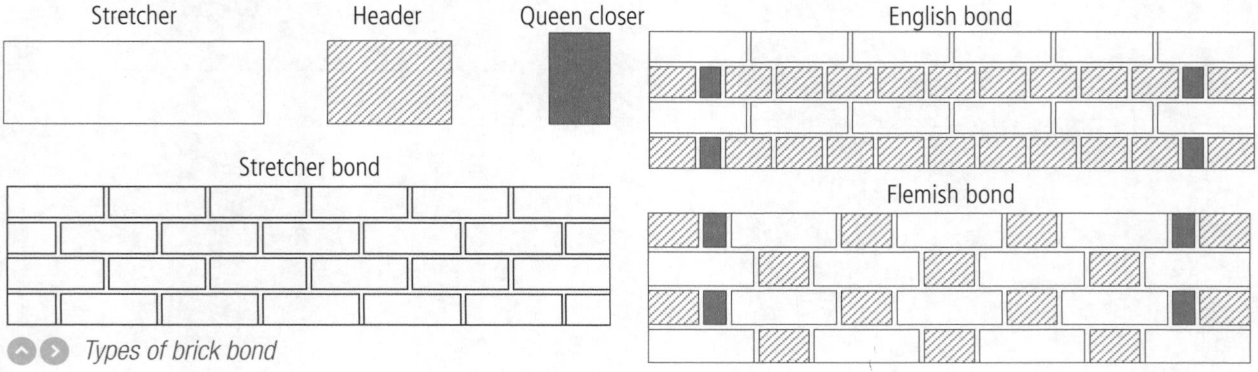

____

____

____

____

Stretcher

Header

Queen closer

English bond

Stretcher bond

Flemish bond

Types of brick bond

☐ CONCRETE CAVITY WALL CONSTRUCTION

17. The wall construction from the foundation to the initial floor level is known as ______________________ ______________________.

18. What is the purpose of cavity infill? Use neat freehand sketches to explain your answer.

____

____

____

____

No cavity infill

Cavity infill

19. Damp-proof course needs to be stepped on a sloped site so that it remains a minimum of 150 mm above ground level. On the diagram, use a coloured pencil or pen to indicate the location of the stepped damp-proof course.

Stepped Damp-proof course

☐ ABOVE DAMP-PROOF COURSE LEVEL AND INTERSTITIAL CONDENSATION

20. (a) Rigid insulation is placed within the cavity to ______________________.

(b) Insulation is able to ______________ due to pre-made grooves at the edges.

21. Wall ties have a drip as shown in the diagram. What is the function of a drip?

Drip in wall ties

____

____

____

22. What is the function of the timber board shown in the diagram?

____

____

____

____

____

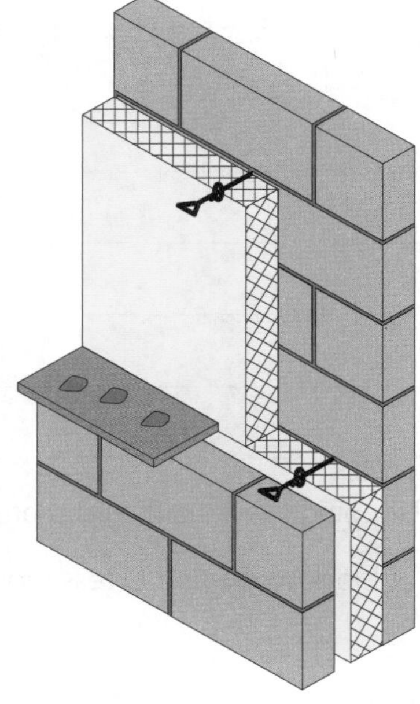

Laying of block work

23. You are a block layer who is training a new apprentice on site. Using notes and neat freehand sketches, explain to your apprentice what interstitial condensation is and how it can be prevented.

THERMAL LOOPING

24. Thermal looping can result from gaps between the inner leaf and the insulation. Explain, using notes and neat freehand sketches, the process of thermal looping.

25. Thermal looping can be difficult to prevent when using ______________________, as the rough surface of block work, and excess mortar can push the ______________ out from the ______________. ____________________________ and/or using ________________ will prevent thermal looping.

☐ WALL TIES

26. Wall ties hold insulation in place and prevent moisture bridging the cavity. Give another function of wall ties. Use neat freehand sketches to elaborate your answer.

____

____

____

____

No wall ties

With wall ties

____

____

27. On the diagram, indicate an appropriate spacing for wall ties for a wall with a 150 mm cavity.

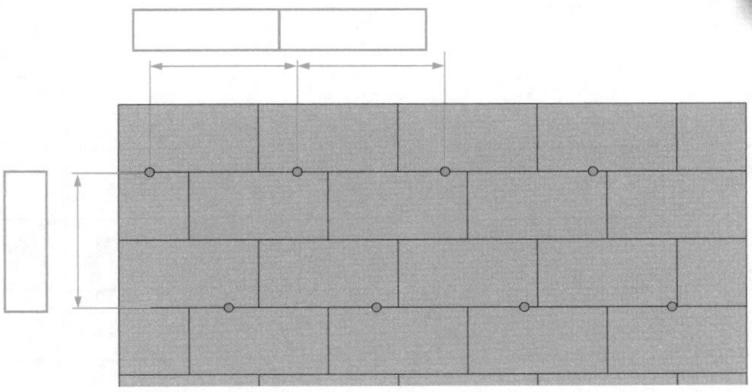

Wall ties spacing

☐ RENDERING

28. What criteria should any external render applied to a building meet?

____

____

____

____

29. The diagram shows the various coats that form an external render. Label each coat, giving a typical thickness for each.

1. ______________________________

2. ______________________________

3. ______________________________

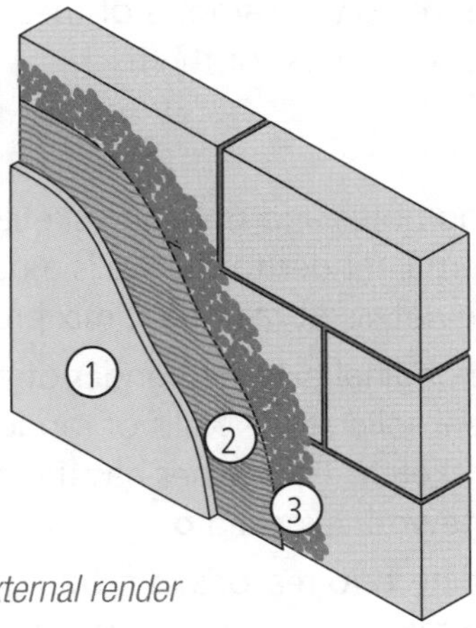

1
2
3

Coats of external render

30. (a) Dyed acrylic render is ______________________________ without paint.

(b) Acrylic render is applied in two coats of approximately ________ thickness.

TRADITIONAL RESOURCES

31. Before cement-based renders became popular, lime renders were used. Give two advantages of a lime render over a cement-based render.

32. You have recently purchased a Georgian farmhouse and have noticed that some of the lime render is in need of repair. Describe the stages involved in reapplying a lime render.

THEORY QUESTIONS

1. One of the primary functions of an external wall is to prevent the penetration of moisture into the dwelling. Describe three different approaches that can be used to achieve this.

2. There are many ways that poor workmanship and installation can lead to the reduced thermal performance of ridged insulation in a cavity wall construction. Explain three ways in which this can occur in a typical cavity wall construction. Outline how they can be prevented.

3. The design of a load-bearing external wall is such that it has to withstand a large number of imposed loads being placed on it from many different directions. Using notes and freehand sketches to illustrate your answer, give examples of these imposed loads and show how the design of a 150 mm cavity wall construction caters for them.

HIGHER LEVEL

4. (a) Using notes and freehand sketches, describe the application of an external render to the walls a new house of concrete block construction. Give details of materials, mix proportions and sequence of coats required.

(b) The original external render of an old house is to be removed to reveal solid stone walls of random rubble construction, as shown on the sketch. The owner has the option of either leaving the external stonework exposed ***or*** of replastering the walls.

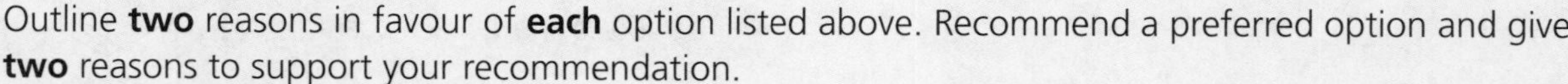

Outline **two** reasons in favour of **each** option listed above. Recommend a preferred option and give **two** reasons to support your recommendation.

(c) If the house is to be replastered, a 1 lime:3 sand mix is recommended for the external render. Give **two** reasons why such a mix is recommended for this house.

2004 Higher Level Q3

OPENINGS IN CAVITY WALLS

1. An opening (ope) is a ______________________ to facilitate windows and doors.

2. Problems caused by opes include:

(a) They create an area of ______________________.

(b) They leave an area from which ______________________ (thermal bridging).

(c) Opes create an area through which __________ can easily spread.

3. The weight above an opening in a wall must be spread to the surrounding wall. Lintels are used to spread this weight. On the diagram, label the lintel. Use arrows to indicate how the lintel spreads the weight above it to the surrounding block work.

Lintel

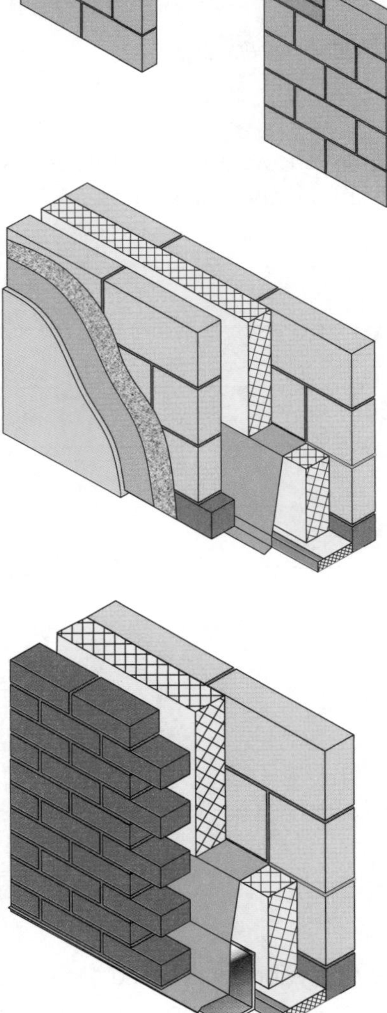

CLOSING THE CAVITY AROUND OPES

4. Where concrete blocks are used, pre-stressed concrete lintels are installed. Prefabricated cavity closers are used to close the cavity, and damp-proof course is placed over the lintel to prevent moisture bridging the lintel. Label the underlined terms on the diagram.

Concrete lintel

5. Where brick work or full fill insulation is used, rolled steel lintels are installed. Steel lintels come pre-packed with insulation, and damp-proof course is placed over the lintel to prevent moisture bridging the lintel. Label the underlined terms on the diagram.

Steel lintel

6. (a) It is important to properly ____________ the cavity space around an ope.

(b) If this is not done correctly, __________ can easily ____________ of the building.

(c) Heat can also escape across solid components by ________________.

7. (a) What is a thermal bridge?

(b) List some problems associated with a thermal bridge.

8. On the diagram, show how thermal bridging can be avoided behind the window-cill.

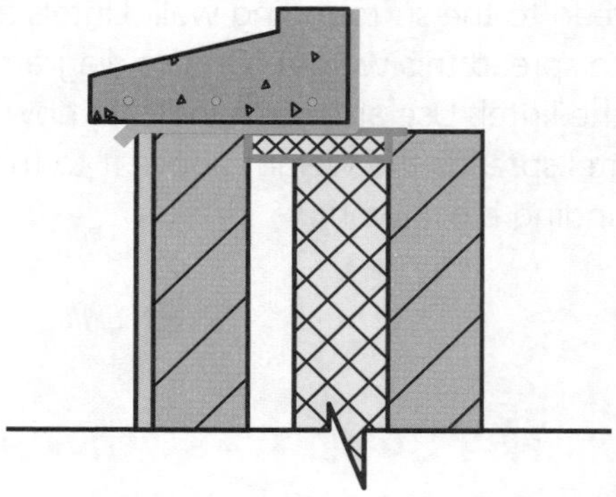

Avoiding thermal bridging

9. The diagram shows a section through a window lintel. Label the section.

1.
2.
3.
4.
5.
6.
7.
8.
9.
10.
11.

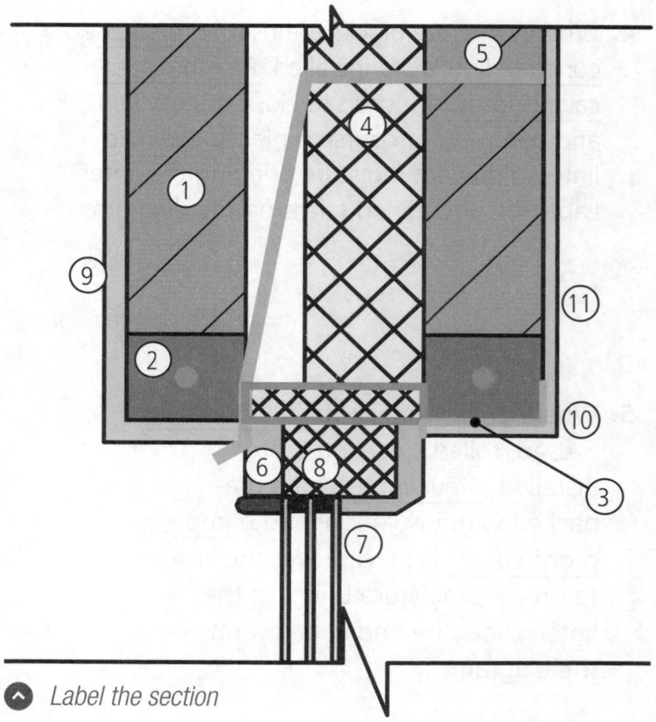

Label the section

10. The base of a window is called the window-cill. What materials is a window-cill made from?

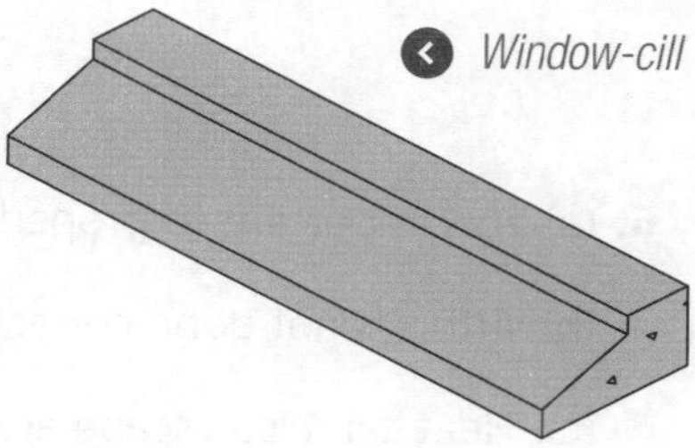

Window-cill

11. What design details ensure moisture resistance around a window-cill? Use notes and neat freehand sketches to support your answer.

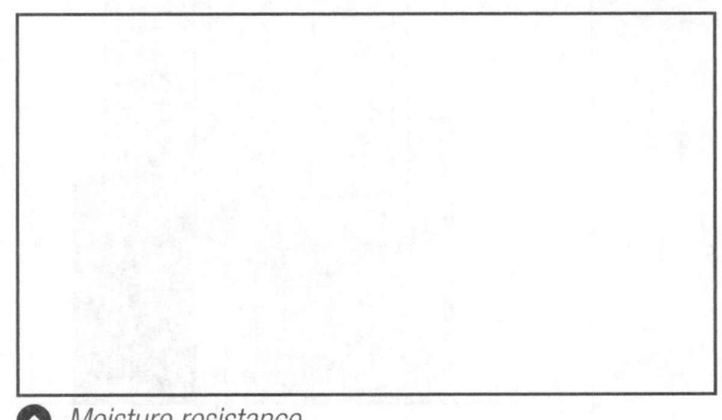

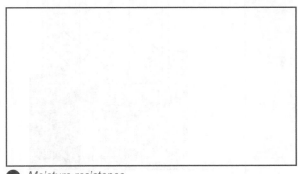

Moisture resistance

Sealing the cavity

12. The diagram shows an isometric view of a window-cill. Label the diagram.

1.
2.
3.
4.
5.
6.
7.
8.
9.
10.
11.
12.
13.

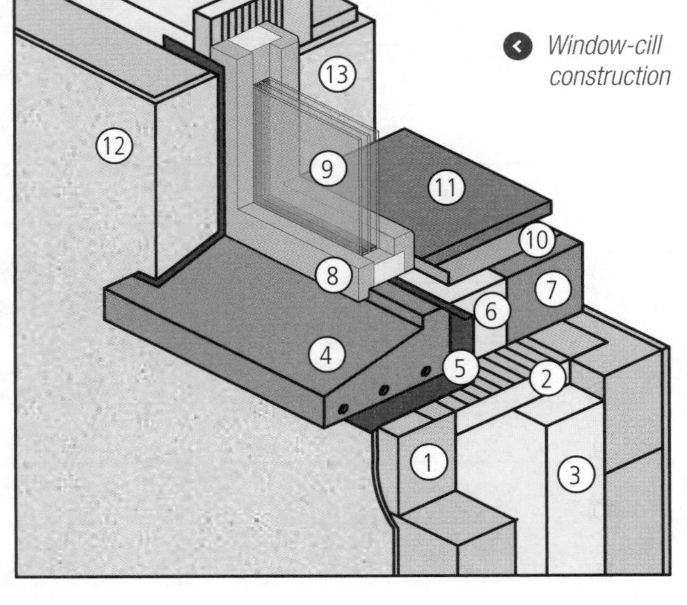

Window-cill construction

13. The diagram shows an incomplete sectional view of a window-cill. Complete the sectional view.

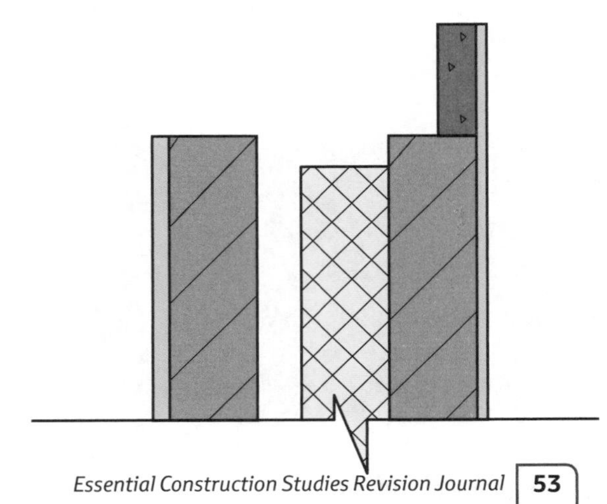

Sectional view of a window-cill

☐ WINDOW JAMBS

14. The side of a window is called the __________ or __________.

15. Following a building inspection, it was found that the existing window jamb detail allowed an excessive amount of heat to escape. Indicate on the diagram the likely path of heat escape.

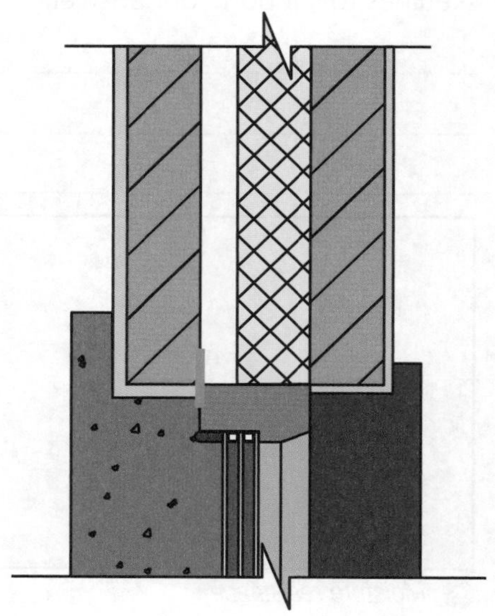

Window jamb heat loss

16. The diagram shows a sectional view of a window jamb. Label the diagram.

1. ______________________________
2. ______________________________
3. ______________________________
4. ______________________________
5. ______________________________
6. ______________________________
7. ______________________________
8. ______________________________
9. ______________________________
10. ______________________________
11. ______________________________
12. ______________________________

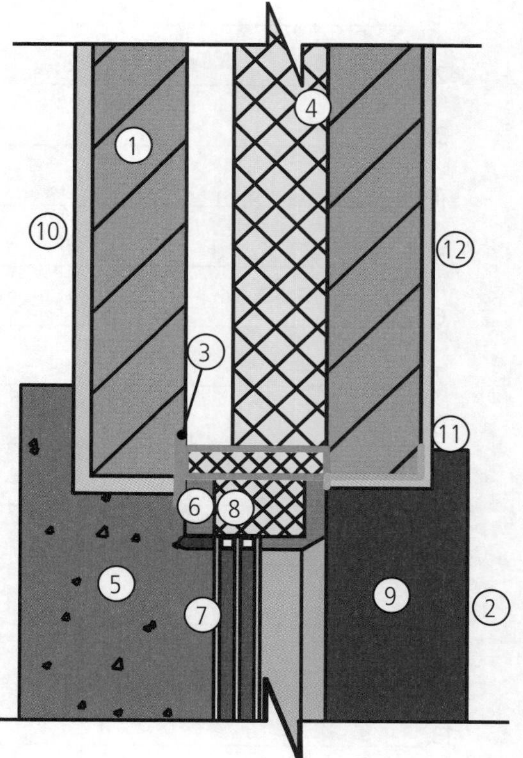

Sectional view of a window jamb

WINDOWS

☐ FUNCTIONS AND DESIGN FEATURES

17. What are the functional requirements of a window?

18. List the design features of windows.

☐ DESIGN FEATURES

1 LIGHT

19. In order to provide enough light, the window area of a room must be at least 10% of the floor area. On the diagram, indicate how 10% of the floor area is calculated and applied to the window area.

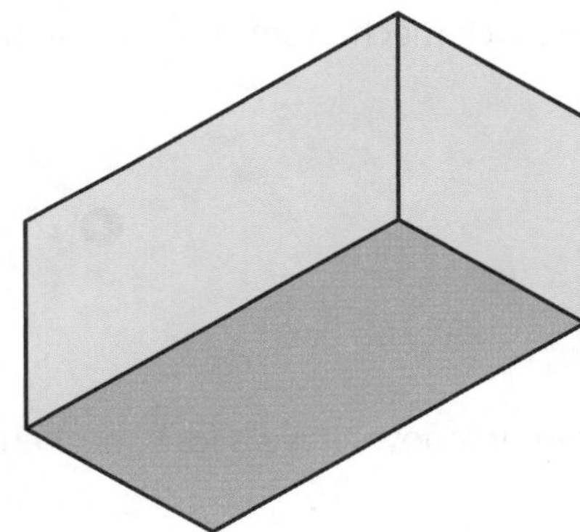

Window area to provide light

2 VENTILATION

20. Opening a window provides rapid ventilation to a room.

This is also known as ________________.

21. Vents in a window frame can also provide ________________.

22. In a habitable room (a room that is used for living or sleeping), the window area able to provide purge ventilation must be equal to at least 5% of the floor area. On the diagram, indicate how 5% of the floor area is calculated and applied to the window area.

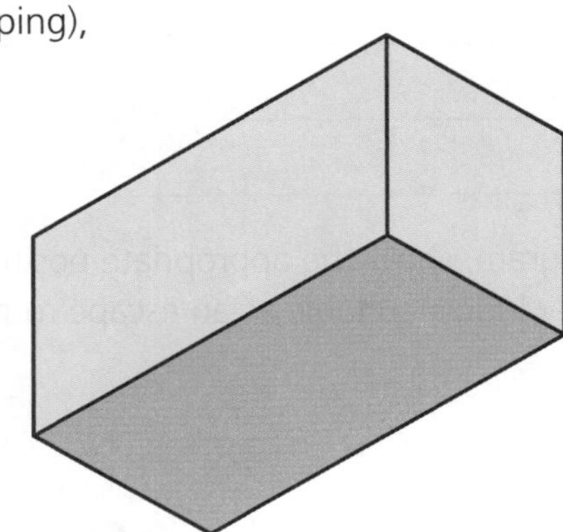

Window area to provide ventilation

3 THERMAL AND ACOUSTIC INSULATION

23. Windows are common areas in a building through which heat can easily escape and sound can easily penetrate. How can this be avoided? Use neat freehand sketches to support your answer.

Method 1: ______

Method 2: ______

Method 3: ______

☐ SECURITY

24. All windows should be able to be locked in the closed position. Highlight the lock mechanisms on the diagram.

Lock mechanisms

25. Many modern windows have a lock mechanism that holds the window open in a ______.

☐ FIRE ESCAPE

26. Building regulations state that a window that can be used as an escape route in the event of a fire must be provided for in:

27. On the diagram, show the appropriate position and sizing of a window suitable as an escape route from a fire.

Fire escape

☐ AESTHETICS

28. (a) Windows have an impact on the overall ____________ appearance of a building.

(b) The type of window chosen (sash or casement), its ___________ and the relationship between the amount of solid wall area to window area is critical in determining this.

(c) ____________ is the term used to describe the arrangement of windows across the façade of a building.

Adjusting window orientation affects the aesthetics of a building

☐ WINDOW TYPES

29. Below is a list of four types of window. Briefly describe each type.

(a) Lights: ______________________________

(b) Casement windows: ______________________________

(c) Sliding sash windows: ______________________________

____

(d) Pivot windows: ______________________________

____

30. A casement window consists of three main parts, as shown in the diagram. Label the diagram.

1. ____________ 5. ____________

2. ____________ 6. ____________

3. ____________ 7. ____________

4. ____________ 8. ____________

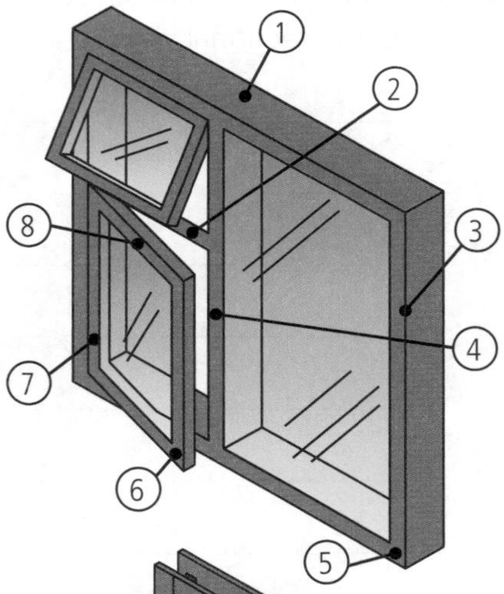

Casement window

31. The diagram shows a sliding sash window. What style of architecture are sliding sash windows typically associated with?

____

____

____

Sliding sash window

32. The diagram shows a pivot window. This type of window pivots about a fixed point. Where might a pivot window be used?

____

____

____

Pivot window

33. Window frames are secured using ____.

34. The diagram shows an incomplete sectional view of a casement window head. Complete the sectional view.

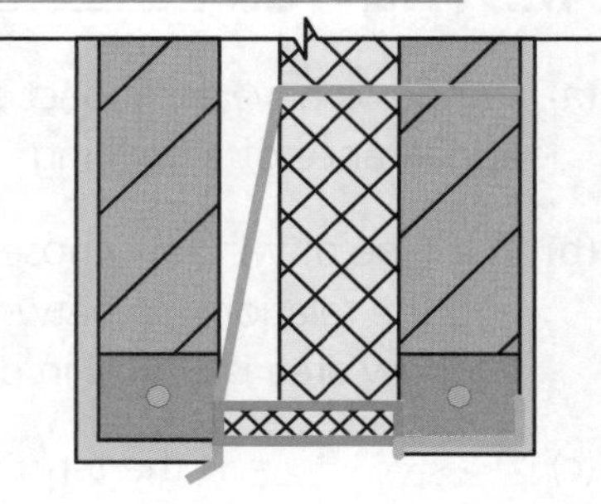

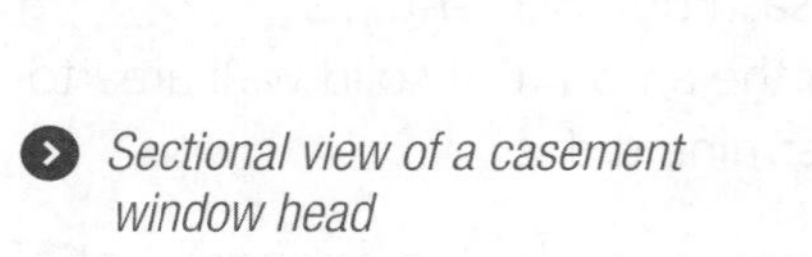

Sectional view of a casement window head

35. Shown is an incomplete sectional view of a casement window-cill. Complete the sectional view.

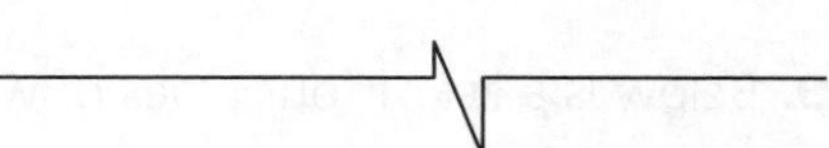

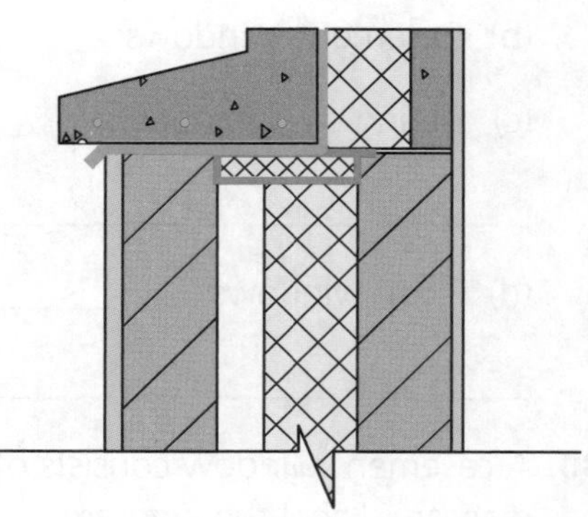

Sectional view of a casement window-cill

36. The diagram shows a sectional view of a casement window jamb. Label the sectional view.

1. ______________________________
2. ______________________________
3. ______________________________
4. ______________________________
5. ______________________________
6. ______________________________
7. ______________________________
8. ______________________________
9. ______________________________
10. ______________________________
11. ______________________________
12. ______________________________
13. ______________________________

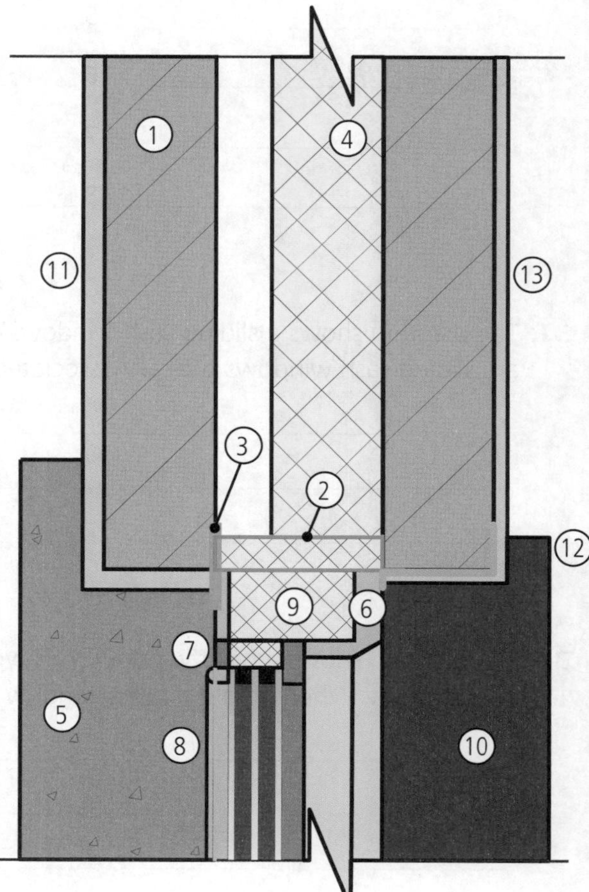

Sectional view of a casement window jamb

☐ OPENINGS FOR EXTERNAL DOORS

37. What are the functional requirements of an external door?

38. List the design features of an external door.

39. (a) Both the head and reveal details for a door are very similar to the details for a window. However, the ___________ (base of the door) is very different to the cill detail for a window.

(b) This is because the threshold must be designed to:

40. The diagram shows a sectional view of a door lintel. Complete the diagram.

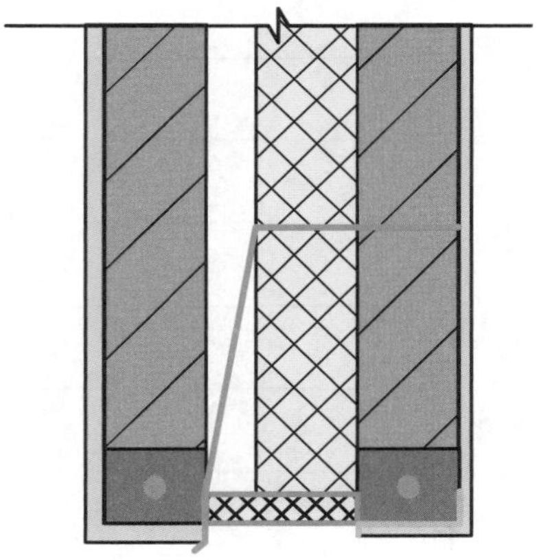

Sectional view of a door lintel

41. The diagram shows an incomplete threshold detail. Complete the detail. Using a coloured pen or pencil, indicate the correct position of Damp-proof course, radon membrane and airtightness tape.

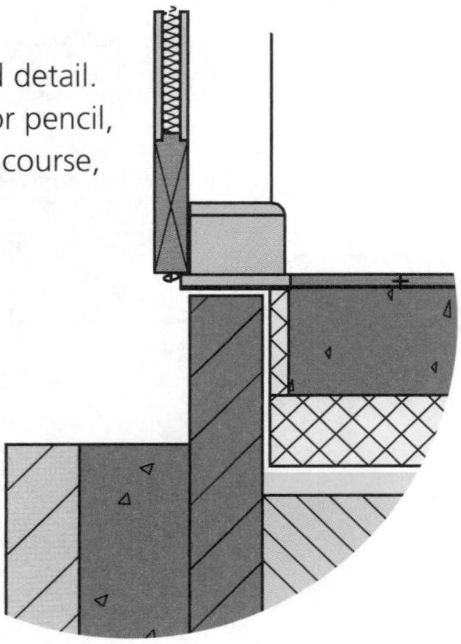

Door threshold detail

42. A door should include an airtight draught excluder under it and rubber seal around the frame. At least one external door should be wheelchair accessible with a maximum slope of 15°. Indicate these key principles on the diagram.

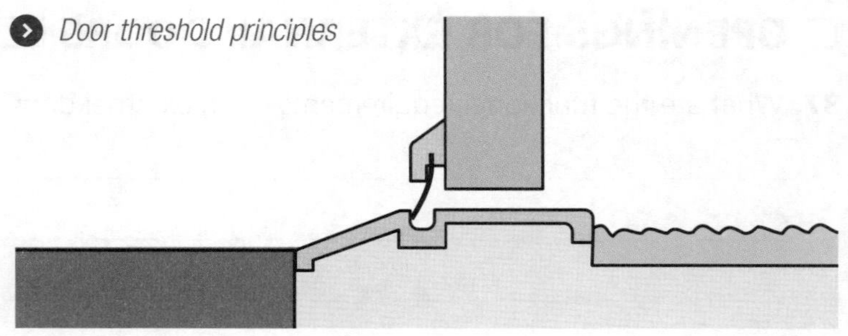

Door threshold principles

43. The diagram shows a storm gully. What is the function of a storm gully and where might it be located?

____

____

____

____

____

____

Storm gully

44. The diagram shows a sectional view of a door threshold. Label the diagram.

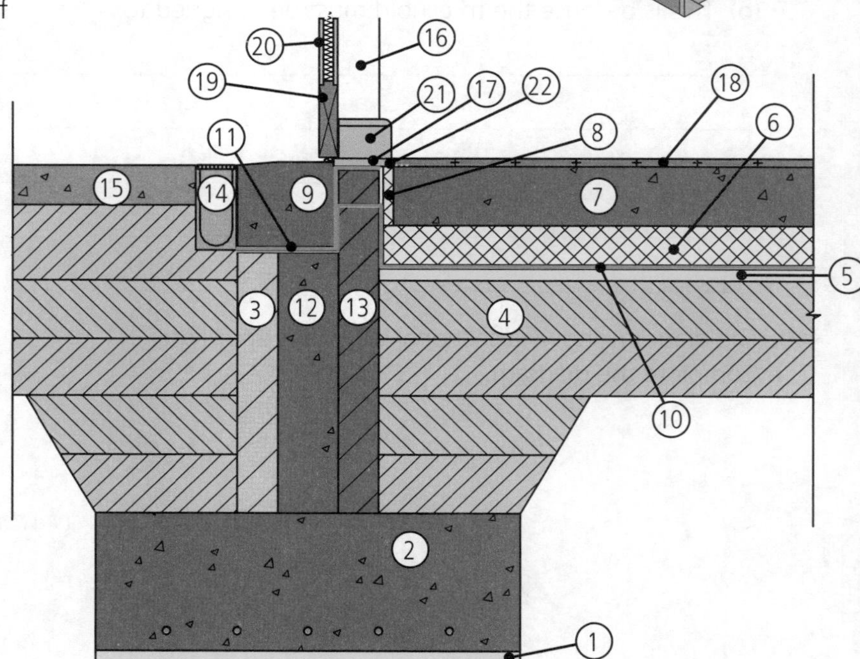

Sectional view of a door threshold

1. ______________________
2. ______________________
3. ______________________
4. ______________________
5. ______________________
6. ______________________
7. ______________________
8. ______________________
9. ______________________
10. ______________________
11. ______________________
12. ______________________
13. ______________________
14. ______________________
15. ______________________
16. ______________________
17. ______________________
18. ______________________
19. ______________________
20. ______________________
21. ______________________
22. ______________________

THEORY QUESTIONS

ORDINARY LEVEL

1. A triple-glazed timber casement window, as shown in the sketch, is fixed in a 350 mm external concrete block wall with an insulated cavity. The fixed frame of the window is 150 mm × 80 mm. The wall is plastered on both sides.

(a) To a scale of 1:5, draw a vertical section through the bottom portion of the window showing the fixed frame of the window and the concrete cill. Show the typical construction details from 300 mm below to a level 250 mm above the concrete cill. Indicate the typical sizes of **three** main components.

(b) Include in your drawing the typical design detailing that would prevent the formation of a thermal/cold bridge at the concrete cill.

2012 Ordinary Level Q5

2. A triple-glazed timber casement window is fixed in the external wall of a dwelling house, as shown in the sketch. The external wall is a 350 mm concrete block wall with an insulated cavity. The wall is plastered on both sides. The fixed frame of the window is 150 mm × 80 mm.

(a) To a scale of 1:5 draw a vertical section through the top portion of the window showing the fixed window frame and the concrete lintels. Show the typical construction details from 300 mm below to a level 400 mm above the concrete lintels. Include **four** typical dimensions.

(b) Show clearly on your drawing the flashing (damp-proof course) and the insulation at the window head.

2011 Ordinary Level Q1

7

HIGHER LEVEL

3. The main entrance door to a two-storey dwelling house is a four-panel solid wooden door. The external wall in which the door is fitted is of timber frame construction with a rendered concrete block outer leaf. This wall supports the first floor joists, as shown in the accompanying outline drawing.

(a) To a scale of 1:5, draw a vertical section through a portion of the external wall, doorframe, door and first floor joists. The section should show the typical construction details from 400 mm below the top of the door to a level 500 mm above the first floor joists. Include typical dimensions.

(b) Show clearly on your drawing the position of the vapour control layer to ensure an airtight structure.

2012 Higher Level Q7

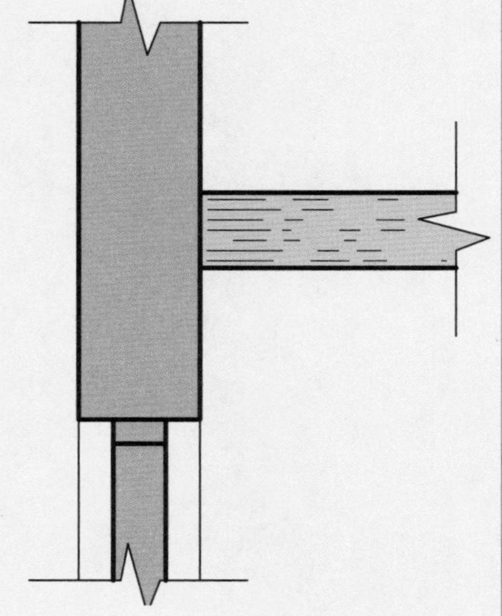

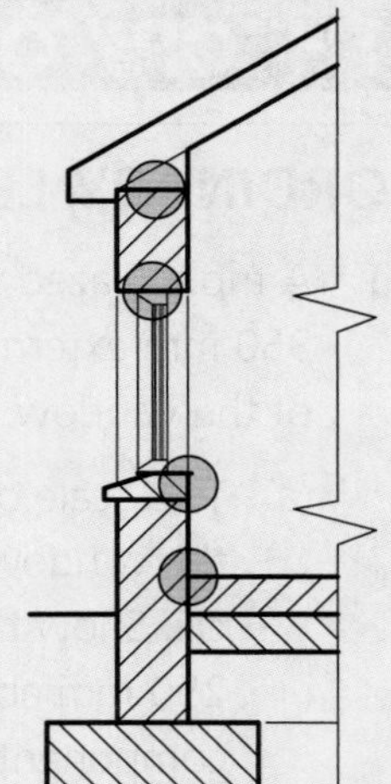

4. Careful design detailing is necessary in order to design a building envelope which is free of thermal/cold bridges. The drawing shows an outline section through a single storey house having a 350 mm external concrete block wall with an insulated cavity. The ground floor is an insulated solid concrete floor.

(a) Select any **three** locations from those circled on the sketch, and show clearly, using notes and annotated freehand sketches, the typical design detailing which will prevent the formation of thermal bridges at each location selected.

(b) Discuss in detail **two** advantages of designing a building envelope which is free of thermal bridges.

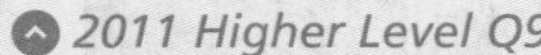
2011 Higher Level Q9

5. (b) Discuss in detail, using notes and freehand sketches, two design considerations for a contemporary window frame and glazing system that will ensure the high thermal performance of both:

- the window frame and
- the glazing system.

(c) Outline two environmental considerations that should be taken into account when recommending a preferred material for the window frame.

2010 Higher Level Q8 (b) and (c)

6. (a) Discuss in detail, using notes and freehand sketches as appropriate, two functional requirements of a contemporary glazing system for a modern dwelling house.

(c) Recommend a preferred window frame and glazing system for a new house and give two reasons in support of your recommendations.

2009 Higher Level Q3 (a) and (c)

UPPER FLOORS

CONSTRUCTION STUDIES

☐ FUNCTIONS AND FEATURES

1. Describe the primary functions of an upper floor.

____

____

____

____

____

2. Describe the primary design features of an upper floor.

______________ ______________

______________ ______________

______________ ______________

3. Draw sketches to show how upper flooring offers restraint to the external walls.

☐ DESIGN FEATURES

1 SUPPORTING THE JOIST

4. (a) Upper floors consist of joists with __________ (i.e. __________ above and ______________ below).

(b) The size of the joist depends on the ________ but realistically __________ is the ____________ size of a joist.

(c) The ____________ forms the ceiling for the downstairs rooms and provides ____________ to the spread of fire.

5. A floor joist's primary function is to support its own weight and any weight placed on it. This is achieved by transferring the load on the joist to the inner leaf. Using notes and the partially completed sketches, describe two common methods used to support a joist.

____

____

Continued

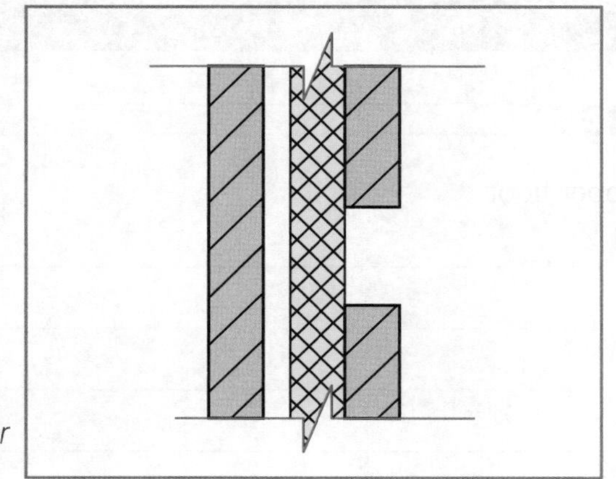

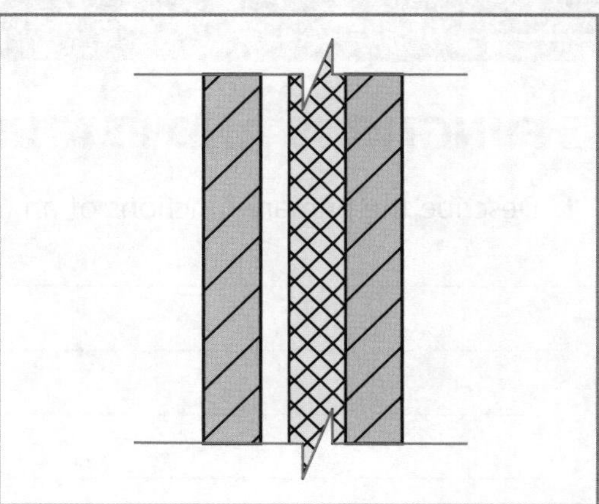

Two methods of supporting upper floor joists

6. Using a clear annotated sketch, show the correct construction arrangement for a direct bearing joist.

7. To prevent the risk of fire spreading between neighbouring houses, no floors joist should cross the party wall between buildings. In the space provided indicate how joists are supported at a party wall.

2 RIGIDITY

8. To prevent movement and twisting in a floor arrangement, it is vital that the entire floor acts as one rigid unit. Using notes and by completing the sketches on the next page, show two methods that are used to achieve this design feature in upper floors.

Continued

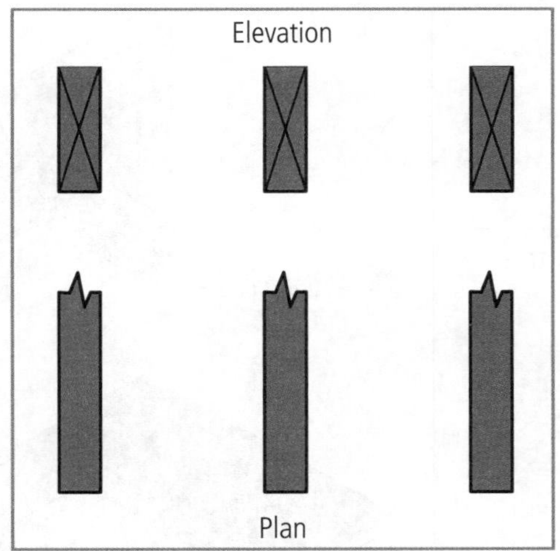

Rigidity in floors method 1

Elevation

Plan

Rigidity in floors method 2

SECURING THE JOISTS

9. (a) Where joists are ____________ to a wall, they must be secured to the wall using steel __________ nailed or ____________ into the wall.

(b) __________________ is used with the bridging to ensure no movement occurs.

(c) It is important to fill the void between the wall and the joist with _______________ and ensure an _____________________.

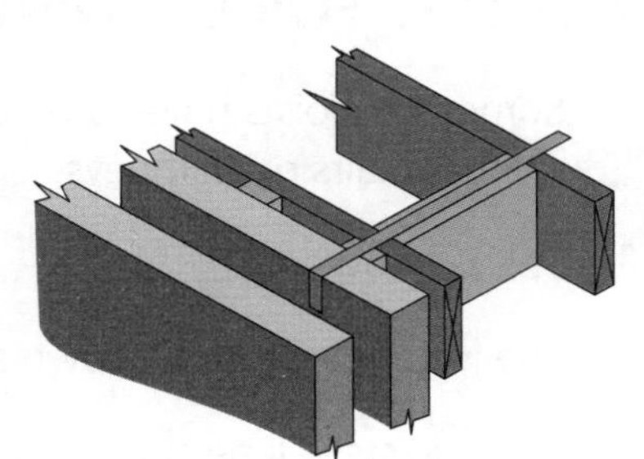

Joists are strapped and packed to adjacent wall

3 ACOUSTIC AND THERMAL INSULATION

10. Upper floors can often be noisy, particularly in apartments. Suggest two methods of improving an upper floor's acoustic and thermal performance.

____

____

____

____

____

Method 1: ______________

Method 2: ______________

4 AIRTIGHTNESS

11. (a) Airtightness is ____________ to achieve with upper floors.

(b) A continuous ______________________________ must be installed between the joists and around the ____________ of the floor.

(c) Particular attention must be paid to where the joist is ______________________________.

(d) ____________________ is used to seal any gaps or spaces between the mortar and the joist.

Airtightness at the wall

Airtightness membrane

Airtightness membrane

TRIMMINGS FOR OPENINGS

12. (a) Sometimes joists have to be cut short to accommodate ______________________________, such as stairs or chimneys.

(b) This is known as ____________ the joists.

(c) The joist being cut is known as the ____________ joist.

(d) These joists will be supported by a ____________ joist.

(e) The weight of the trimming joist will be carried by the ____________ joists.

13. Describe, with the aid of notes and neat freehand sketches, two methods for transferring the weight of the trimming joist onto the trimmer joist.

____

____

____

____

____

Method 1: ____________________

Method 2: ____________________

ACCOMMODATING SERVICES

14. In order to accommodate services, joists can be __________ and __________ to allow for pipes and cables.

15. Safety is a major concern when constructing an upper floor. The floor must not be weakened in any way by the addition of services. Likewise, electrical services must be positioned so as not to pose a risk to any person working with the floor (for example, when nailing a floorboard).

Describe, using notes and neat freehand sketches, the relevant building regulations that deal with such risks.

____

____

____

THEORY QUESTIONS

1. Outline three design features of a typical timber upper floor construction. Using notes and freehand sketches, explain how each of these features is accommodated for in the floor construction.
2. The accommodation of plumbing and electrical services in upper floor construction can pose a large risk if not properly carried out. Outline some of these risks and describe the regulations put in place to minimise them.
3. The layout for a first floor plan is shown in the sketch. Running through the floor is a double chimney breast. Using notes and freehand sketches, deign an appropriate layout for the floor joists for this plan. In your answer, indicate how you would account for the chimney breast.

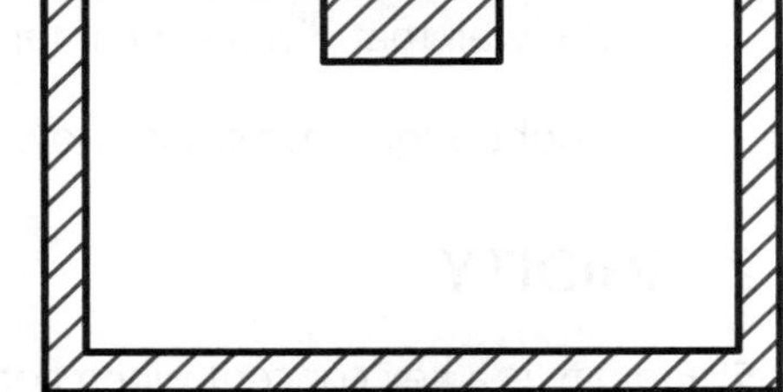

ORDINARY LEVEL

4. The accompanying sketch shows the first floor of a dwelling house which consists of wooden joists, tongued and grooved flooring boards with a plasterboard ceiling beneath.

(a) Show, by means of a neat freehand sketch, herringbone bridging for the floor structure.

(b) Discuss **two** advantages of using herringbone bridging instead of solid bridging.

(c) Using a large freehand sketch, show the tongued and grooved joint between two flooring boards and list **one** advantage of this method of jointing.

2007 Ordinary Level Q9

9

INTERNAL PARTITIONS

☐ FUNCTIONS AND FEATURES

1. What is the function of an internal partition wall?

____

2. List the design features of internal partitions.

____

3. What can external walls be constructed from?

____

☐ DESIGN FEATURES

1 SUPPORT

4. (a) Internal walls can be either __________ or __________.

(b) Load-bearing walls require a __________ to support the __________ on the wall.

(c) The wall that divides the internal space between two neighbouring houses is known as a __________ wall.

Load-bearing and non-load-bearing walls

2 RIGIDITY

5. Rigidity is a key concept when constructing a partition wall. Using notes and neat freehand sketches, show how rigidity is achieved in a standard stud wall partition.

____

6. Draw an annotated sketch to show the design differences between a load-bearing stud wall and a non-load-bearing stud wall.

3 ACCOMMODATION OF SERVICES

7. (a) Additional __________ may be added between studs to provide a backing to fix electrical sockets or switches to.

(b) As with floor joists, provision must be made for ____________________ and ____________________ in the studs.

(c) No holes should be made in the first _______ or central _______ of the studding.

(d) Likewise, all notching should be located in the first ______ of the studding.

(e) The maximum thickness for the holes is ______ the width of the stud.

(f) The maximum allowable depth of the notching is ______ the width of the stud.

8. Insert suitable measurements to show how the building regulations for accommodation of services apply to a stud partition.

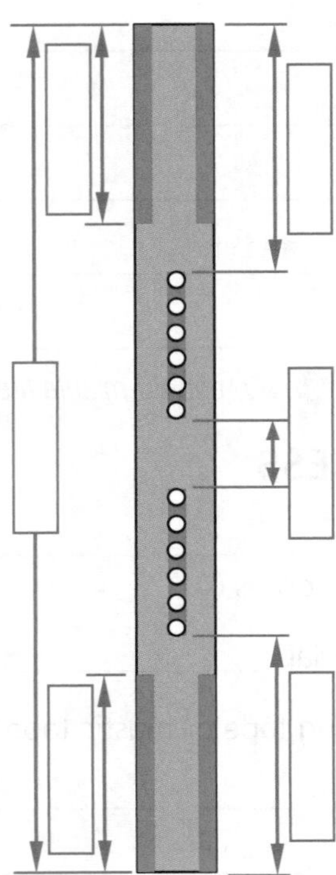

Accommodation of services in a stud partition

9

4 FIRE RESISTANCE

9. The spread of fire in a building is a major cause for concern. Using notes and neat freehand sketches, describe two simple design considerations that can be used to prevent the spread of fire through a timber partition and around a door detail.

10. Label the incomplete details of the 30- and 60-minute fire doors. Add appropriate measurements.

1.
2.
3.
4.
5.
6.
7.
8.

30- and 60-minute fire doors

5 AIRTIGHTNESS

11. (a) An ______ is attached to the studs in order to reduce the movement of air between rooms ( ).

(b) This is a special ______ that does not allow air to pass through it.

(c) Special sealing tape or mastic tape is used around the following joints:

6 THERMAL AND ACOUSTIC INSULATION

12. (a) __________ is __________ between the studs to improve the thermal and acoustic performance of the stud wall.

(b) __________ or __________ can be used.

☐ CONSTRUCTING A TIMBER PARTITION

13. After the birth of a new child, a family want to further divide their house by splitting an existing room into two smaller bedrooms. As their builder, you must describe the process of erecting a timber partition to subdivide the existing room. Use the headings and spaces provided to explain and illustrate your answer.

(a) Fixing the header plate

____

____

____

____

____

____

(b) Setting out the sole plate

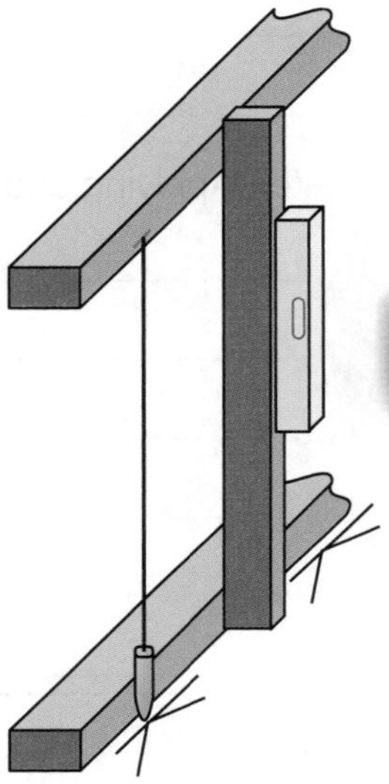

____

____

____

____

____

____

Setting out the sole plate

Methods of securing the sole plate to the floor

(c) Fixing the studs

- Each stud should be measured ____________ as the height of a room may vary along the length of the room.
- Each stud is ___________ and ____________.
- The spacing of each stud will be determined by the size of the ______________________ being used.
- ____________ wide plasterboard ___________ thick should be located at ___________ centres.
- ___________ plasterboard can be located at ___________ centres.

Stud template

(d) Fixing the noggins

(e) Applying and finishing the plasterboard slabs

14. Label the diagram.

1. ________________
2. ________________
3. ________________
4. ________________
5. ________________

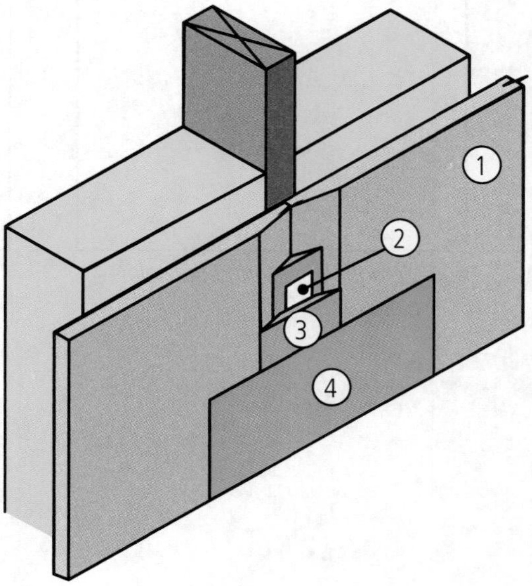

Label the above diagram

THEORY QUESTIONS

HIGHER LEVEL

1. A new two-storey house has load-bearing and non load-bearing timber stud partitions. The house has a solid concrete ground floor and a suspended timber first floor.

(a) Using notes and detailed freehand sketches, compare the design detailing for the construction of each of the following:

(i) a load-bearing partition to support the first floor joists.

(ii) a non load-bearing partition on the first floor.

2005 Higher Level Q4 (a)

2. A load-bearing, timber stud partition with a plaster finish separates a dining room and a living room in the ground floor of a two-storey house.

(a) Using notes and freehand sketches, describe in detail the construction of the partition.

(b) Show clearly the design details necessary to accommodate a standard flush panel door.

(c) Label and give the sizes of each of the components of the partition.

(d) Discuss in detail the advantages and disadvantages of using either a timber stud partition or a concrete block partition wall.

2002 Higher Level Q9

3. Compare an internal non load-bearing stud partition with a solid concrete block non load-bearing partition, with plaster finish to both. Refer to the general construction involved, from ground floor to first floor level, and discuss the advantages and disadvantages of each type of partition.

1995 Higher Level Q2

www.educateplus.ie
Teacher resources
username : 61570M
Password : K61570M

ROOFING

☐ FUNCTIONS AND FEATURES

1. What are the functions of a roof?

• To keep heat in a building
• To protect a building from the weather

2. What are the design features of a roof?

Strength and Stability	Ventilation
Weather resistance	Fire resistance
Thermal and acoustic Insulation	Aesthetics

☐ DESIGN FEATURES

1 STRENGTH AND STABILITY

3. (a) A roof must be able to withstand:

- the weight of the Slates/tiles and other building materials in a roof.
- the weight of Snow, ice and rais that might collect on a roof.
- the force of driving wind
- decay.

(b) All timber used in roof construction must have a moisture content of less than 20%.

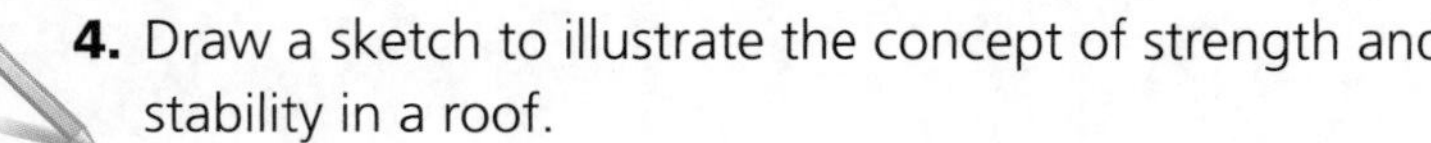

4. Draw a sketch to illustrate the concept of strength and stability in a roof.

2 WEATHER RESISTANCE

5. (a) A roof must be waterproof.

(b) This is achieved by using waterproof materials and ensuring a high quality of workmanship.

(c) A roof must resist Snow, Ice and water collecting. The Slope of a roof can help to achieve this.

6. Draw a sketch to illustrate the concept of weather resistance.

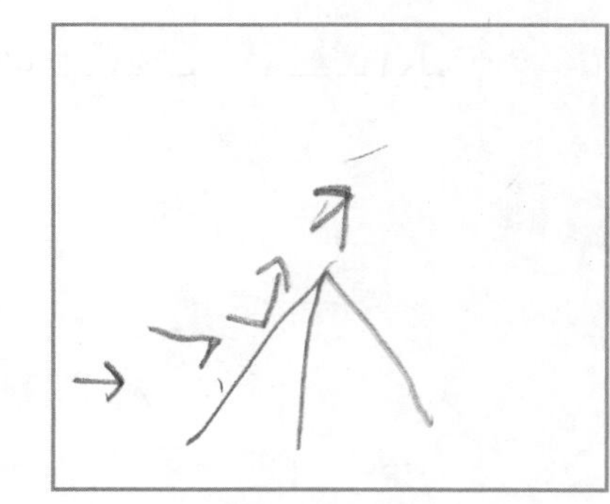

3 THERMAL AND ACOUSTIC INSULATION

7. (a) Hot air rises, which means a lot of heat can be lost through a roof.

(b) To reduce this, the attic space should be insulated with quilted insulation.

(c) A minimum insulation of 250 mm should be used.

8. The structure should also resist the ________ of ________ from outside the building.

9. (a) Draw a sketch to illustrate the concept of thermal insulation.

(b) Draw a sketch to illustrate the concept of acoustic insulation.

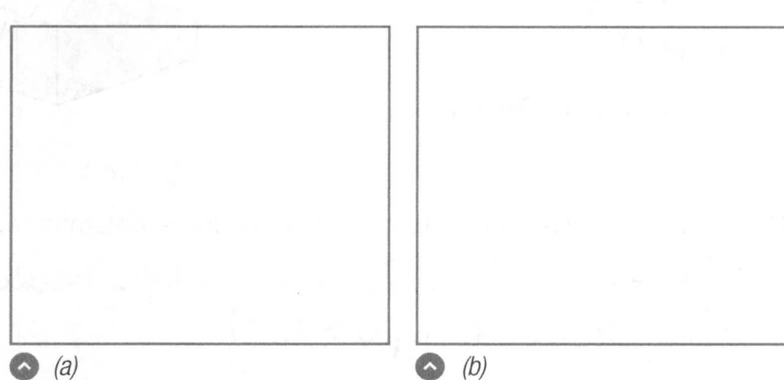

(a) (b)

4 VENTILATION

10. A roof must be adequately ventilated in order to prevent fungoi attack and build up of condensation

11. Draw a sketch to illustrate the concept of ventilation.

5 FIRE RESISTANCE

12. A roof should resist the spread of fire so as to allow time for occupants to escape.

13. Draw a sketch to illustrate the concept of fire resistance.

6 AESTHETICS

14. The shape, size and slope of a roof and the materials used to construct it will affect the overall appearance of a house.

15. (a) Shape and form: Too many dormers will make the house look off ballance and cluttered

(b) Slope: Too steep a slope will make the house look off balance.

(c) Materials: The choice of slates or tiles and the quality of finish will have a big impact on the overall appearance of the house.

☐ ROOF TYPES

16. Label the diagram of a roof.

1. Hipped end
2. Valley
3. Ridge
4. Hip
5. common rafter

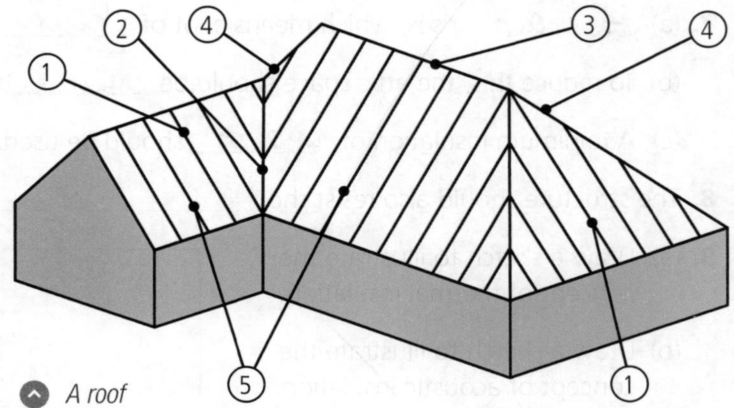

A roof

17. What are the two categories of roof? How do we determine which category a roof falls into?

• Pitched roofs (roofs with a slope between 10° and 70°)
• Flat roofs (slope > 10°)

18. Pitched roofs can be either:

(a) traditional cut roof. This is:

- a roof that is cut on site.
- typically used for one off houses and in rural areas.

(b) trussed roof. This is:

- a roof that is premade in a factory.
- typically used for housing schemes where lots of identical roofs are being made.

TRADITIONAL CUT ROOF

19. Every part of a traditional cut roof is cut and assembled on site using hand tools and power tools

20. A couple building a one-off house want a traditional cut roof. List the advantages and disadvantages of a traditional cut roof.

Advantages	Disadvantages
- It is cheaper than a prefabricated roof for a one off house as set-up costs are reduced and a crane is not required to hoist up the roof - The attic space is more ~~ex~~ accessible and easier to convert	- Construction can be slow. - It can be quite difficult to calculate certain cuts - The quality of the roof components and workmanship cannot be "Factory controlled"

21. Label the parts of a cut roof.

1. Ridge board
2. collar
3. purlin
4. wallplate
5. common rafter
6. binder
7. Hanger
8. Load-bearing internal wall
9. Strut
10. Joist

A cut roof

ROOF COMPONENTS 1

22. Rafters form the main structure of a roof. Outline the typical size and spacing for rafters on a traditional cut roof.

- rafters are generally spaced at 400mm centres

23. (a) Rafters are supported by purlins

(b) A purlin prevents the rafters sagging in the middle.

(c) Purlins are typically 200mm by 75mm.

(d) Purlins can be arranged either vertically or at 90° to the rafter (known as a cant purlin).

24. (a) Draw a sketch of a vertical purlin.

(b) Draw a sketch of a cant purlin.

(a)

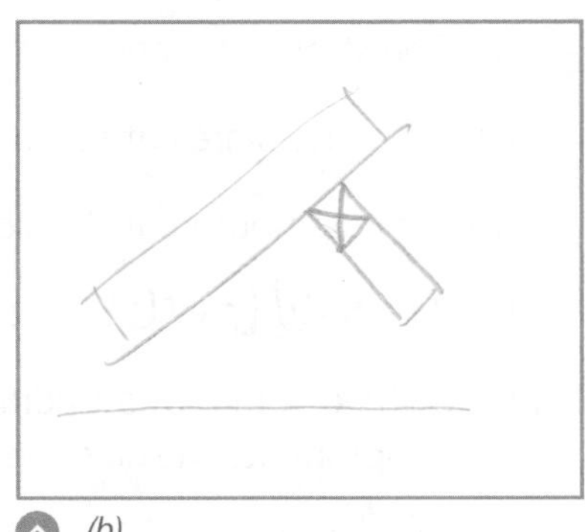

(b)

ROOF COMPONENTS 2

25. (a) Purlins are supported by Struts.

(b) Struts are roof members held in compression.

(c) Struts are typically 150mm by 50mm.

(d) The struts are supported by internal Loadbearing walls or specially designed ceiling joists.

(e) Spreader plates are used to prevent the strut from slipping.

26. Draw and label a sketch of a purlin, a strut and a spreader arrangement.

ROOF COMPONENTS 3

27. (a) collars and hangers are used to keep a roof rigid.

(b) Collars and hangers break up the roof from one big triangle into several small triangles

(c) This is called triangulation

(d) Collers prevent the rafters from spreading apart

(e) Hangers prevent the ceiling joist from Sagging.

(f) Collars and hangers are typically 150mm by 50mm.

28. On the diagram, show the correct placement of collars and hangers.

The correct placement of collars and hangers

ROOF COMPONENTS 4

29. (a) A roof is fixed to the walls by attaching it to a wallplate.

(b) A wallplate is a length of timber that runs the length of the inner leaf.

(c) A wallplate is typically 100mm by 100mm.

(d) The wallplate is fixed onto the inner leaf using express nails and galvanised steel straps

(e) The straps are spaced at 2m centres, and are at least 1m long.

(f) The rafters are cut to sit on a wallplate using a birds mouth cut

(g) A birds-mouth cut should be a maximum of $\frac{1}{3}$ the thickness of the rafter.

(h) The wallplate and the ends of the rafter must be treated with preservative

30. Label the diagram of a traditional cut roof at wallplate level. Add appropriate measurements.

1. Wallplate
2. Birds-mouth
3. Pitch line
4. Galvanisheel steel strap

$\frac{2}{3}$

$\frac{1}{3}$

Traditional cut roof at wallplate level

CLOSING THE CAVITY

31. To prevent the spread of fire and to improve thermal insulation, it is important to properly close/seal the wall cavity.

32. There are two common ways to close a cavity. Using notes and neat freehand sketches, identify both methods and show how thermal bridging was reduced or avoided.

____

____

____

Method 1: ____________ Method 2: ____________

THE EAVES

33. (a) The eaves is the area located at the base of a roof.

(b) The end grain of the rafters, which extends past the external leaf, is faced with a timber fascia.

(c) The underside is finished with a plywood sofit nailed to a timber batton

(d) Mineral wool insulation in the rafter space must ____________ over the ____________.

(e) ____________ over the insulation and ________ in the ____________ provide ventilation.

34. Label the diagram of a completed eaves detail.

1. ______________________
2. ______________________
3. ______________________
4. ______________________
5. ______________________
6. ______________________

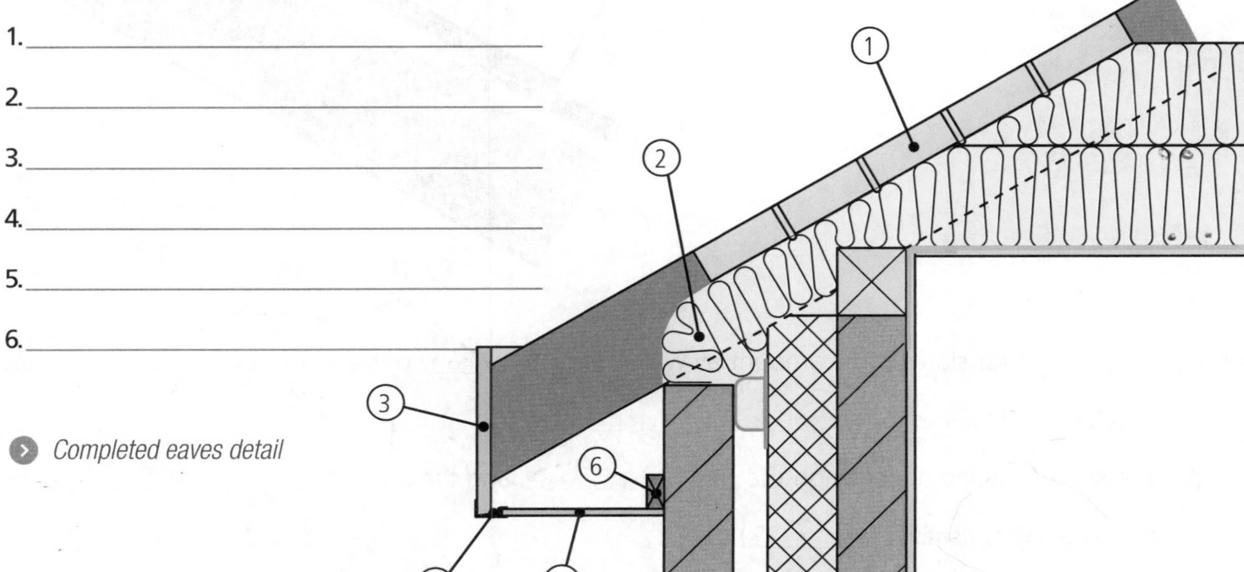

Completed eaves detail

ROOF COVERING

35. (a) Once the roof timbering is in place the roof can be coverd.

(b) Slate and tile are the most common covering used in Ireland.

(c) The type of covering chosen usually depends on:

- visual aesthetics of the house.
- the roof coverings used on surrounding houses
- the exposer of the house to the elements
- the cost of the roof covering.

36. (a) Type 1F sarking felt is first tacked to the rafters before the roof covering is put on.

(b) This acts as a moisture barrier.

(c) A heavier gauge 5u Sarking felt is used at the eaves, where a more durable material is needed.

(d) The felt is typically 500mm in length.

(e) This should overlap into the gutter by 50mm.

(f) A tilting fillet is used to support the felt. This prevents water ponding where the felt meets the fascia.

37. (a) Timbe batten (50mm x 25mm) are nailed to the rafters.

(b) The spacing of these battens is known as the batten gauge.

(c) The margin is the exposed portion of the slate.

38. Label the diagram of a slated roof.

1. batten gouge
2. lap
3. margin

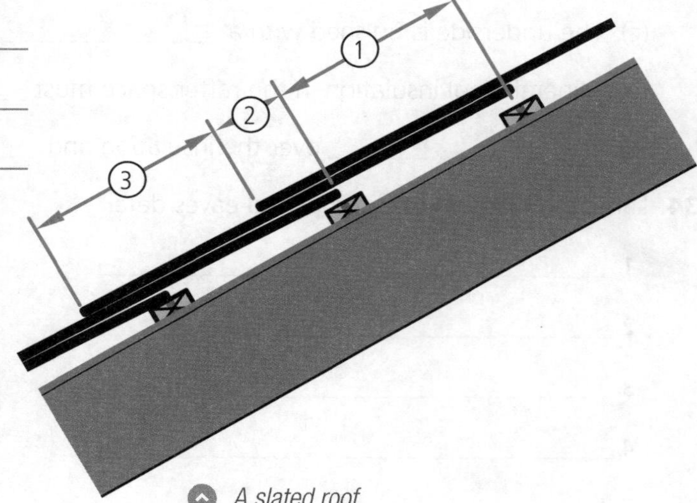

A slated roof

39. (a) the lap for slates is the amount by which the tails of slates in one course overlap the heads of slates in the next course.

(b) The size of the lap depends on the the slates used, and the level of weather exsposer in the area (the lap is usually 100mm).

(c) Each slate must include a side lap of half the the slate's width.

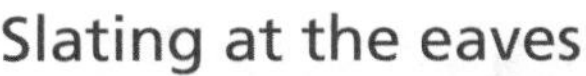

Slating at the eaves

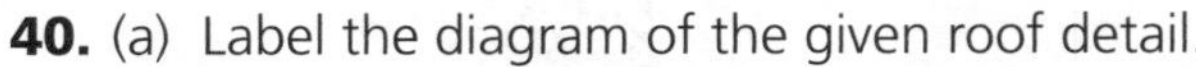

40. (a) Label the diagram of the given roof detail.

1. Gutter
2. fascia
3. Sofit
4. cavity barrier
5. wall plate
6. felt
7. battens
8. Rafter

Roof detail

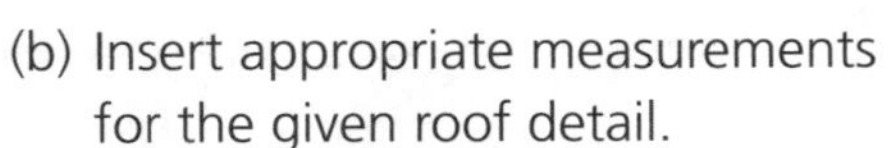

(b) Insert appropriate measurements for the given roof detail.

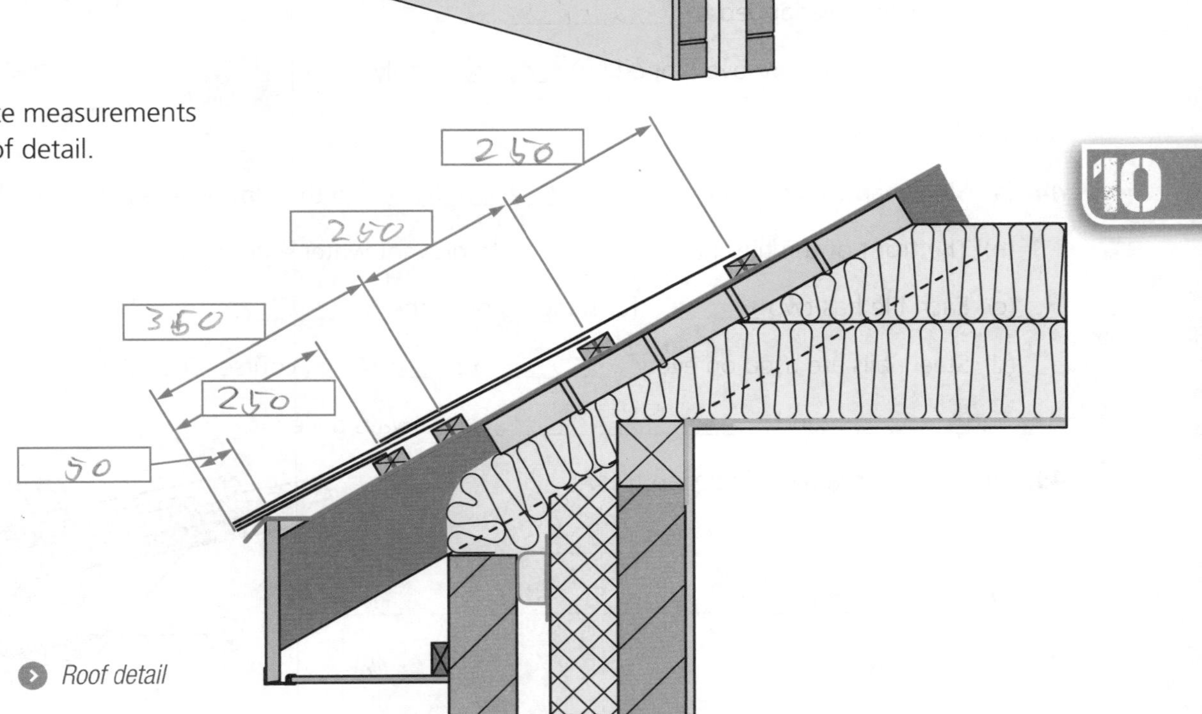

Roof detail

41. (a) To add strength at the eaves, three courses of slate are used.

(b) Slates must overhang the fascia by 50mm.

(c) The initial two courses are cut slates rather than full length slates.

(d) This ensures that the lap is maintained along the entire roof, up to the gutter.

(e) The length of the first courses is equal to the batten (usually 250mm).

(f) The length of the Second course is equal to the gauge the lap (250+100 = 300).

Slating at the gable

42. (a) A typical slate size is ____________________.

(b) ____________________ are used at the gable edge of the roof.

(c) This avoids having to use thin half slates which

____________________.

Slating at the gable

Tile covering

43. (a) Tiles are made of concrete or clay.

(b) Tiles come in a variety of colour, shapes and sizes.

(c) Tiles can be either double or Single lap.

(d) Double lap tiles overlap in a similar way to slates, with each tile being overlapped by two tiles.

(e) Single lap tiles are overlapped by one tile only.

Single lap tiles

Single lap tiles

44. (a) Single lap tiles have an interlocking Side lap, so the tiles only require a single overlap.

(b) The front of the tiles has a drip to prevent water entering by capillary action.

(c) Each tile has two nips for hanging onto the battens.

(d) Steel nails are used on every third or fourth course. Tiles at the eaves, verges, top and bottom are always nailed.

45. Label the diagram of single lap tiles.

1. nails
2. clips

Single lap tiles

RIDGE DETAIL

46. (a) The top of a roof is known as the ridge.

(b) The roof is capped with a prefabricated ridge Slate, which is either nailed in place or bedded in morter.

(c) Sarking felt at the ridge should have a minimum overlap of 225mm.

47. Draw a neat freehand sketch of a slated ridge detail.

VERGE DETAIL

48. (a) The area where a roof meets the gable end of the house is known as the ______________.

(b) At the verge, the __________ and ____________________ and run along the slope of the gable.

(c) This is known as the __________________.

(d) The fascia and soffit are fixed to _________________ that are __________ into the wall.

(e) The cavity space is closed using __________ that are __________ into the __________.

(f) The maximum overhang for the ladder is __________.

(g) The entire ladder should not be longer than __________.

(h) The edge of the __________ slate is sealed using either:

- ________________ on a slate undercloak.
- a prefabricated ________________.

49. Insert appropriate measurements on the diagram of the verge detail.

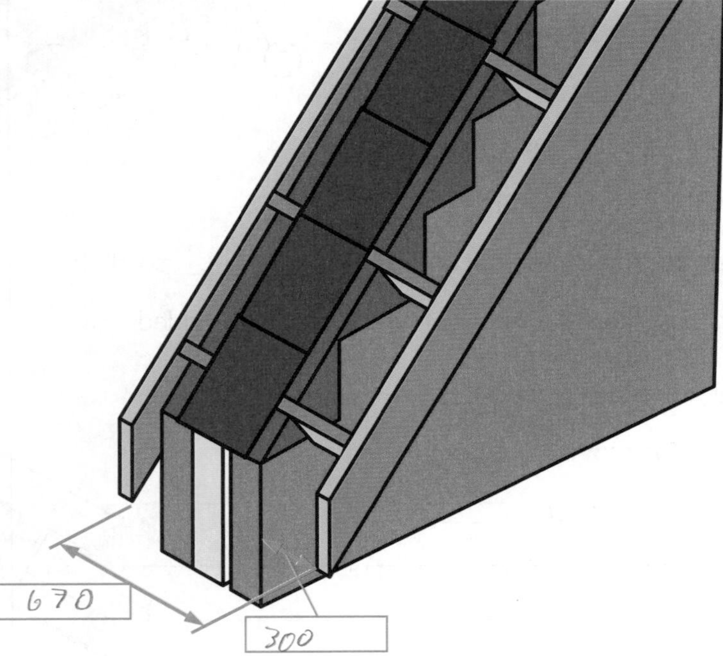

Verge detail

VALLEY DETAIL

50. Identify a problem typically associated with valley details and describe how this problem is overcome.

a problem is leaking
to prevent your youse lead.

51. The flashing in a valley is supported by plywood valley boards. Using notes and neat freehand sketches, outline three methods for supporting the plywood valley board.

____

____

____

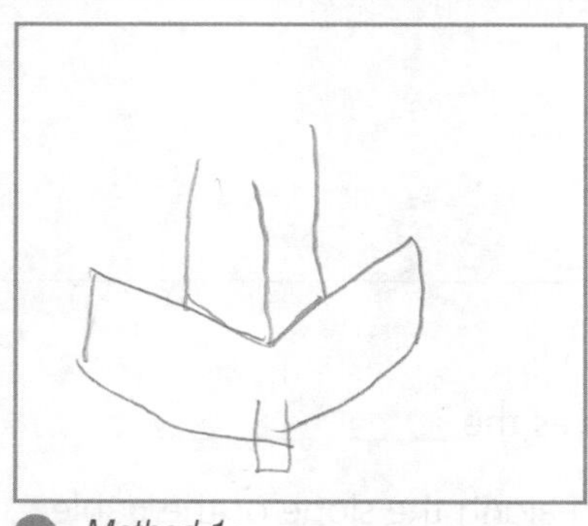

Method 1: __________

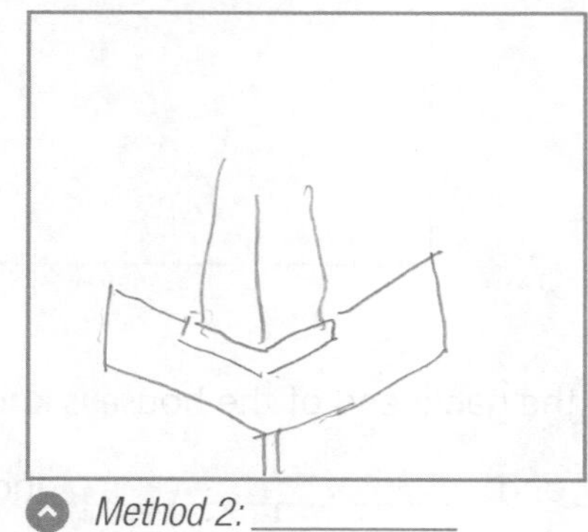

Method 2: __________

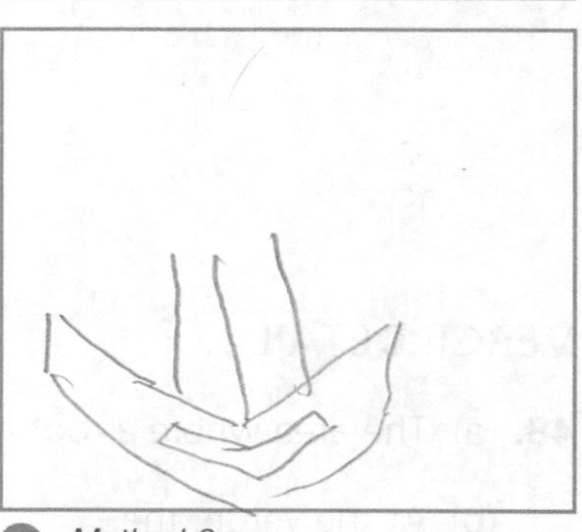

Method 3: __________

52. ______________ form the sides of the valley gutter and prevent ______________.

PREFABRICATED TRUSS ROOF

53. Label the diagram of a prefabricated roof.

1. Gang nail plate
2. wall plate (100mm x 100mm)
3. rafter 170x 45mm
4. bracing 100mm x 25mm
5. Tention webs
6. compression webs
7. ceilling tie

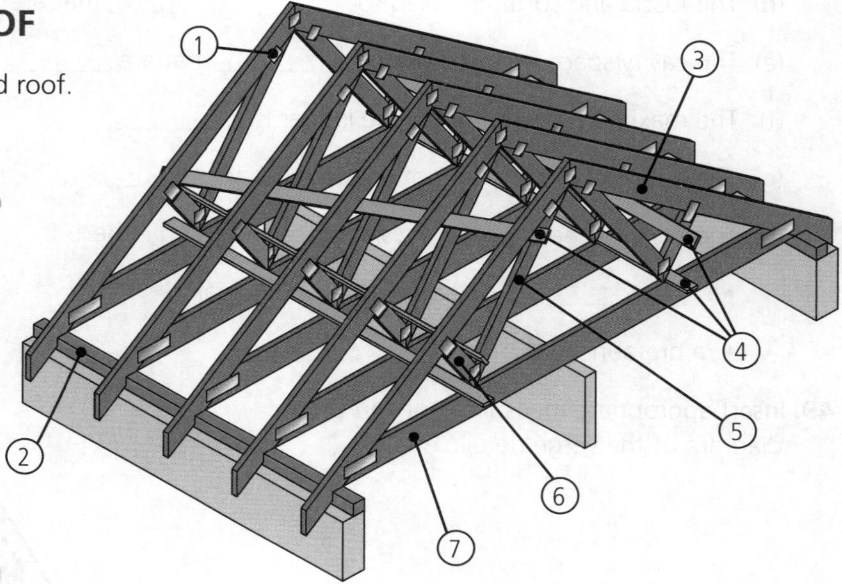

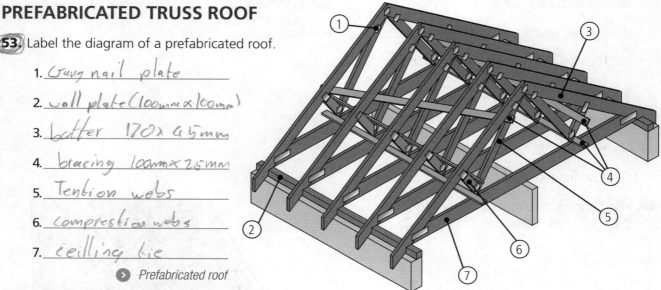

Prefabricated roof

BRACING THE ROOF

54. (a) Bracing is used to connect each truss so all the trusses act as one unit.

(b) List the areas of a roof where bracing is added.

ceiling level

rafter level

diagonally from eaves to ridge

ridge level

additional cheevron bracing

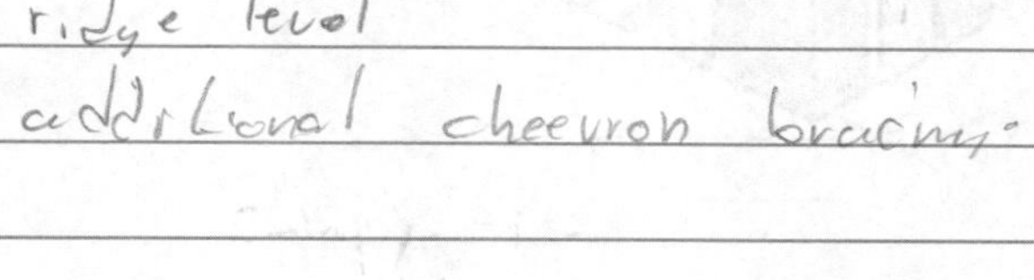

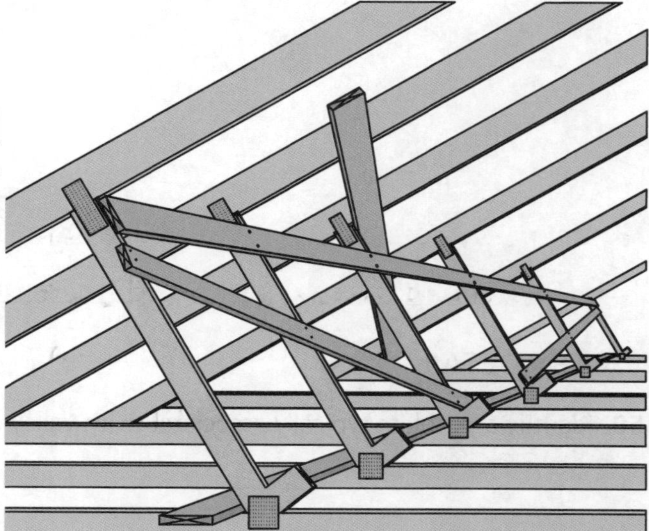

Bracing

GABLE LADDER

55. (a) The gable ladder is fixed to the ____________.

(b) Timber battens, at a maximum spacing of ____________________, support the ladder.

(c) All timber used for the gable ladder must be treated with ____________.

(d) The ladder should not be longer than ___________.

(e) The ladder should not project more than ___________ from the wall.

Gable ladder

COMPARISON OF ROOF TYPES

56. A couple building a new house are trying to decide whether to install a traditional cut roof or a prefabricated truss roof. In the table below, compare the advantages of each roof type.

Traditional cut roof	Prefabricated trussed roof online
• A traditional cut roof can be designed s that it can easily be coverted into a living space. • A traditional cut roof does not require specilist machinery such as cranes and teleporters to erec it. • A traditional cut roof allows for the easy design of attic storage space. • local labour can be employed in both the cutting and erection of the roof • A tracinal cut roof does not require specialist equipment to manufacture it.	

FLAT ROOF

57. (a) Flat roofs are classified as any roof with a pitch of less than 10 °.

(b) They must have a minimum fall of 1:40 to adequately drain off water.

(c) Flat roofs are not generally recommended for large spans as water tends to pond on the surface. This will result in the roof covering sagging, and the roof will eventually leak

(d) Flat roofs are often used for lean-to roofs, and can be fixed to the wall in a variety of ways.

COMPONENTS OF A FLAT ROOF

58. (a) The slope of a flat roof is created by a firring piece.

(b) The firring piece can be tapered along the length of the joist.

(c) The slope can also be created by diminshing the size of the firring piece along consecutive joists in the direction of the slope.

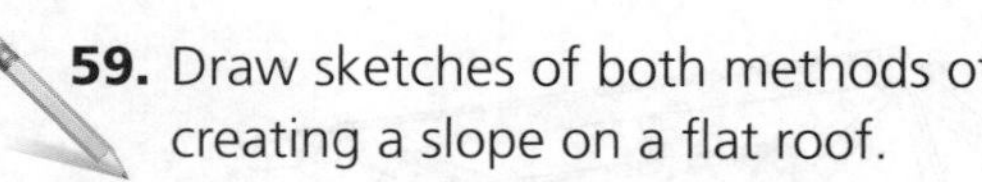

59. Draw sketches of both methods of creating a slope on a flat roof.

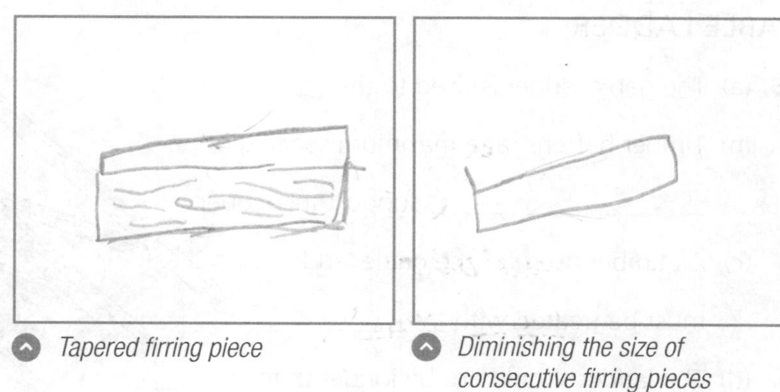

Tapered firring piece

Diminishing the size of consecutive firring pieces

60. (a) Exterior grade plywood, OSS or tongued and grooved boarding is laid onto the firring pieces.

(b) 3 layers of felt are used to weatherproof the roof.

(c) The joints are laid so that they are staggered between layers.

(d) Each sheet should have a minimum of 100m overlap

(e) Hot bitumen is used to bond the felt.

(f) White stone chippings or a reflective coating are placed on the covering to reduce the effects of continuous expansion and contraction due to weather.

LAYOUT OF A FLAT ROOF

61. There are two types of layout for a flat roof:

(a) Cold deck construction: This method has insulation between the joist under the boarding. It requires additional ventilation

(b) Warm deck construction: This method has insulation above the boarding. It does not require additional ventilation. warm deck construction is the preferred method as it reduces the effects of thermal expansion and contraction on the boarding.

62. Label the diagram of warm deck components.

1. chippings
2. Three layers of felt
3. 100mm insulation
4. Vapour barrier
5. 25mm plywood decking
6. firring piece
7. 150mm Joist
8. 15mm Plasterboard Slab

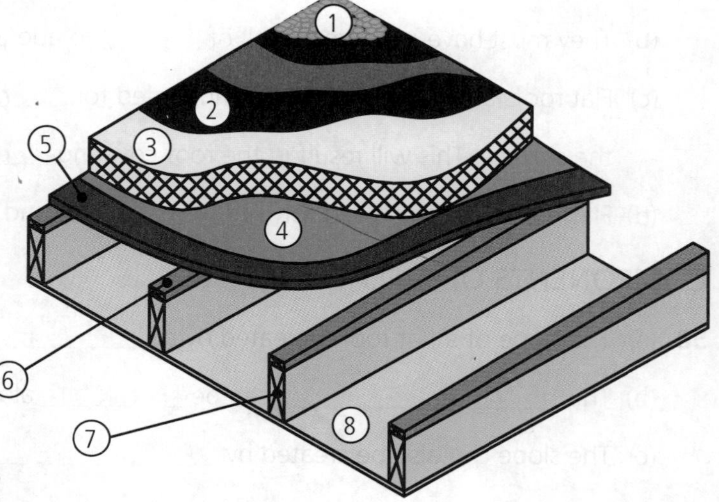

Warm deck

63. Label the diagram of cold deck components.

1. Chippings
2. Three layers of bitumnious Felt (asphalt)
3. Vapour barrier
4. 100m insulation
5. 15mm plasterboard slab
6. 25mm plywood decking
7. firring piece
8. 150mm Joist

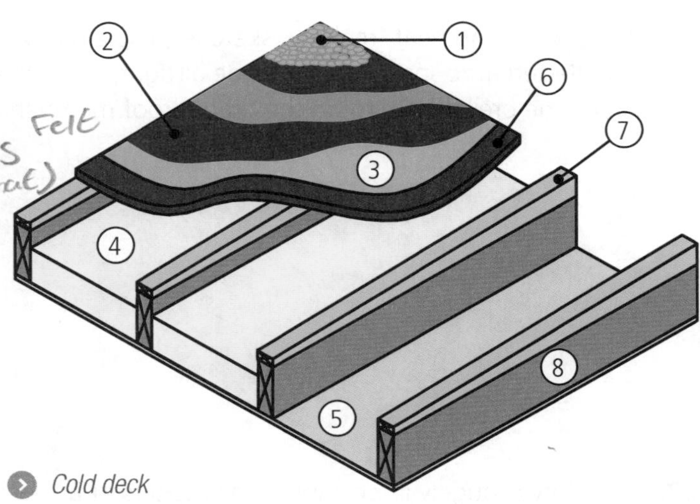

Cold deck

Abutment detail (warm deck)

64. (a) Where a flat roof meets a wall, each layer of felt should be wrapped up along the wall

(b) A lead cover flashing built into the wall is dressed over the felt.

(c) A tilting fillet is used to prevent any damage to the corner of the felt.

(d) A damp proof fillet is built across the cavity.

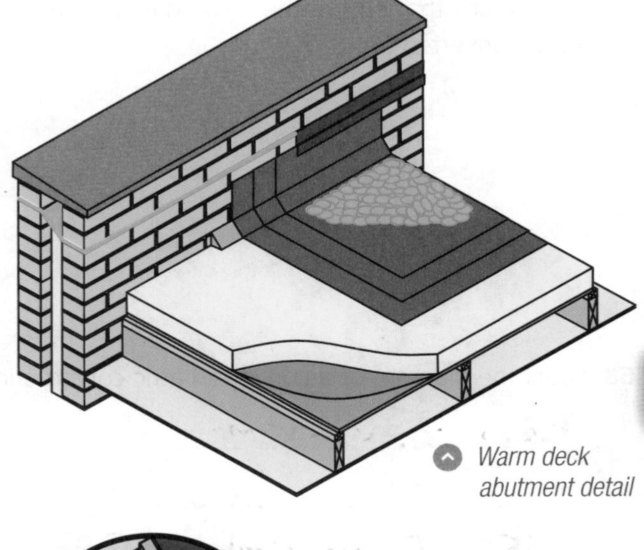
Warm deck abutment detail

Abutment detail (cold deck)

65. (a) The felt and cover flashing are dressed as for a warm deck roof.

(b) Additional ventilation is achieved with a proprietary vent.

(c) A clear air space is created behind the vent using a sheet of 12mm plywood sheeting, which is fixed to 25mm x 50mm timber battens

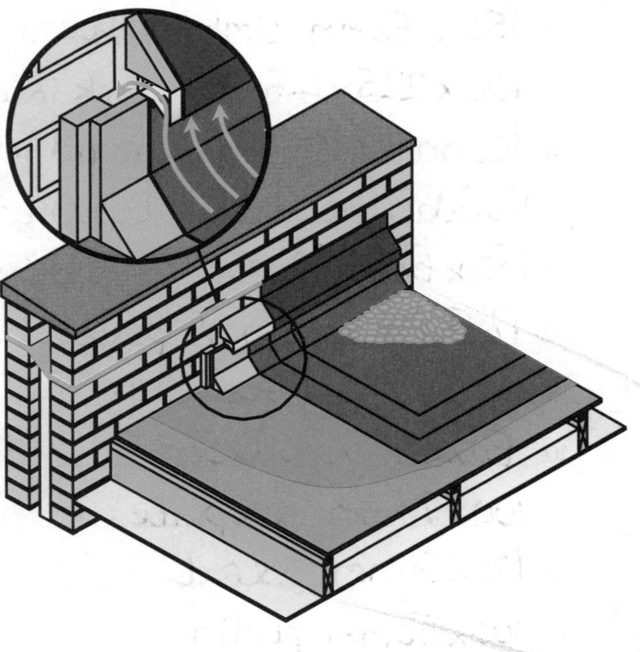
Cold deck abutment detail

66. Using notes and neat freehand sketches, explain how a converted attic space can be made airtight, yet at the same time prevent dry rot in the timber roof members.

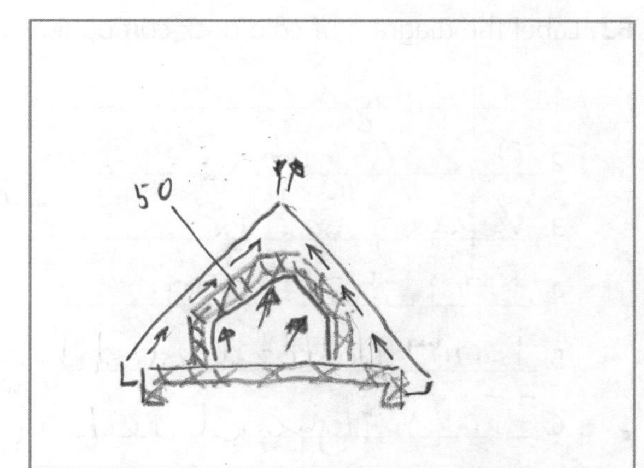

67. Fire safety is hugely important for all aspects of a building's construction. Outline the key building regulations that ensure these standards are maintained for a converted attic.

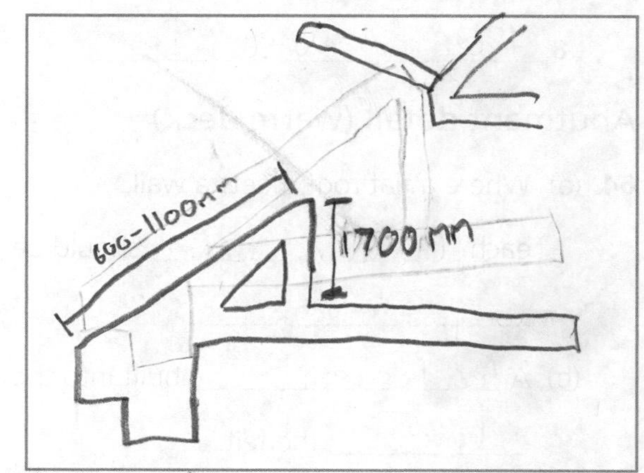

68. Label the diagram of a converted attic construction.

1. 100 x 225 x 450mm block inner leaf
2. 100 x 100mm wall plate
3. 150 x 50mm timber rafters
4. 100 x 225 x 450mm block inner leaf
5. 100mm foil backed rigid insulation
6. Prefabricated cavity closer
7. 150 x 50mm timber Joist with quilted Insulation
8. 12.5mm internal plaster
9. 12.5mm plaster slab
10. Eaves ventilator
11. 100 x 75mm soleplate
12. 100 x 50mm strut
13. 100 x 50mm purlin
14. 100 x 50mm brace
15. 100mm minium urethane board lining the habitable space
16. 12.5mm internal plaster
17. 20mm fascia

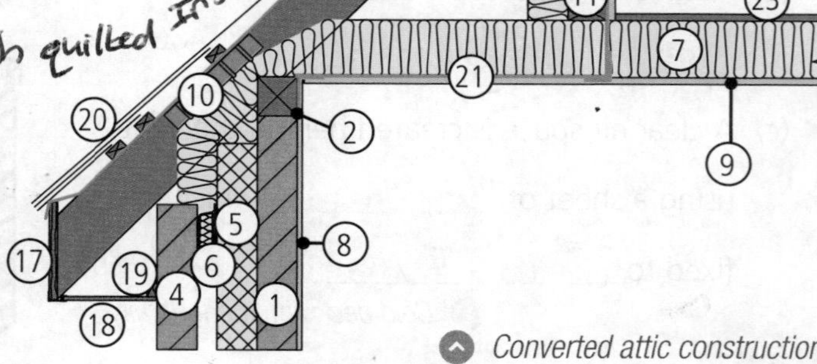

Converted attic construction

18. 12mm soffit with ventilation
19. 50 x 25mm timber battens
20. 600 x 300mm slates on timber battens on breather membrane
21. Airtightness membrane
22. Airtightness sealing tape
23. 20mm ~~T&G~~ T and G flooring

THEORY QUESTIONS

ORDINARY LEVEL

1. A dwelling house has a traditional cut roof with a pitch of 45 degrees, as shown in the sketch. The roof, which is insulated, is covered with concrete roof tiles which are supported on 200 mm × 50 mm rafters. To a scale of 1:5, draw a vertical section through the portion of the roof at the ridge, as shown within the circle in the sketch. Show all the construction details from the top of the ridge to 150 mm below the collar tie and include three courses of tiles at the ridge. Label the roof components and give their typical sizes.

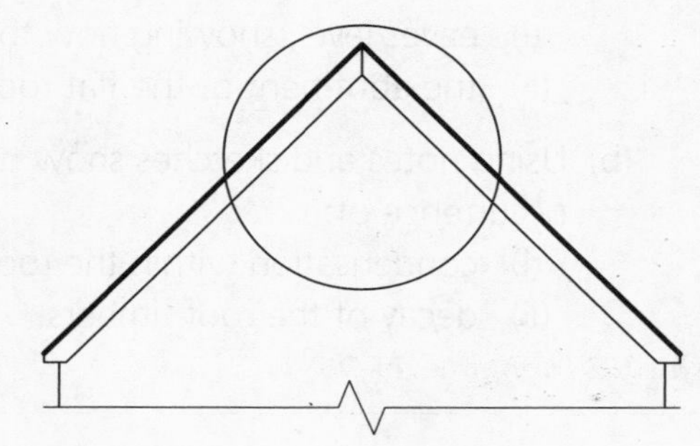

2009 Ordinary Level Q5

HIGHER LEVEL

2. A triple-glazed bay window projects 1.5 metres from the external wall of a dwelling house, as shown in the accompanying sketch. The external wall is a 350 mm concrete block wall with an insulated cavity. The lean-to roof is an insulated slated roof and has a pitch of 30°. Insulated plasterboard is fixed to the underside of the rafters to form a sloped ceiling.

(a) To a scale of 1:5, draw a vertical section through the window, roof and front wall of the house. The section should show the typical construction details from 400 mm below the concrete lintels of the bay window, through the fixed frame of the window, wallplate and rafter to a level 400 mm above the abutment of the lean-to roof and the front wall of the house.

(b) Indicate on your drawing the design detailing that ensures moisture does not penetrate at the abutment of the roof and the wall of the house.

2012 Higher Level Q1

3. (a) Discuss in detail, using notes and freehand sketches, **three** functional requirements of a roof suitable for a dwelling house.

(b) Using notes and freehand sketches, show **two** different types of pitched roof structure suitable for a dwelling house having an internal span of 6.0 metres and one internal load-bearing wall.

For each roof type, indicate the design detailing that ensures the structural stability of the roof and include the typical dimensions of **three** structural members.

(c) Recommend a preferred roof structure for a dwelling house and give **two** reasons in support of your recommendation.

2011 Higher Level Q2

4. (a) To a scale of 1:10, draw a vertical section through the window, the external wall and the roof of a timber-framed house. The external leaf is of concrete block construction with a rendered finish.

The roof has prefabricated trussed rafters, is slated and has a pitch of 45 degrees. Show all the constructional details from 300mm below the window head, through the eaves and include three courses of slate.

(b) On the drawing, label and indicate the typical dimensions of four main structural members.

2006 Higher Level Q7

5. It is proposed to extend the kitchen area of an existing two-storey house. This requires the construction of a timber flat roof to the extension. The external wall of the house is a 300 mm insulated cavity wall.

(a) To a scale of 1:5, show the design details of the roof construction at:
  (i) eaves level, showing how the rainwater is to be removed.
  (ii) the abutment of the flat roof with the wall of the existing house.

(b) Using notes and sketches show two design considerations in the roof construction which prevent the occurrence of:
  (i) condensation within the roof structure.
  (ii) decay of the roof timbers.

2002 Higher Level Q8

FIREPLACES AND CHIMNEYS

☐ FUNCTIONS AND FEATURES

1. What are the functions of a fireplace and chimney?

____

____

____

____

____

2. List the key features of a chimney.

____

____

____

____

____

____

3. Label the components of a typical fireplace.

1. ______________________________
2. ______________________________
3. ______________________________
4. ______________________________
5. ______________________________
6. ______________________________
7. ______________________________

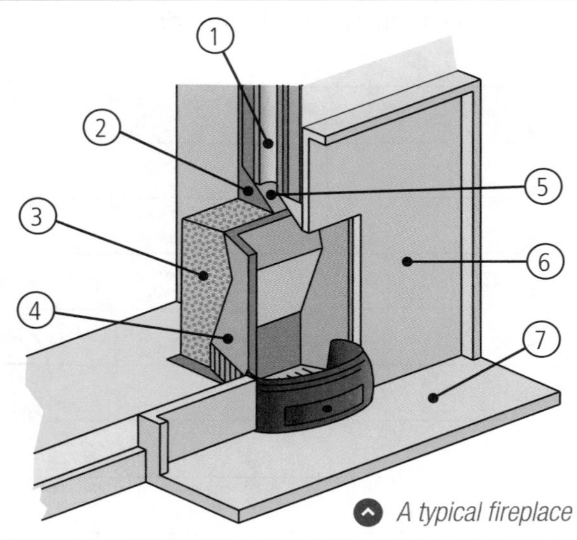

A typical fireplace

☐ DESIGN FEATURES

1 FIREPLACE PROPORTION AND DESIGN

4. (a) Due to the huge __________ of a fireplace and chimney system, it must have its own __________.

(b) The __________ of a standard foundation are maintained around the fireplace __________.

(c) For structural integrity, the jambs should be a __________.

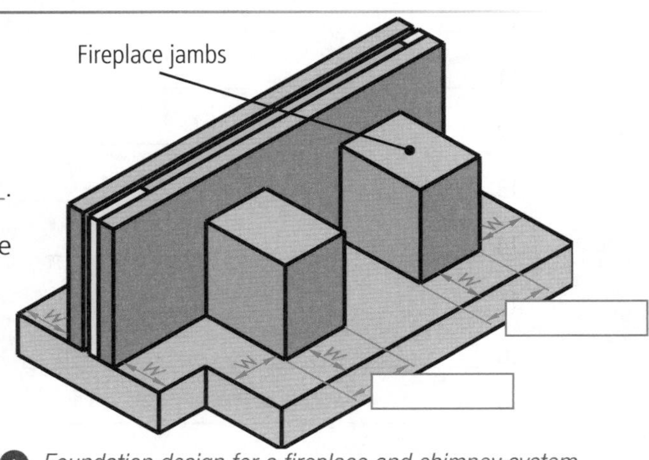

Foundation design for a fireplace and chimney system

5. What is the function of the chimney gather in a fireplace?

A typical prefabricated chimney gather and chimney lintel

6. A fire hearth contains an open flame, and it is vital that no combustible material comes into contact with the flames. Explain how this is achieved around a typical fireplace. Insert appropriate minimum projections on the diagram.

Preventing combustible material from coming into contact with flames

7. Label and add appropriate measurements to the diagram of a fire hearth detail.

1.
2.
3.
4.
5.
6.
7.
8.
9.
10.
11.
12.
13.
14.
15.
16.
17.
18.
19.
20.
21.
22.
23.
24.

Fire hearth detail

2 COMBUSTION AND HEATING METHODS

WOOD PELLET BURNERS

8. (a) Wood pellet stoves burn wood pellets made from the woody ________________ plant (also known as ____________________).

(b) They are ____________________ as the carbon created when __________ the pellets was ________________ during the ____________________.

(c) The pellets are automatically fed into the burner by an ________________.

(d) Pellets must be kept dry at all times and stored in a ______________________________.

9. Draw a labelled sketch of a typical wood pellet burner.

WOOD BURNING STOVES

10. Wood-burning stoves are generally considered to be more energy efficient and environmentally sustainable than a conventional open hearth fireplace. Discuss the design features that make wood-burning stoves more efficient.

RETROFITTED STOVES

11. House owners with an existing traditional fire hearth want to insert a modern wood-burning stove into the original space. The diagram shows a section of the existing layout. Using notes and by completing the sketch, show how a new stove can be installed.

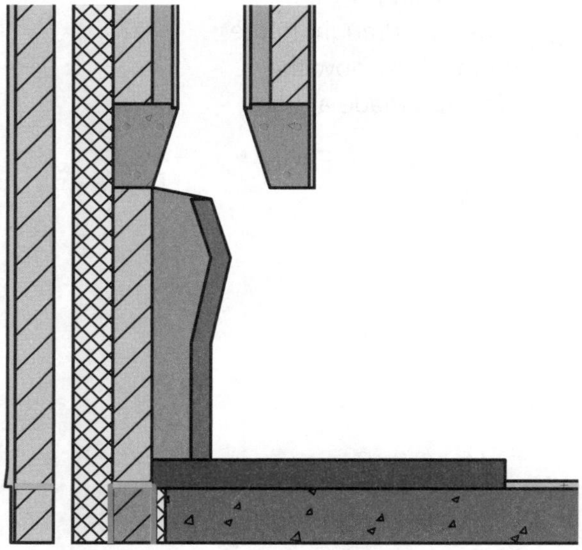

How a retrofitted stove is installed

12. (a) An alternative design for a stove is to link the ______________________ with the existing ______________________.

(b) When connecting the stove to the flue pipe, it is recommended that a ______________ mm should be allowed immediately above the appliance before any change of ______________ ______________.

(c) A ______________________ should continue up the ______________________ of the clay flue pipe.

13. Indicate on the diagram how a stove can connect with an existing chimney flue.

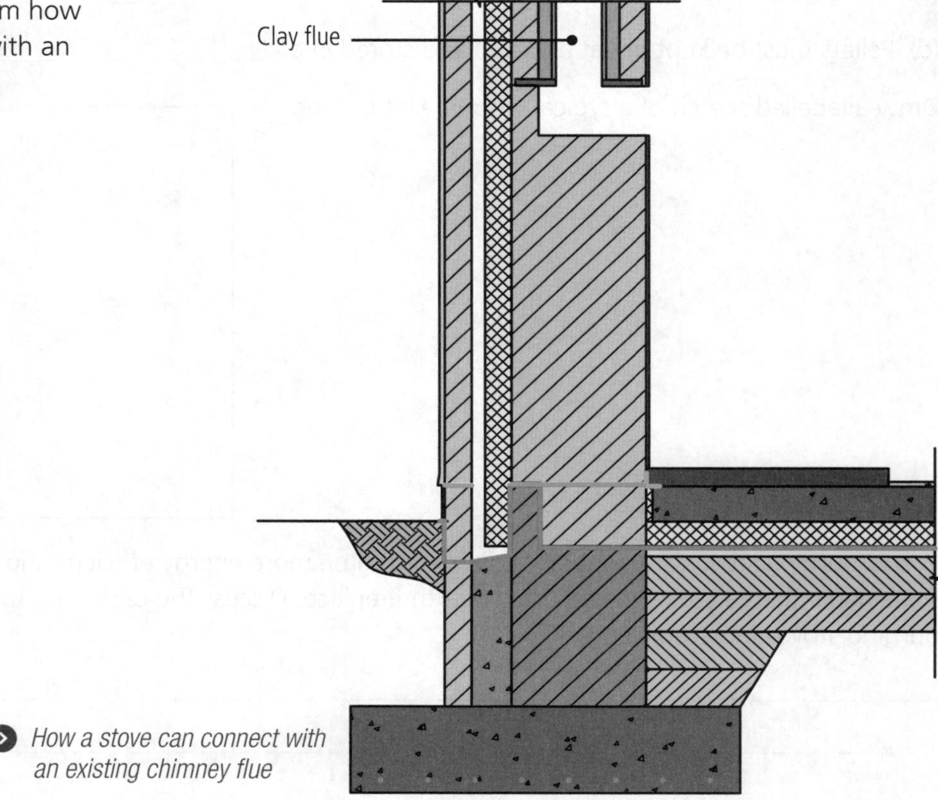

How a stove can connect with an existing chimney flue

14. On the diagram, show how a room sealed stove draws air from outside the building without causing a draught in the room. Show how the system is made airtight.

Room sealed stove

NEW STOVES

15. (a) New stoves do not require an

_______________________ or __________.

(b) Instead __________ or __________ lined stove pipes transfer the exhaust to the outside.

(c) A _____________________________ is fitted to the joists to ensure the stove pipe is secure and that it is not in contact with

any ______________________________.

(d) A plaster slab surround can be built on upper levels to hide the

___________________.

(e) An insulation and radiation

___________________ provides support and ensures that the pipe does not come into contact with any combustible material.

(f) A _____________________ and

_____________________ ensures that the system is watertight.

Installing a new stove

3 FIRE SAFETY

16. Preventing the spread of fire throughout a house is possibly the most important design feature for any chimney. Using notes and neat freehand sketches, discuss how this can be achieved for a typical chimney stack.

____

____

____

____

____

CHIMNEYS BETWEEN PARTY WALLS

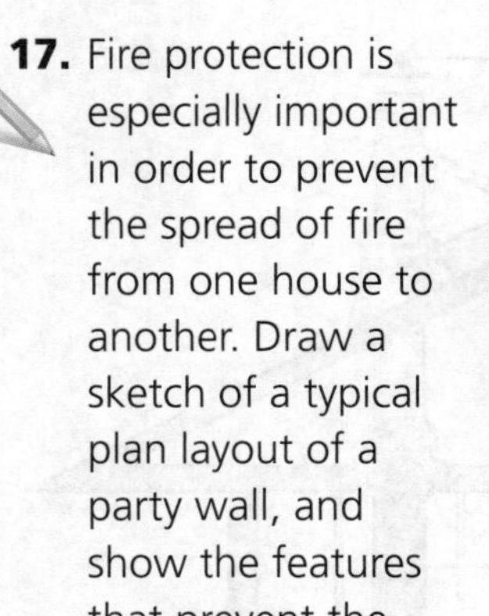

17. Fire protection is especially important in order to prevent the spread of fire from one house to another. Draw a sketch of a typical plan layout of a party wall, and show the features that prevent the spread of fire between buildings.

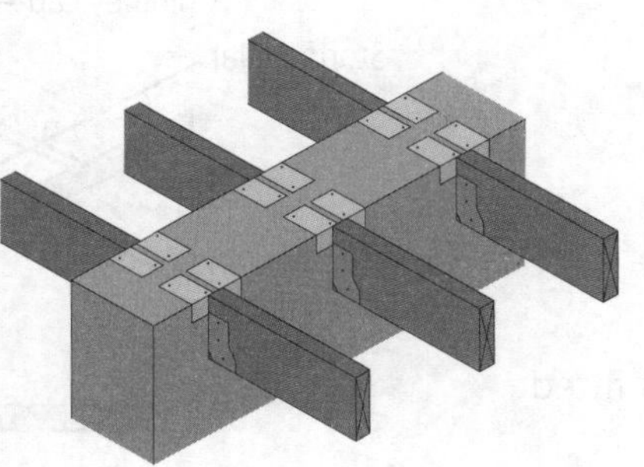

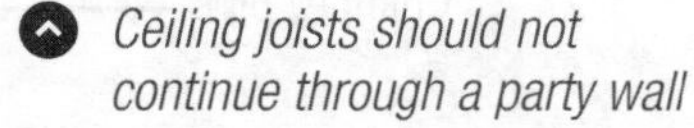

Ceiling joists should not continue through a party wall

CARBON MONOXIDE

18. Carbon monoxide has been described as a 'silent killer'. Explain what carbon monoxide is and how it is created within a home.

____

____

____

____

____

____

____

19. (a) Carbon monoxide build-up can be prevented by:

- ensuring all boilers are ______________.
- ensuring the fire has ______________.
- installing ______________ vents.
- installing ______________ vents.
- installing ______________ vents.

(b) All homes should have a ______________ in the same ______________ as the ______________.

4 WIND STABILITY

20. (a) Chimneys must be designed to withstand the __________.

(b) The ______________ is the most important design factor to achieve this.

(c) Because wind is different in different parts of the country, a guideline map is used to determine the __________ of the chimney.

21. On the map, indicate the correct chimney proportions for each region in Ireland.

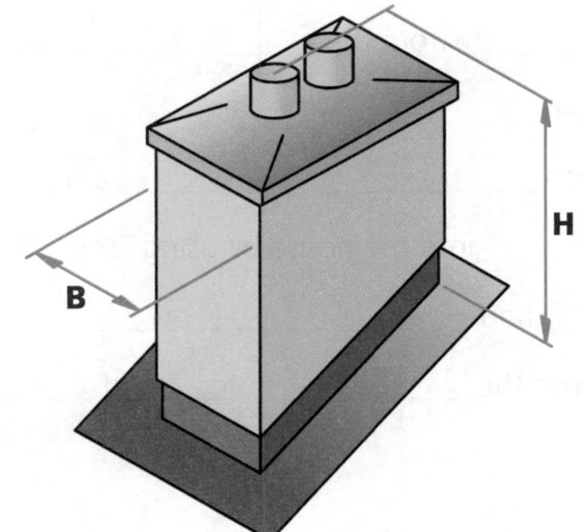

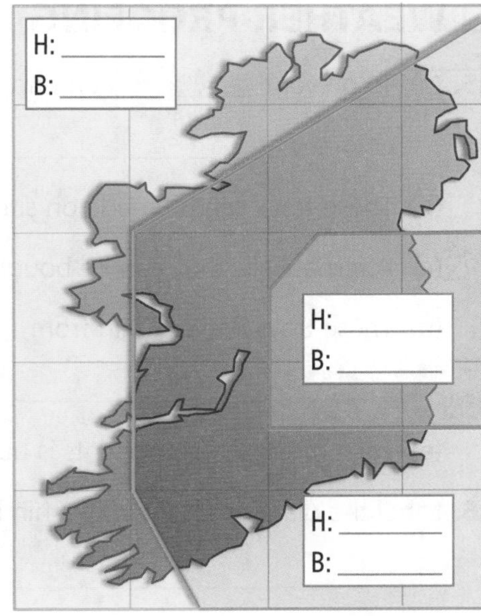

The correct chimney proportions for each region

BACK DRAFT

22. (a) When the wind blows against a roof, it creates zones of __________ and zones of __________.

(b) Exiting smoke from chimneys in the zone of __________ can be __________________ into the chimney. This is known as ___________.

(c) Chimneys in the zone of __________ can be excessively __________.

(d) Chimneys must be ______________________ to prevent either problem occurring.

23. On the diagram below, indicate (a) the zone of pressure and (b) the zone of suction.

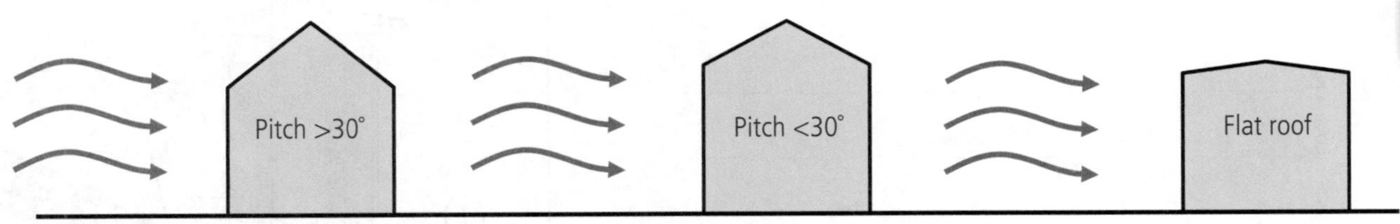

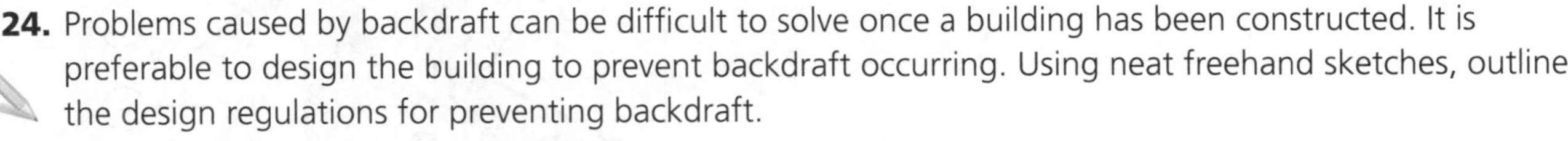

The zone of pressure and the zone of suction

24. Problems caused by backdraft can be difficult to solve once a building has been constructed. It is preferable to design the building to prevent backdraft occurring. Using neat freehand sketches, outline the design regulations for preventing backdraft.

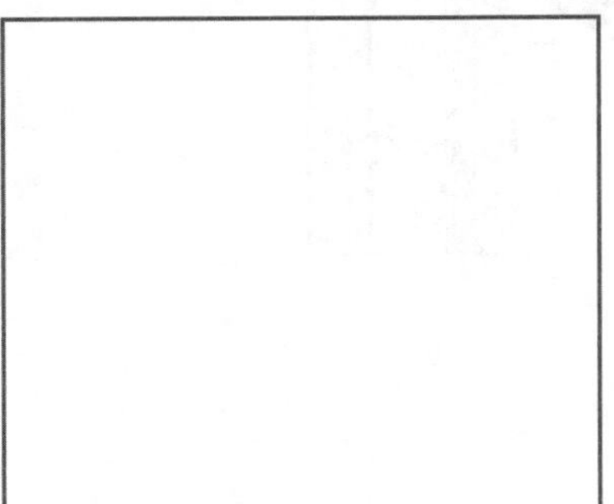

☐ WEATHER-PROOFING A CHIMNEY

25. (a) To prevent __________ entering a house, a __________ is used to separate the portion of the chimney ______________________________ from the ____________________ of the chimney.

(b) These trays can be made on site from __________.

(c) Alternatively, they can be bought as _________________________ with _________________________.

(d) These trays prevent rain from __________ into the house by using:

________________________________ and ________________________________.

(e) Each of these components is built into the __________________ and __________________.

26. Label the diagram of a typical chimney.

1. ________________________________
2. ________________________________
3. ________________________________
4. ________________________________
5. ________________________________
6. ________________________________

Typical chimney

27. Label and add appropriate measurements to the sectional diagram of a chimney detail.

1. ________________________________
2. ________________________________
3. ________________________________
4. ________________________________
5. ________________________________
6. ________________________________
7. ________________________________
8. ________________________________
9. ________________________________

Sectional view of a chimney detail

THEORY QUESTIONS

HIGHER LEVEL

1. A chimney is designed to accommodate a modern wood-burning stove, as shown in the accompanying sketch. The chimney is located on an internal 215 mm solid concrete block wall between the living room and the kitchen. The flue from the stove to the main flue liner is 150 mm in diameter. The floor is an insulated solid concrete ground floor with a 20 mm floating hardwood finish. The dimensions of the stove are: height 700 mm, width 550 mm, depth 450 mm.

(a) To a scale of 1:5, draw a vertical section through the ground floor, hearth and chimney. The section should show the typical construction details from 400 mm below the finished floor to a level 300 mm above the top of the flue from the stove, and include the connection to the main flue liner in the chimney. Include **three** typical dimensions on your drawing.

(b) Indicate clearly on the drawing how the flue liners in the chimney are joined to ensure the safe removal of smoke and flue gases.

Note: Show an outline of the stove only; it is not necessary to show a detailed drawing of the stove.

2013 Higher Level Q7

2. A concrete block chimney stack with a sand/cement render passes through a cut roof which is slated and is pitched at 45°, as shown in the sketch.

(a) To a scale of 1:5, draw a vertical section through the chimney stack and roof, showing the typical details of the chimney stack, flue, chimney capping and portion of the roof structure.

Show clearly the design details necessary to prevent the penetration of water between the chimney stack and the adjoining roof surface.

(b) On your drawing, show **two** design details that will help prevent the occurrence of a downdraught in a chimney as shown. Include dimensions as appropriate.

2011 Higher Level Q7

3. An open fireplace is located on the party wall between two semi-detached houses. The party wall is a 300 mm solid block wall and the ground floor is a concrete floor with a 25 mm woodblock finish.

(a) To a scale of 1:5, draw a vertical section through the ground floor, hearth and fireplace. The section should show all the construction details from the bottom of the foundation to the top of the second flue liner.

Include four typical dimensions on your drawing.

(b) Indicate clearly on the drawing how the flue liners are joined to ensure the safe removal of smoke and gasses from the fireplace.

2008 Higher Level Q1

4. The accompanying sketch shows two semi-detached houses.

(a) Using notes and freehand sketches, show **two** design details that would help restrict the spread of fire between the houses.

(b) Using notes and freehand sketches, show **two** design details that would facilitate escape from a domestic dwelling in the event of an outbreak of fire.

(c) A smoke detection system is compulsory in all new residential dwellings. Outline **two** considerations to be observed when fitting a smoke detection system in a house.

2006 Higher Level Q9

5. To a scale of 1:5 draw a vertical section through an open fireplace in a ground-floor room with a suspended timber floor. Show all constructional features and give sizes of all component parts of the fireplace and the floor. Explain briefly the reasons why a chimney might not efficiently remove the smoke from such a fireplace.

1995 Higher Level Q1

TIMBER FRAME CONSTRUCTION

☐ FUNCTIONS AND FEATURES

1. What is the function of a timber frame house?

____

____

2. What are the design features of a timber frame house?

____

____

____

____

____

____

3. (a) Which design features do timber frame construction and block cavity construction share?

____

____

____

(b) These features are achieved using the same methods as concrete cavity construction, such as

____________________, ____________________ and ____________________.

4. Name three design features used in timber frame construction that are different to those used in block cavity construction.

____

____

____

☐ CONSTRUCTION METHODS

5. A couple want to build a new home. They are unsure of the construction methods available to build their new home. Outline the difference between a block cavity construction and a timber frame construction. In the boxes provided on the following page, sketch a sectional view through the external wall of both construction methods to support your answer.

Block cavity construction	Timber frame construction

Continued

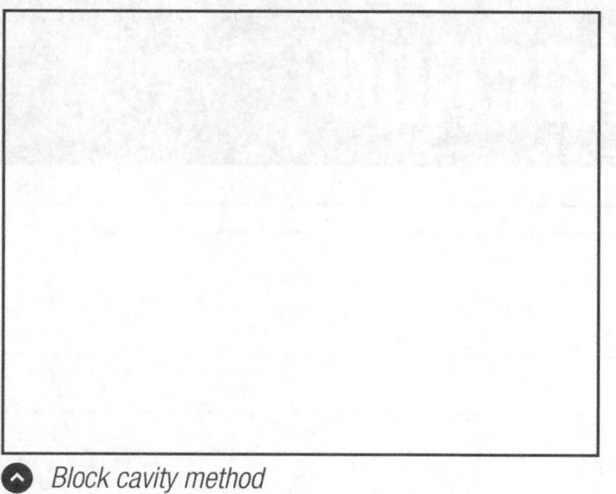
Block cavity method

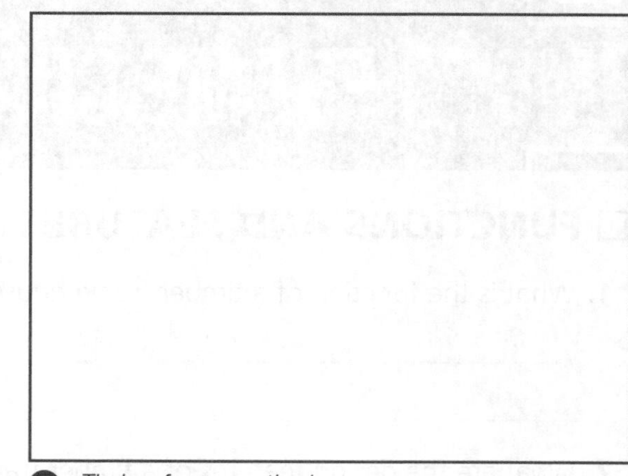
Timber frame method

TIMBER FRAME CONSTRUCTION

6. A typical timber frame wall consists of:

(a) an outer __________ leaf, which acts as a _____________ layer.

(b) a _________________________________.

(c) 12 mm of __________ sheeting.

(d) 120 mm of quilted __________ between softwood timber frame studs.

(e) a ____________________ membrane.

(f) 19 mm of a _____________ slab.

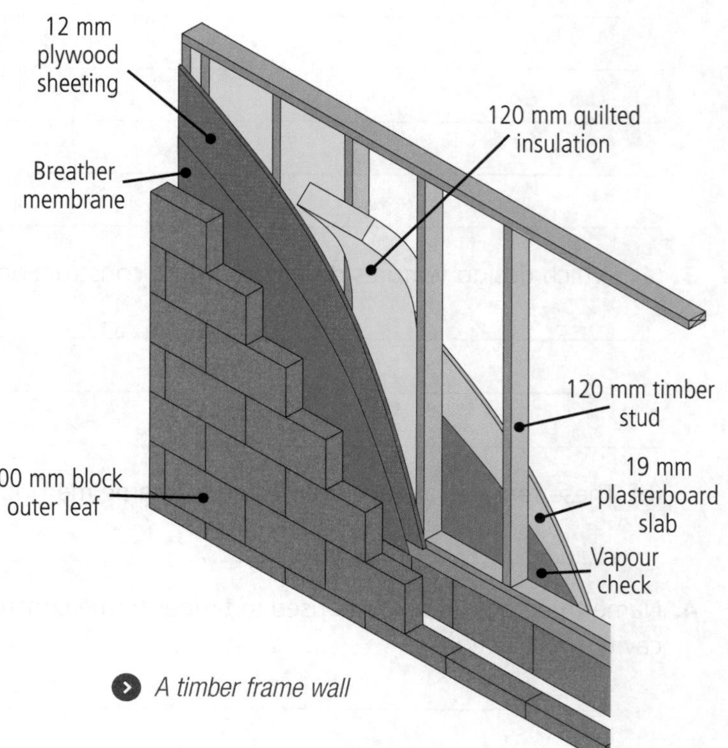

A timber frame wall

COMPARISON OF CONSTRUCTION METHODS

7. A couple want to build a new home. They are unsure whether they should build a timber frame house or a block cavity house. Compare the advantages and disadvantages of traditional block cavity construction and timber frame construction.

Block cavity construction	Timber frame construction

☐ DESIGN FEATURES OF TIMBER FRAME HOUSES

1 MOISTURE RESISTANCE

8. When using timber as a construction material, take the following characteristics into account:

(a) ______________ when in ___________ and _______________________ environments.

(b) Timber ___________ if overly ________.

(c) To prevent these occurring, the cavity should be ____________________ using _____________________ in the ____________________.

(d) This allows ____________ to circulate and remove ____________, and allows the building to ___________.

9. On the diagram, use arrows to indicate the movement of air through a proprietary vent.

The movement of air through a proprietary vent

10. (a) To prevent water vapour entering the timber frame from inside the house, a ____ membrane is attached to the ____________ of the inner leaf. This acts as a barrier to prevent any moisture vapour/droplets entering the stud wall.

(b) To assist in the removal of any moisture build-up due to _____________________________ from inside the stud, a _____________________________ is placed on the ____________ of the inner leaf. This allows water _________________________ to pass from inside the stud out through the cavity but does not allow water _____________ to return from the outer leaf back inside the house.

12

11. On the diagram, draw the vapour check and breather membrane. Using arrows, show the movement of moisture that the breather membrane and vapour check permit.

The vapour check and breather membrane

2 TIMBER MOVEMENT

12. (a) Timber is a natural material which will ___________ and ___________.

(b) This must be ______________ in the ___________ of the building.

(c) ____________________ should be fixed only to the ______________ to maintain an ________________.

(d) ______________________ should be catered for at the ____________, ____________ and ____________.

(e) ______________________ sealant should be used to allow for ______________.

13. On the diagram, indicate the design considerations that allow for the movement of timber around the eaves.

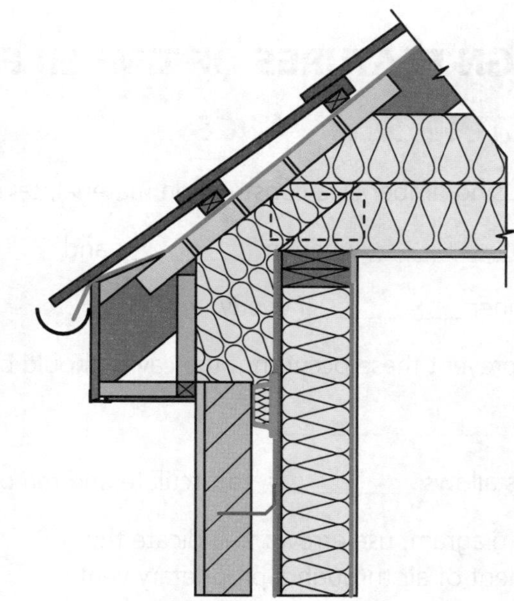

Movement of timber around the eaves

3 FIRE RESISTANCE

14. (a) Timber is a ______________________________.

(b) As the timber inner leaf ______________ the __________ of the ________________,

maintaining its ______________________________ during a fire, and __________ the __________ of fire is a primary concern.

(c) Using timber treated with __________________ preservative, __________, __________ and

______________________________ assists in resisting the passage of fire.

15. On the diagram, indicate the features of a timber frame wall that resist the passage of fire.

Features of a timber frame wall that resist the passage of fire

16. The diagram shows a timber frame party wall. Draw the mineral wool fire stop and the vertical fire barriers.

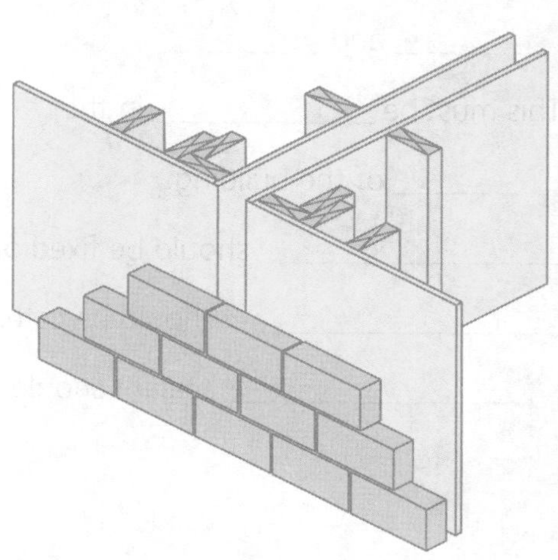

Timber frame party wall

☐ TIMBER FRAME CONSTRUCTION PROCESS

STEP 1: FOUNDATIONS

17. (a) The ____________________, ___________ and ___________________ of a timber frame building are constructed using the same methods as a ______________________ building.

(b) The inner leaf of the rising wall is thicker, as it has to accommodate the timber frame (__________mm).

(c) The timber frame is __________ to the site on __________ and __________ into place using a __________.

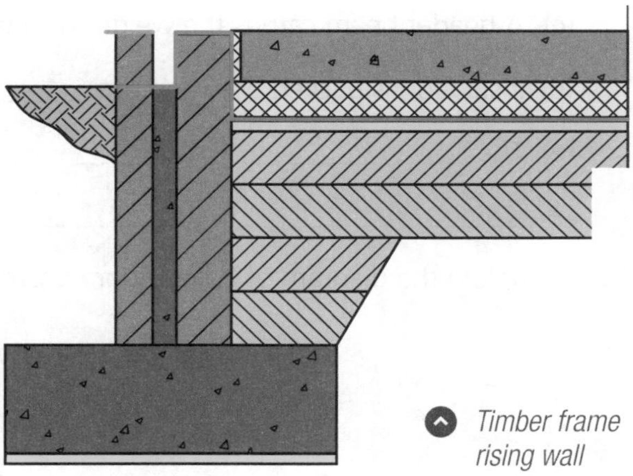

(d) It is then __________ to ensure the frames are __________ and __________.

Timber frame rising wall

STEP 2: SECURING THE FRAME

18. Describe how the timber frame is secured to the rising wall.

____

____

____

____

____

19. Label the diagram of a timber frame set-up.

1. ____
2. ____
3. ____
4. ____

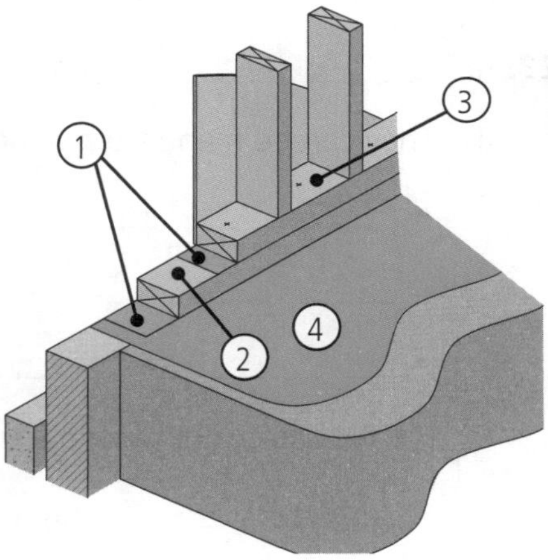

Timber frame set-up

20. Label the diagram showing how a timber frame is connected to a rising wall.

1. ____
2. ____
3. ____
4. ____
5. ____

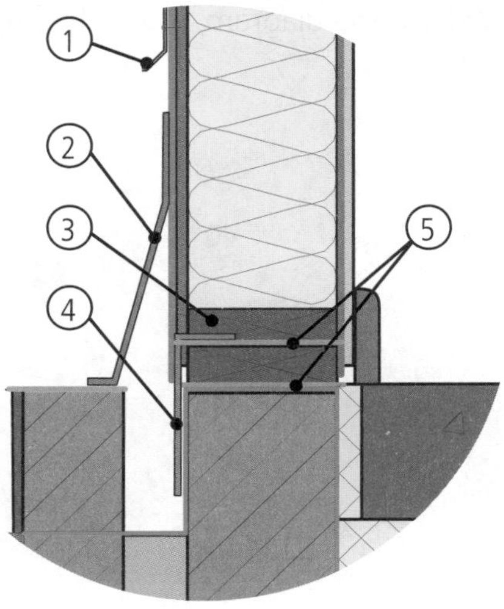

Connecting a timber frame to a rising wall

12

STEP 3: UPPER FLOOR CONSTRUCTION

21. (a) The first floor is __________ into place to rest on ______________________________.

(b) A ______________________________ is used to evenly transfer the __________________.

(c) A header beam carries the weight of the ______________.

(d) Insulation is packed between the ________________ and the _______________.

(e) The ______________________________ is continued across the floor between the __________ and ______________________________.

22. Complete the diagram of a first floor construction.

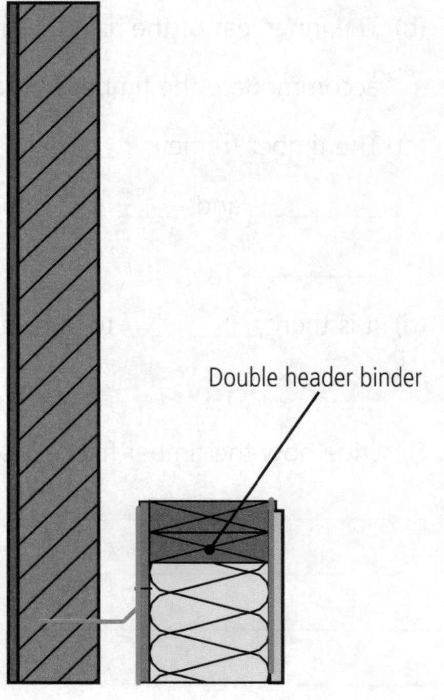

First floor construction

STEP 4: OPENINGS

CAVITY BARRIERS

23. (a) ________________ prevent fire entering into a cavity.

(b) They can be made from either:

- _________________________ (usually _______x_______) that are pressed tightly against the ________________.
- ___________________________ stuffed in __________________.

(c) For fire safety, the window frame should be fixed to the ________________ only, and not to the __________________.

24. On the diagram, insert the fire barrier around the ope.

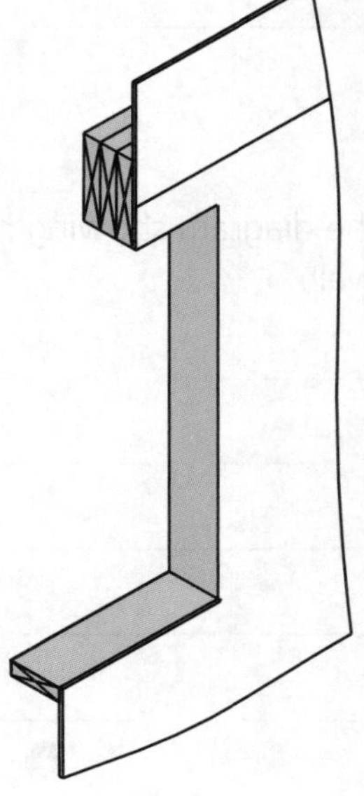

The fire barrier around the ope

LINTELS

25. (a) ____________________ are used over any openings in the ________________.

(b) __________________________ or _____________________ are used to support the __________________

(c) The cavity is __________ using a _____________________ around the ope.

(d) Vents are added over the ope to ________ the timber frame.

(e) The ____________________ is __________ with __________ to prevent ____________________ the ope.

(f) This damp-proof course must under lap the existing _____________________.

26. Label the lintel details on the diagram.

1. ____
2. ____
3. ____
4. ____
5. ____
6. ____
7. ____
8. ____

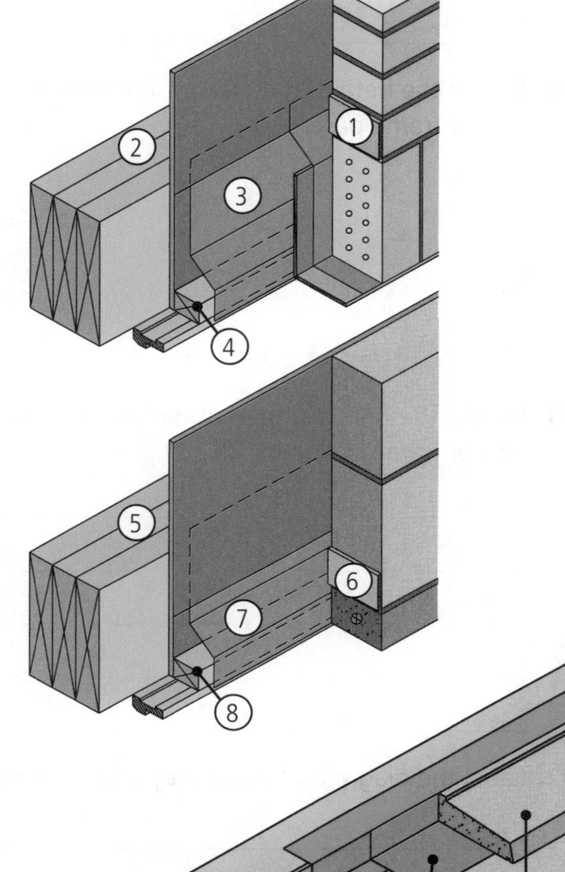

Lintel details

Timber frame cill

WINDOW-CILLS

27. (a) The window-cill rests on the __________________ and the __________________.

(b) ________ is wrapped around the cill to prevent ______________ entering the cavity.

(c) A second damp-proof course layer is also ______________ over the top of the _________________ and along the ____________ of the ________________ ________________.

28. Using a coloured pen, show the Damp-proof course lapped over the cavity barrier and wrapped around the cill.

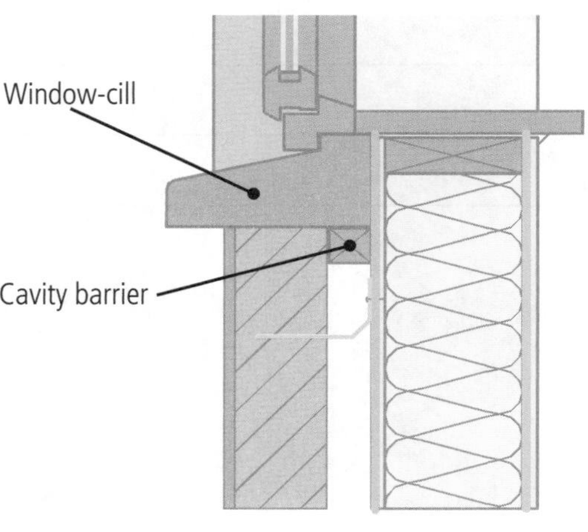

Damp-proof course lapped over the cavity barrier and wrapped around the cill

STEP 5: PARTY WALLS BETWEEN BUILDINGS

29. What measures are taken to ensure that a fire in one building does not spread to a neighbouring building through the party wall?

30. Sketch the details that prevent fire spreading through a timber frame party wall.

STEP 6: CHIMNEYS

31. How is the fire risk inherent with chimneys reduced in a timber frame building?

32. Label the diagram of a chimney arrangement.

1.
2.
3.
4.
5.
6.
7.
8.

Chimney arrangement

STEP 7: ROOF LEVEL

33. (a) Between party walls, ________________ of plasterboard are used up to ____________________.

(b) The inside layer is ___________ plank type plasterboard fixed ____________________.

(c) The outside layer is ___________ plaster slab fixed ____________.

(d) ___________ and ________________________________ are used to prevent the spread of fire through the external cavity.

(e) A ____ is laid between the adjoining walls.

(f) ______________________ is placed along the roof between the ___________.

(g) ______________ is fixed to the adjoining ______________________.

34. Label the diagram of how a party wall is made fire resistant.

1. ____________________________________
2. ____________________________________
3. ____________________________________
4. ____________________________________
5. ____________________________________

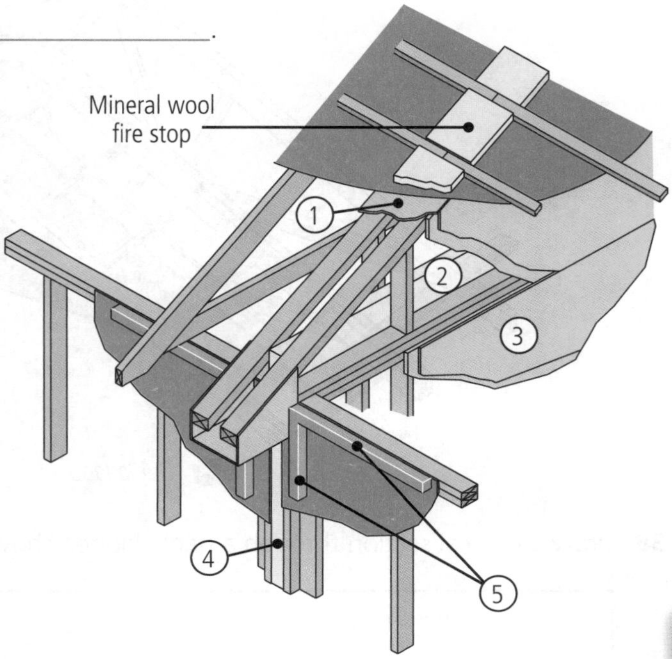

Making a party wall resistant to fire

EAVES DETAIL

35. (a) The weight of the roof is carried entirely by the ____________________.

(b) ______________________ in the ___________ and between the rafters ensure that the roof space is well ______________________.

(c) A ______________________________ is used to ensure that _______ cannot spread to the roof space.

36. Label the eaves detail.

1. ____________________________________
2. ____________________________________
3. ____________________________________
4. ____________________________________

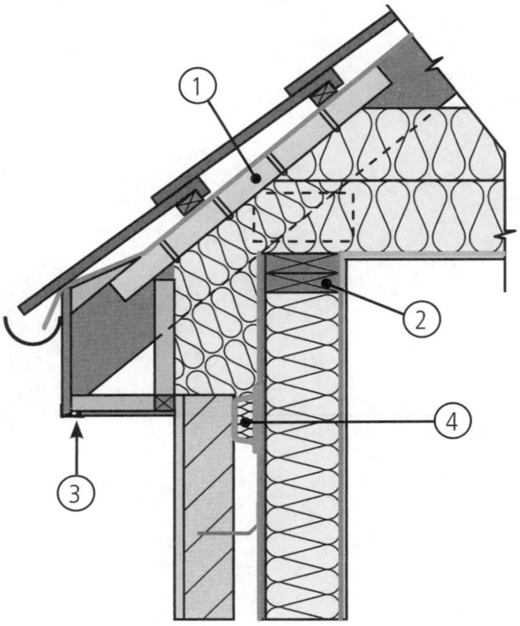

Eaves detail

GABLE LADDER

37. (a) The ________________ is fixed to the last truss.

(b) Timber battens, at a maximum spacing of __________________________, support the ladder.

(c) All timber used for the gable ladder should be treated with ________________.

(d) The gable ladder should not be longer than _______________________.

(e) The ladder should not project more than __________________________.

(f) A fire barrier is placed between the ______________along the _______________ of the roof.

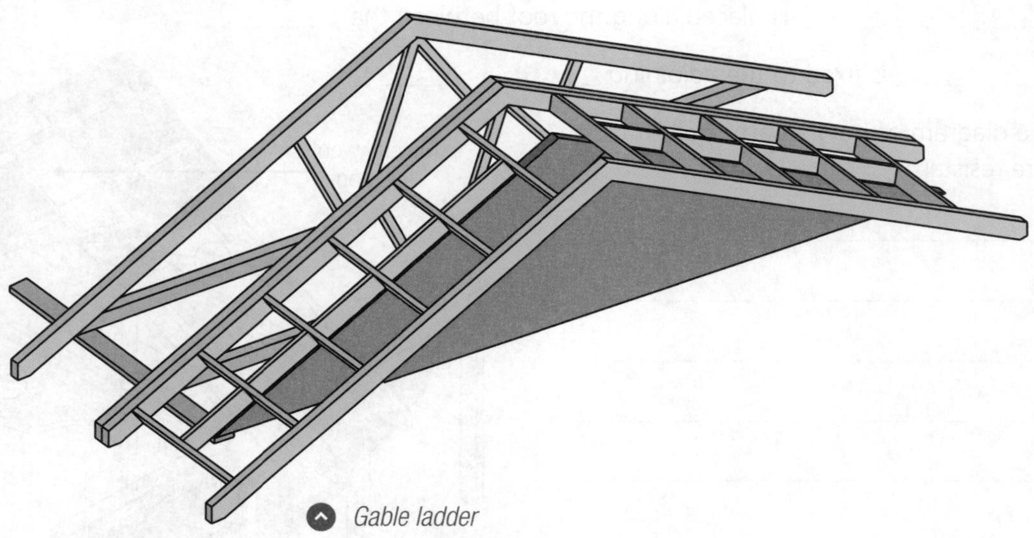

Gable ladder

38. Draw a vertical section through a gable ladder, showing key building regulations.

THEORY QUESTIONS

HIGHER LEVEL

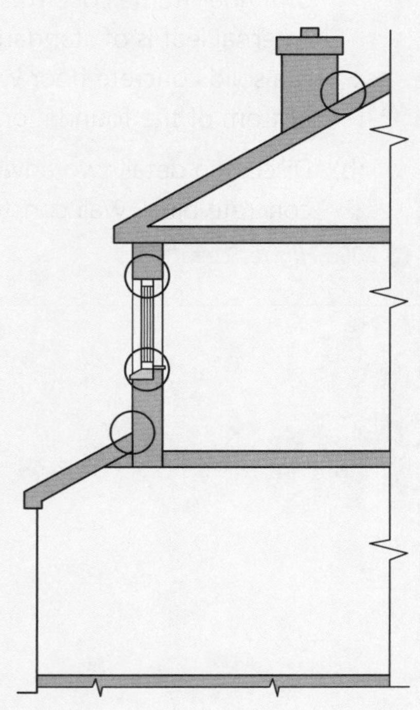

1. A two-storey house, as shown in the drawing, is of timber frame construction with a rendered concrete block outer leaf. The chimney is also of rendered concrete block construction and both roofs are slated. Careful design detailing is required to prevent the penetration of dampness at the critical junctions circled in the drawing.

(a) Select any **three** locations from those circled on the drawing and show, using notes and freehand sketches, the typical design detailing which will prevent the penetration of dampness at each location.

(b) Select any **two** junctions and specify a damp-proofing material suitable for each junction. Discuss the advantages of each material for the specified junction.

(c) Discuss in detail the importance of ensuring that moisture does not penetrate to the inner leaf of a wall of timber frame construction.

2013 Higher Level Q9

2. A four-panel wooden door is fixed in the external wall of a two storey timber-frame house, as shown in the sketch. The external wall, which supports the first floor joists, has a concrete block outer leaf with a rendered finish.

(a) To a scale of 1:10, draw a vertical section through the external wall, door and floor joists. The section should show the typical construction details from 400 mm below the head of the door frame to 400 mm above the first floor joists.

Show clearly the external wall, the door, door frame and the first floor joists. Indicate the typical dimensions of four main structural members.

(b) On the drawing, show clearly how the first floor joists are supported at the timber-frame inner leaf of the external wall.

2007 Higher Level Q7

3. (a) To a scale of 1:10, draw a vertical section through the window, the external wall and the roof of a timber-framed house, as shown in the sketch. The external leaf is of concrete block construction with a rendered finish. The roof has prefabricated trussed rafters, is slated and has a pitch of 45 degrees.

Show all the constructional details from 300 mm below the window head, through the eaves and include three courses of slate.

(b) On the drawing, label and indicate the typical dimensions of four main structural members.

2006 Higher Level Q7

12

4. Timber frame construction is now widely used for domestic dwellings in Ireland.

(a) To a scale of 1:10, draw a vertical section through the external wall and ground floor of a house of timber frame construction. The top of a window-cill is positioned 900 mm above floor level, the external leaf is of standard concrete block construction with a rendered finish and the ground floor is a solid concrete floor with 20 mm quarry tile finish. Show all the constructional details from the bottom of the foundation to the top of the concrete cill.

(b) Discuss in detail two advantages of timber frame construction and two advantages of standard concrete block wall construction and recommend a preferred wall type for a new house.

2005 Higher Level Q9

STAIRS

☐ FUNCTIONS AND FEATURES

1. What are the main functions of a stairs?

____

____

2. Outline the key design features that should be taken into consideration when designing a stairs.

____

____

____

____

____

____

____

____

____

____

____

____

☐ PARTS OF A STAIRS

3. (a) Stairs: a ______________ and ______ leading from one floor level to another.

(b) Stairwell: ______________ by the stairs.

(c) Flight: ______________ from one floor to another or to a landing.

(d) Landing: a ________ between ________.

It provides a ________ and can also be used to change ________ of stairs.

(e) Tread: the upper surface ______ of a step (where the foot is placed).

(f) Riser: the upper ______ between two treads.

(g) String: a ________ at the sides of the stairs that ______ the tread and the riser.

(h) Handrail: a ________ and ______ for a person climbing the stairs.

(i) Baluster: the timber that ________ the ________ and prevents people from

______________.

(j) Balustrade: the term for both the ________ and ________.

(k) Newel post: the ______ at the ______ and ______ of a flight of stairs which supports the

______ and ______.

4. Label the parts of a stairs.

1. ____________________
2. ____________________
3. ____________________
4. ____________________
5. ____________________
6. ____________________

The parts of a stairs

5. Explain the following:

(a) Total rise: ____________________

(b) Total going: ____________________

(c) Rise: ____________________

(d) Going: ____________________

(e) Nosing: ____________________

(f) Pitch line: ____________________

6. The edge of the ________ should be a maximum of ________ away from the pitch line.

7. Using annotated sketches, show the total rise, total going, rise, going, nosing and pitch line.

☐ CONSTRUCTING A STAIRS

8. Describe the process of constructing the steps for a timber stairs.

9. Label the parts of a stairs.

1. ______________________
2. ______________________
3. ______________________
4. ______________________
5. ______________________
6. ______________________

Stairs

10. Draw a neat annotated sketch of how a string is attached to a newel post.

11. Draw annotated sketches showing the bottom three steps and the top three steps of a straight flight, closed string stairs.

Bottom three stairs

Top three stairs

☐ STAIR REGULATIONS

12. A well-designed stairs should take into consideration the user's natural stride. Using notes and neat freehand sketches, describe how the building regulations take a user's stride into account.

Stair regulation 1

Stair regulation 2

13. Whenever a person is at a height, there is a risk of them falling and injuring themselves. Using notes and neat freehand sketches, outline how this risk is reduced for a standard stairs.

Method 1

Method 2

14. Other stair regulations include:

(a) A maximum of __________ is permitted without a __________.

(b) __________ must project a minimum of ________ beyond the riser.

(c) The handrail must be located ______________ above the pitch line.

(d) Stairs can have a minimum width of __________.

(e) A minimum of ________ headroom, measured vertically from the pitch line, must be provided.

(f) A __________ must be provided at the _______ of every __________.

(g) Where a door opens out onto a landing, a minimum space of ________________,

free of ____________________ must be left for safety.

15. Insert the recommended dimensions for the given stairs.

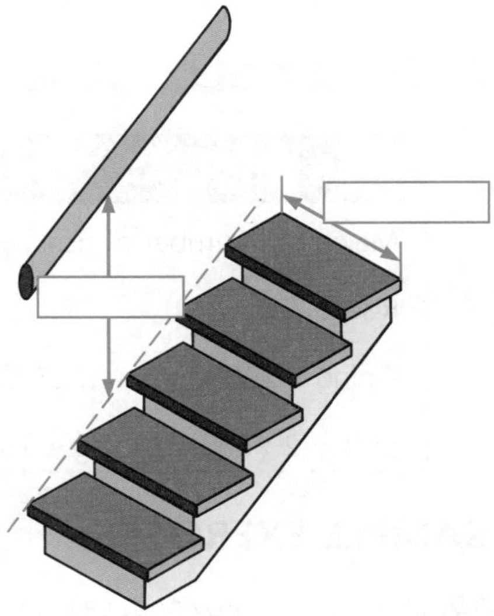

Recommended dimensions for stairs

16. Insert the recommended dimensions for the clearance space from the given door.

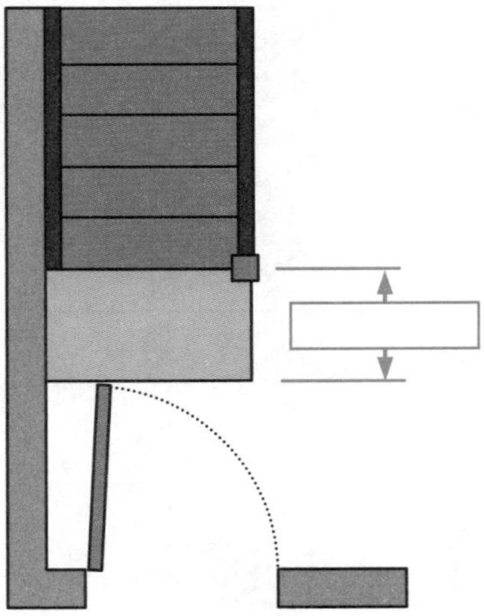

Recommended dimensions for clearance space from door

17. (a) Draw a sketch of head clearance.
(b) Draw a sketch of nosing detail.

(a)

(b)

13

☐ TAPERING/WINDER STEPS

18. For safety reasons, tapering or winder steps should be avoided. If this is not possible, close adherence to the building regulations will ensure the tapering steps are as safe as possible. Outline the key regulations governing the design of tapering steps.

☐ STAIR CALCULATIONS

REMEMBER!

Maximum number of risers = 16

Rise ≤ 220

Going ≥ 220 (optimum 250)

550 ≤ (2 × rise) + going ≤ 700

SAMPLE EXERCISES

19. In the space provided, calculate an appropriate rise and going for the overall stairs details shown in the diagram.

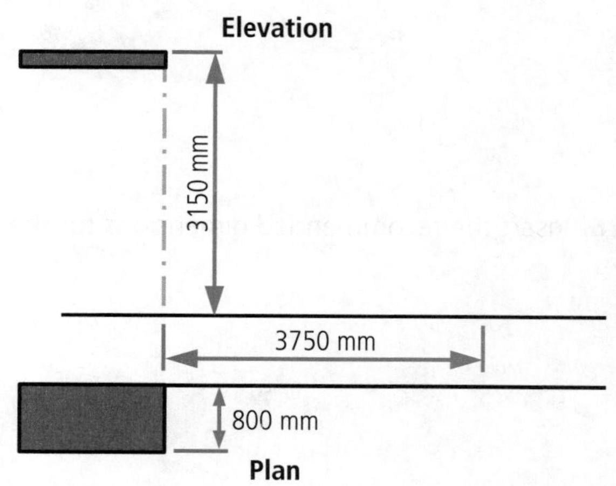

Overall stairs details

20. In the space provided, calculate an appropriate rise and going for the overall stairs details shown in the diagram.

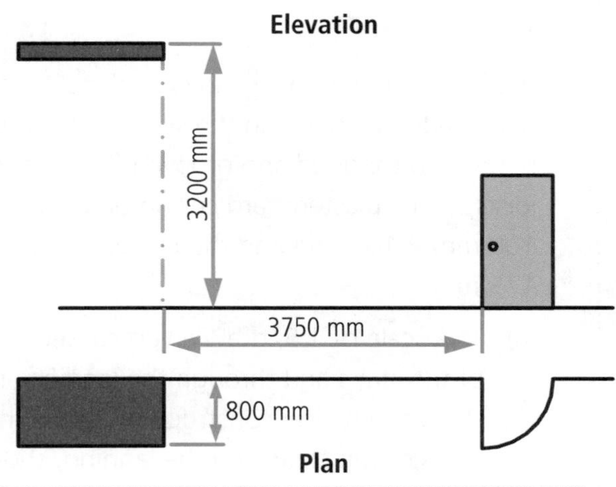

Overall stairs details

THEORY QUESTIONS

ORDINARY LEVEL

1. The sketch shows a portion of a closed string timber stairs suitable for a dwelling house.

(a) To a scale of 1:5, draw a vertical section through the bottom three steps of the stairs. Show the string, treads and risers and give their typical sizes.

(b) Show on your drawing **one** design detail which will ensure that the stairs does not creak when in use.

2011 Ordinary Level Q5

HIGHER LEVEL

2. A closed-string wooden stairs leads to a landing with balustrade, as shown in the sketch. The landing has a hardwood tongued and grooved floor, on 200 mm × 50 mm joists with a plasterboard ceiling beneath. The newel post is 100 mm × 100 mm and the rise of a step should not exceed 175 mm.

(a) To a scale of 1:5, draw a vertical section through the centre of the stairs and through the landing. The section should show the typical construction details through the top three steps of the stairs and the landing, showing the newel post, balusters and handrails to the stairs and landing. Include the typical dimensions of three structural members of the stairs. Show the typical handrail height to stairs and landing.

Note: On your drawing, show a 500 mm length of landing.

(b) Indicate on your drawing **two** design features that ensure that the stairs is safe for all users.

2013 Higher Level Q1

3. A cut-string timber stairs suitable for a domestic dwelling is shown in the accompanying sketch.

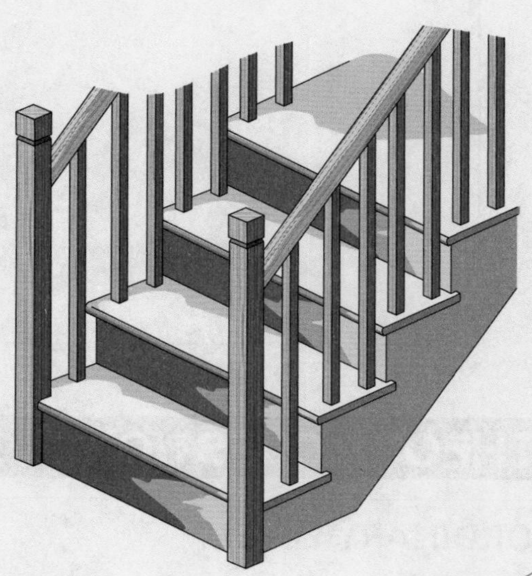

(a) To a scale of 1:5, draw a vertical section through the bottom four steps of the stairs. Include the newel post and balustrade and show the typical dimensions of **four** main structural members of the stairs.

(b) Using notes and freehand sketches show **two** design features that ensure that the stairs is safe for all users.

2008 Higher Level Q7

PLUMBING

☐ FUNCTIONS AND FEATURES

1. What are the functions of a domestic plumbing system?

____

____

2. What are the key design features of a domestic plumbing system?

____

____

____

____

____

☐ PLUMBING COMPONENTS

TAPS AND VALVES

3. Taps and valves are used to control the supply of water around a building. Using notes and neat freehand sketches, outline the difference between a tap and a valve.

____

____

____

____

Sketch of a section through a tap

Sketch of a section through a valve

DRAIN-OFF VALVE

4. (a) A drain-off valve is used to ______________ a water system when ______________, ______________ or ______________ are taking place.

(b) Drain-off valves contain a built-in ______________ or ______________.

(c) They are placed at the ______________ possible point in a water system.

COLD WATER CISTERN

5. (a) A cold water cistern is a ______________________________ that supplies outlets that do not require ______________________, such as toilets.

(b) A cold water cistern typically holds __________ litres.

(c) It contains a stop valve known as a ________________ or ________________.

☐ COLD WATER SUPPLY

6. Describe how cold water typically enters a dwelling from a mains water supply.

____

____

____

____

____

____

____

7. Complete the diagram showing how water enters a building from a mains water supply.

Water mains

How water enters a building from a mains water supply

HARVESTING RAINWATER

8. (a) As water ________________ is introduced and people are charged for their ________________________, people are beginning to look at ways to either:

- ____
- ____

(b) One way to do this is to harvest the free ________________ that runs off roofs.

(c) Generally, rainwater is ________________ (not ________________) but is suitable for flushing toilets, gardening, washing machines and so on.

(d) Up to __________% of all household water can be sourced from harvesting rainwater.

(e) As well as being free, rainwater does not contain any ______________, which can be a problem in some ________________ areas.

9. Describe the process of harvesting and treating rainwater collected from the roof surface of a dwelling.

____

____

____

____

____

____

____

____

____

____

10. Label the components of a typical rainwater harvesting system.

1. ____________________
2. ____________________
3. ____________________
4. ____________________
5. ____________________
6. ____________________
7. ____________________
8. ____________________

A typical rainwater harvesting system

COLD WATER SYSTEMS

11. There are two main types of cold water supply systems used for domestic houses.

(a) ____________________:

- Water is fed __________ into every __________ in the house.
- This water system is ____________________.
- If there is ever a ____________________ from the water mains, there is a risk that the water from toilets and other appliances would ____________________ into the water supply (the mains).

(b) ____________________:

- In this system, the only outlet fed directly from the service pipe is the ____________________ and other outlets that ____________________ is taken from.
- The rising main feeds water to a ____________________ in the __________.
- From here, the ____________________ are supplied.

12. Complete the schematic of an indirect cold water supply.

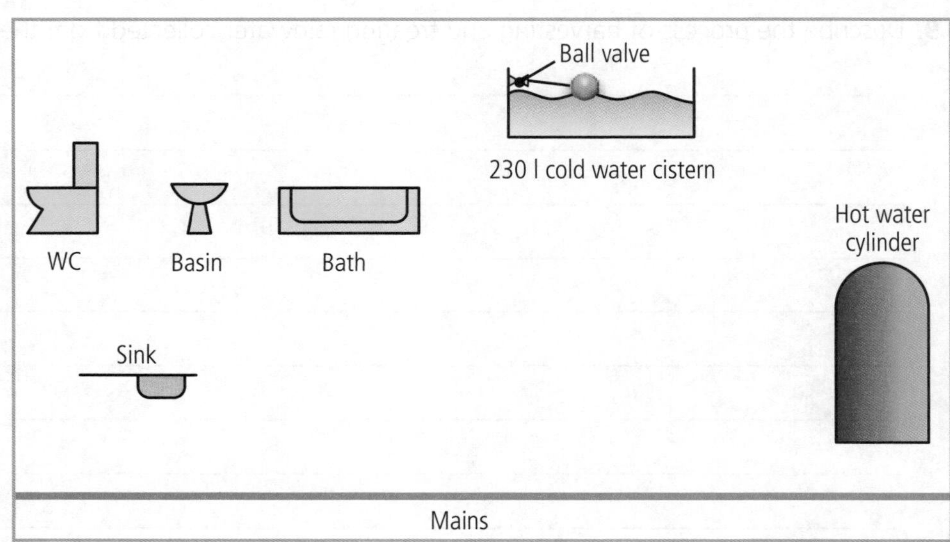

Indirect cold water supply

13. Compare a direct and an indirect cold water system.

Direct cold system	Indirect cold system

HOT WATER SUPPLY

14. Every house requires a hot water supply for everyday activities, such as washing and showering. Hot water is supplied in the home in different ways, such as by (a) immersion heating, (b) direct hot supply and (c) indirect hot supply. Explain the difference between the hot water cylinder designs for each system. Support your answer by completing the diagrams.

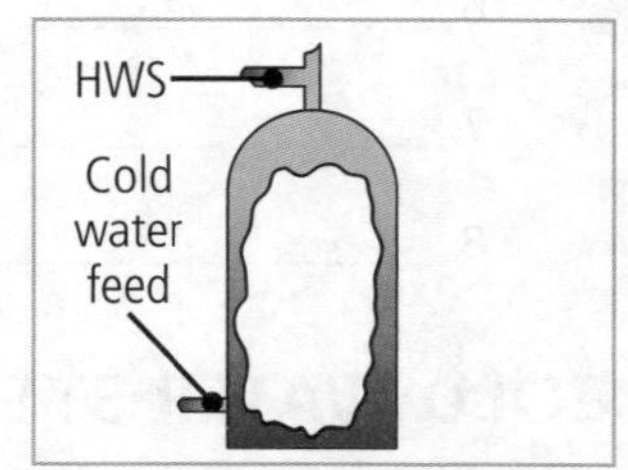

(a) Immersion cylinder

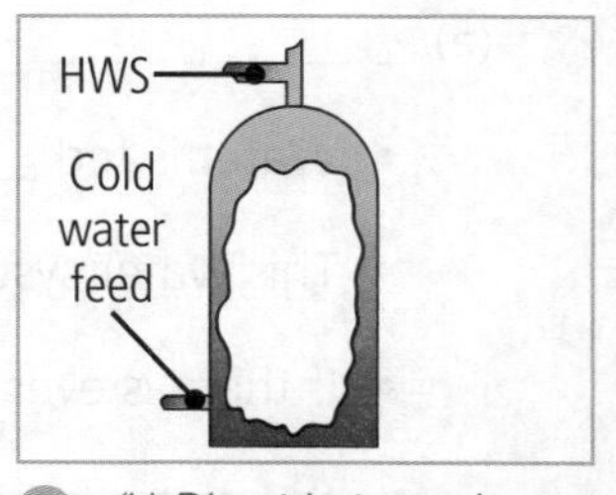

(b) Direct hot supply cylinder

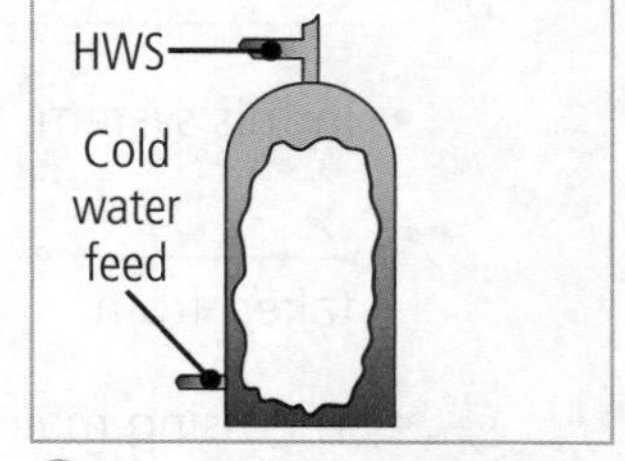

(c) Indirect hot supply cylinder

15. You have been contacted by a couple who have just purchased an old building. They have been experiencing problems with blocked pipes due a build-up of limescale. Upon investigation, you discover that the house has a direct heating system. Explain to the couple why their existing system is causing limescale blockages and how installing a new indirect system will solve this problem.

16. Complete the schematic of an indirect hot water supply system for a typical dwelling, correctly labelling all components and control valves. Use a red pen to indicate hot water and a blue pen to indicate cold water.

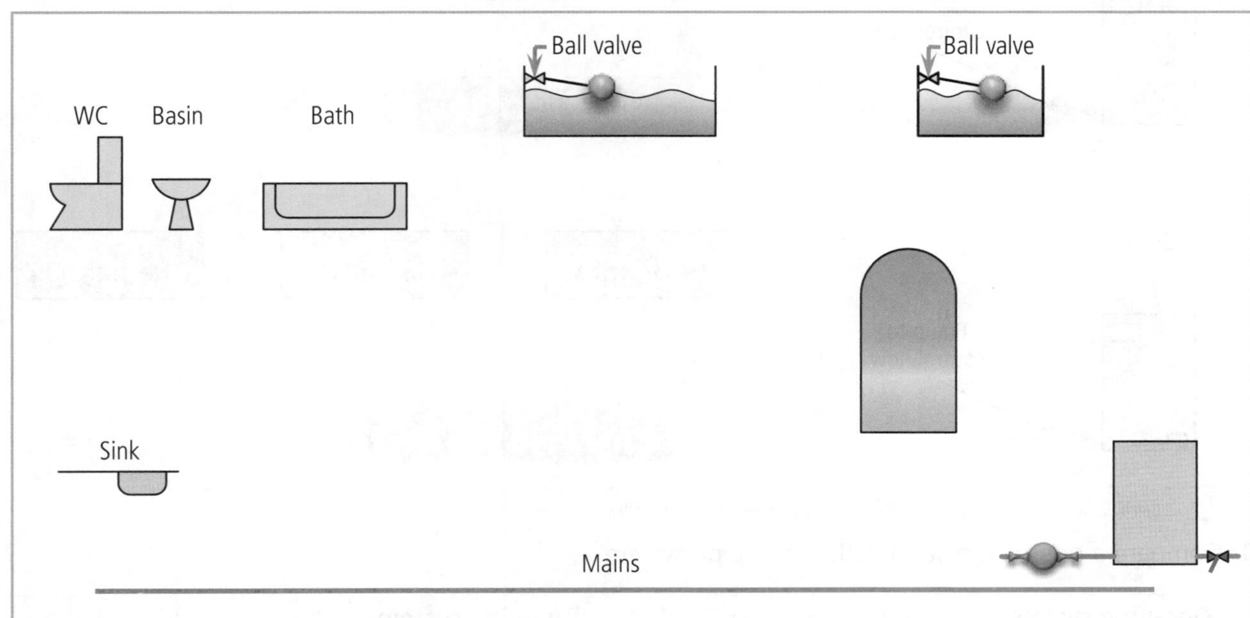

Schematic of an indirect hot water supply system

☐ CENTRAL HEATING

17. Describe, using notes and neat freehand sketches, how a typical radiator works to heat a room.

CENTRAL HEATING SYSTEMS

18. (a) There are many different types of systems used to heat a home. The most common methods are the ________________ system and the ________________ system. In both systems, hot water flows from the ______________ to heat the ________________.

(b) In a one-pipe system, the water flows sequentially from ________________ to the ______________ until it returns to the boiler.

(c) In a two-pipe system two pipes are used. One pipe carries ________ water _______ the radiators, and the other pipe carries ________ water ________ from the radiators.

19. Complete the schematics of a one-pipe and a two-pipe heating system.

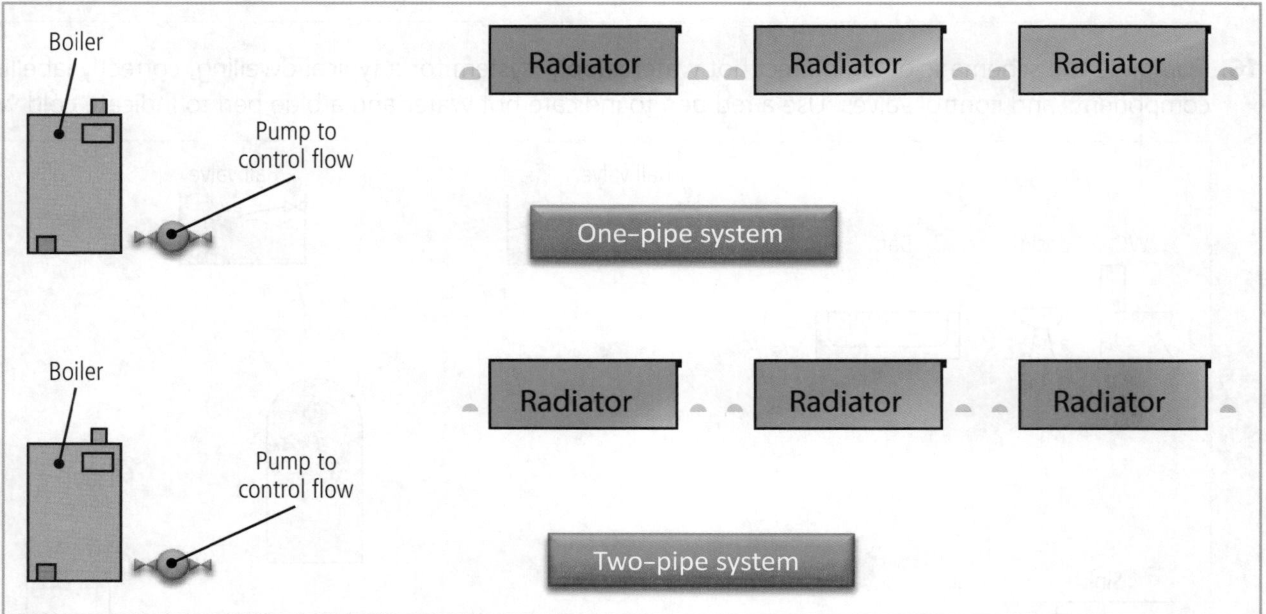

Schematics of a one-pipe and a two-pipe heating system

20. Compare a one-pipe system with a two-pipe system.

One-pipe system	Two-pipe system

ZONED HEATING SYSTEM

21. (a) A zoned heating system uses ______________________________ attached to the hot water flowing from the boiler.

(b) This allows the heating system to be divided into ______________________________, which can act independently of each other.

(c) Different zones can be set to come on at ______________________________ (for example, upstairs late at night and downstairs in the evening).

(d) Zones are set using a ______________________________.

22. Draw a labelled sketch of a zoned two-pipe hot water system.

23. Complete the table listing the advantages of zoned heating systems.

Advantages of zoned heating systems	
	Allows for different ideal temperatures to be maintained in different zones of a dwelling
Comfort	
	Allows isolation of zones for periodic maintenance
Maintenance	
	Allows the heating system to interface with sophisticated digital control technology
Remote setting	

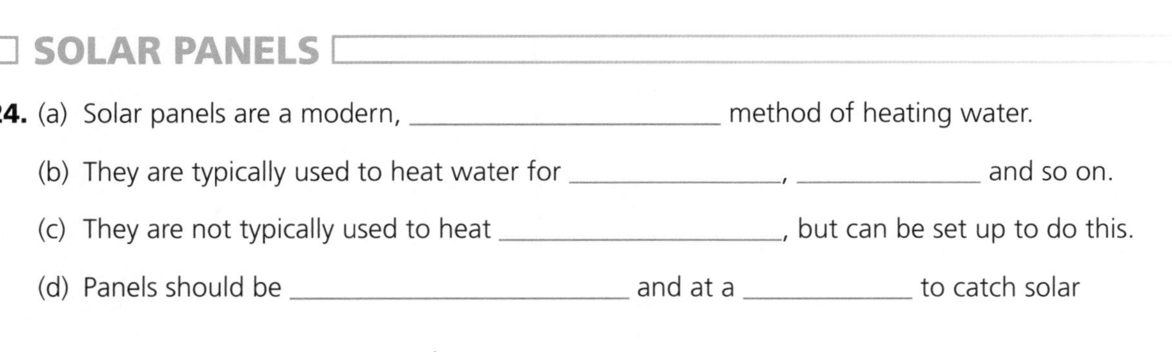

☐ SOLAR PANELS

24. (a) Solar panels are a modern, ______________________ method of heating water.

(b) They are typically used to heat water for _______________, _____________ and so on.

(c) They are not typically used to heat ____________________, but can be set up to do this.

(d) Panels should be ________________________ and at a ____________ to catch solar

________________________.

25. A family want to install a solar panel system in their house to supplement their conventional boiler heating system. Describe, using notes and neat freehand sketches, how the family can incorporate the new solar panel set-up into the pre-existing plumbing system.

26. Name two types of solar panel.

27. Using notes and neat freehand sketches, describe how an evacuated tube captures the sun's heat and transfers it into the home.

FLATBED SOLAR PANELS

28. Flatbed panels are the most common type of solar panel used in Ireland today. They are made up of:

(a) a protective ______________ sheet.

(b) an array of ______________ containing ______________.

(c) an ______________ behind the pipes to absorb the sun's ______________.

(d) ______________ to ensure the panel is ______________.

29. Label the flatbed solar panel components.

1. ______________

2. ______________

3. ______________

4. ______________

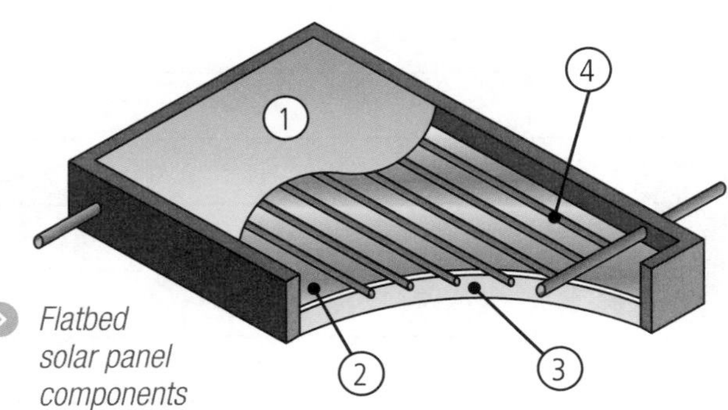

Flatbed solar panel components

30. The pipes can either be arranged in:

(a) a  ______________.

(b) an  ______________.

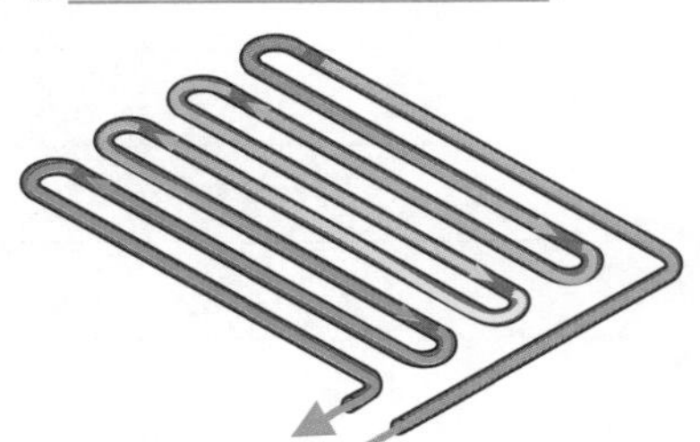

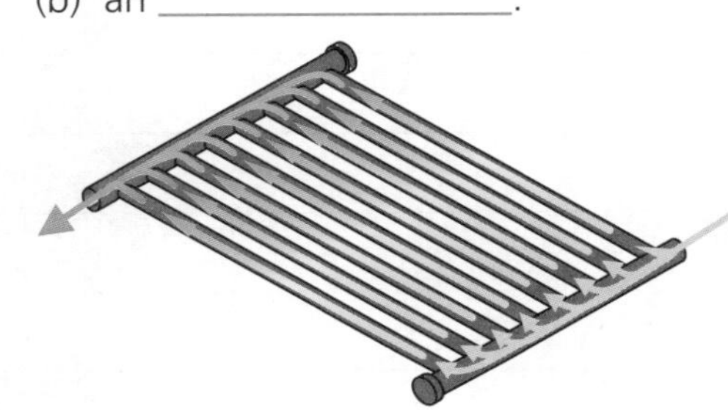

☐ GEOTHERMAL HEATING

31. (a) Geothermal heating uses the concept that the temperature below the earth is ______________.

(b) It operates on a temperature ______________ between ______________ the ground and ______________ the ground.

(c) A liquid with a low ______________ (usually water mixed with ______________, or glycol) is pumped through a pipe under the earth.

(d) The pipe can be a:

- ______________ loop (spaced __________ apart, __________ deep).
- ______________ loop (laid in holes up to __________ deep).
- ______________ loop (buried __________ deep).

32. Complete the diagrams of the three most common ground source pipe layouts used for geothermal heating.

The three most common ground source pipe layouts for geothermal heating

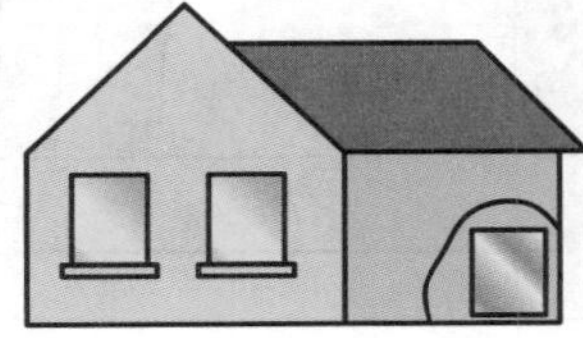

33. A geothermal heating system does not require the ground to be very warm to absorb enough heat to operate. Discuss how a heat compressor converts relatively small differences in heat into large, more useable levels of heat.

Geothermal heat compressor

Compressor
Evaporator
Condenser
Expansion valve

____

____

____

____

____

____

____

____

____

____

____

____

____

____

____

____

____

UNDERFLOOR HEATING

34. (a) Conventional radiators have the disadvantage of ______________ heating a room.

(b) The room is ______________ near the radiator and ______________ further away from the radiator.

(c) Underfloor heating prevents this occurring by evenly heating the room from the __________ up.

(d) In underfloor heating, ______________ pipes are laid over ________________________ in the floors.

(e) The pipes are covered over with a smooth ______________ finish.

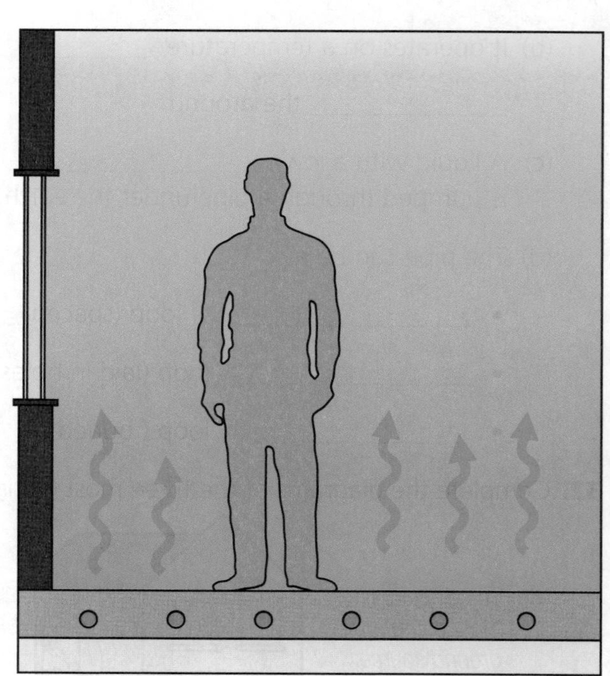

Underfloor heating gives a more even heat than radiators

BOILERS

35. A school wants to replace its old conventional boiler with a new condensing boiler to reduce the annual heating bill. Describe the differences between the two systems, explaining why the condensing boiler is a more efficient choice.

Radiator
Exhaust
Baffle
Burner
Inlet feed
Air intake

A conventional boiler

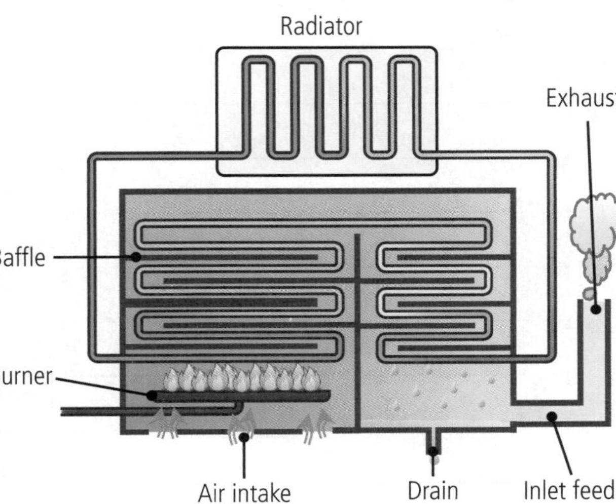

A condensing boiler

THERMOSTATIC RADIATOR VALVE (TRV)

36. (a) A thermostatic radiator valve (TRV) is a valve that ________________ the temperature of a radiator.

(b) Inside the TRV is a ________________ material that ________________ when heated.

(c) When the material expands, it closes a valve ________________ the flow of hot water to the radiator.

(d) When the radiator cools down, the material shrinks and the valve ________________ to allow the hot water to flow.

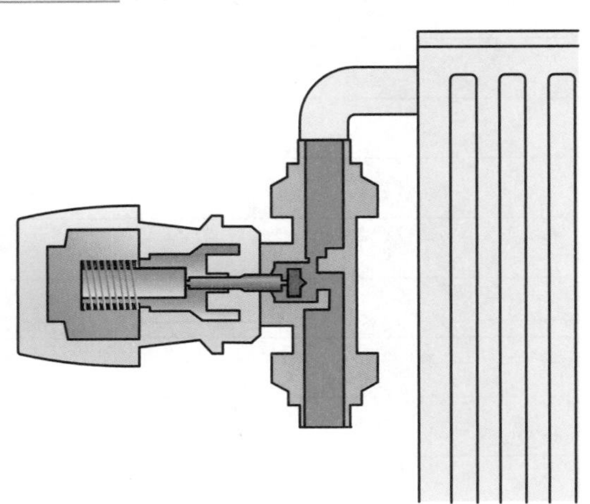

A cross-section through a TRV

HOW A TRV WORKS

37. Installing TRVs on the radiators in a house can help to reduce the cost of heating the house, along with maintaining more control over the heating. Discuss how the TRV can achieve this in a typical home.

38. There are many safety risks associated with a conventional heating system in a dwelling. Discuss what these key risks are and how they may be prevented using the correct safety control fittings.

THEORY QUESTIONS

ORDINARY LEVEL

1. (a) Using a single-line labelled diagram, show the pipework necessary to supply hot and cold water to a wash hand basin and a bath, as shown in the sketch.

Include the following in your diagram:

- water storage tank and overflow.
- rising main.
- hot water cylinder and pipework.
- insulation to the water storage tank and to all pipework.
- location of all necessary valves.

(b) Show, using notes and neat freehand sketches, a design for a tap which will be easy to use by a person with limited hand mobility.

2013 Ordinary Level Q3

2. A dwelling house is connected to the public water supply system to provide clean, treated water for the household.

(a) Using a single-line labelled diagram, show the pipework required to supply cold water to a kitchen sink, as shown in the sketch. Include the following in your diagram:

- pipework from public mains to kitchen sink.
- location of valves.
- material and typical size of pipework.

(b) Include in your sketch **two** design details that would prevent the water in the mains supply from freezing during very cold weather.

(c) Outline **two** ways in which the household could reduce the use of treated water from the public water supply.

2012 Ordinary Level Q3

3. The sketch shows an outline of a single storey-house, an underground rainwater storage tank and a separate rainwater storage tank in the attic of the house.

(a) Using notes and neat freehand sketches, show the pipework necessary to pump the rainwater from the underground storage tank to the tank in the attic. Label the components and give their typical sizes.

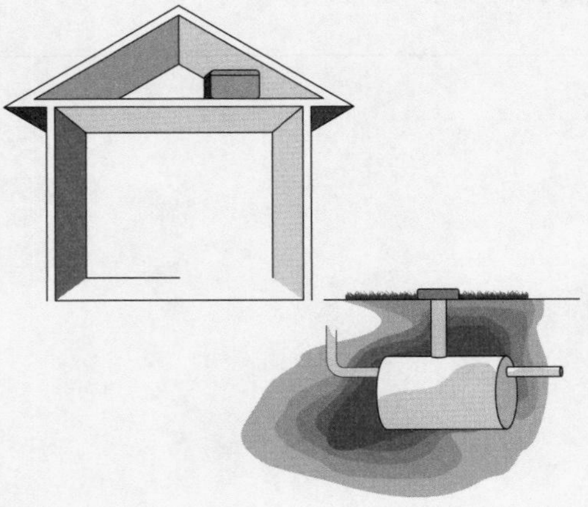

(b) Stored rainwater may be used in both a toilet and a washing machine. Show, using notes and neat freehand sketches, the pipework necessary to connect **one** of these appliances to the storage tank in the attic. Show the necessary valves.

(c) Discuss **one** reason why the rainwater is stored in a separate storage tank in the attic.

2011 Ordinary Level Q7

HIGHER LEVEL

4. It is proposed to use a wood-burning stove combined with a solar collector to provide central heating and hot water for a two-storey house.

(a) Using notes and a single-line diagram, show a typical design layout for the heating system and the domestic hot water system. Show **two** independently controlled heating zones, one on each floor, and include three radiators on each floor. Indicate the location of the control valves and give the typical sizes of the pipework.

(b) Using notes and freehand sketches, discuss **two** design considerations that should be taken into account when siting a solar collector, as shown, to ensure maximum efficiency.

(c) Discuss in detail **two** advantages and two disadvantages of the heating system outlined at 4 above.

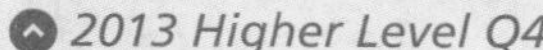

2013 Higher Level Q4

5. (a) A wood-burning stove, as shown in the sketch, is used to heat two independently controlled heating zones, one on each floor, in a two-storey dwelling house. Using notes and a single-line diagram, show a typical design layout for the pipework necessary to independently heat each zone. Show three radiators on each floor, indicate the control valves and give the typical sizes of the pipework.

(b) It is proposed to connect a solar collector, as shown in the sketch opposite, to this system to heat domestic water. Show a design layout for the pipework necessary to connect the solar collector to the existing system and outline the modifications required to the existing system to accommodate the solar collector.

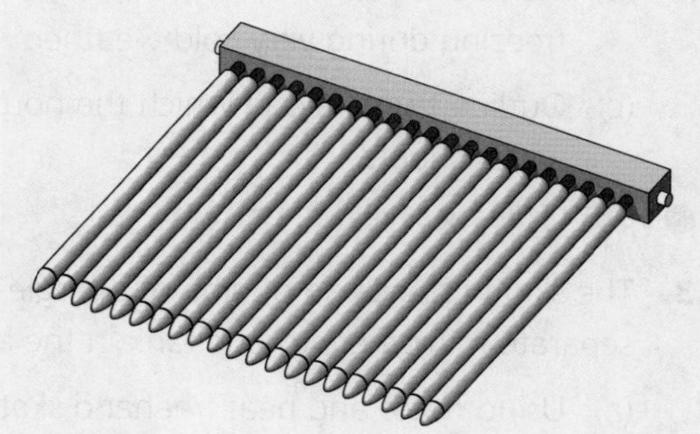

(c) Using notes and freehand sketches, show a preferred location for the solar collector and discuss in detail **two** factors that influenced your choice of location.

2011 Higher Level Q8

15 DOMESTIC ELECTRICITY

☐ ELECTRIC CURRENT

1. (a) Electricity can be defined as the ______________ of ____________ through a conductive material.
   (b) Electric current is measured in ____________ (__________). Its symbol is ______.

VOLTAGE

2. (a) In order for a current to flow, there must be a ____.
   (b) This force is created by ______________________ in charge between various points in the circuit.
   (c) It is measured in ____________. Its symbol is ________.
   (d) A _____________ is a common source of potential difference in a circuit.

CONDUCTORS AND INSULATORS

3. (a) Conductors are materials that are good at _______________ electricity.
   (b) _______________ is a good conductor; it is used for electrical wiring.
   (c) _______________ are materials that do not allow electricity to flow easily.
   (d) _____________ are good insulators. This is why _______ are made from __________ and why electrical cable is wrapped in _______________.

Conducting material

Insulating material

Conductors and insulators

☐ RESISTORS

4. (a) Resistors are components that ______________ the flow of ________________________.
   (b) They have many applications such as in __________ and ____________.
   (c) There are two types of resistor:

   ____________________________________ ____________________________________

   (d) Variable resistors can alter the ______________________________.
   (e) A ____________________________ is an example of a variable resistor.
   (f) The symbol for resistance is ______. It is measured in _________.
   (g) 1 ________ of resistance = 1 ________, which is needed to drive 1 _______ of current.

IMPORTANT EFFECT OF CURRENT

5. (a) When ______________ flows through an area of high resistance, __________ is generated.

(b) ________________________ and ______________ make use of this effect.

6. (a) Electricity ___________________ if the path is ________________.

(b) Electricity always takes the path of _________________________________.

☐ POWER

7. (a) Electrical energy is known as ________________.

(b) Power = ________________ x ________________

(c) Power is measured in ________________. Its symbol is ______.

(d) Energy consumption is measured in ___________________. Its symbol is ______________.

(e) The SI unit of energy consumption is the ______________.

(f) 1 ______________ = 1 ______________________________

POWER SUPPLY

8. (a) The most common method to generate electricity is by a process known as ____.

(b) Electricity is generated by moving a conductive material inside a ________________.

(c) Most generators operate by rotating a conductive coil, called a ______________, inside the magnetic field, called a ______________.

(d) Different sources of energy are used to drive the rotor by turning a large ____________.

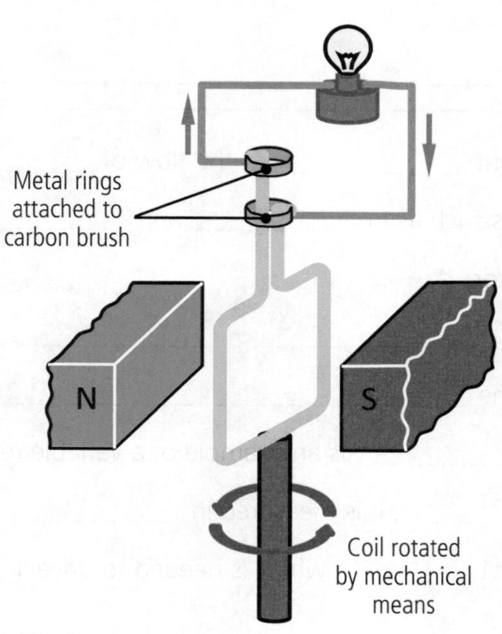

Electromagnetic induction

9. Using annotated sketches, explain how electricity is generated in an induction generator.

☐ ELECTRICITY GENERATION AND DISTRIBUTION IN IRELAND

10. What three types of power station are used in Ireland? Describe what force powers each station.

11. Complete the diagram showing how electricity is generated in a typical thermal power station.

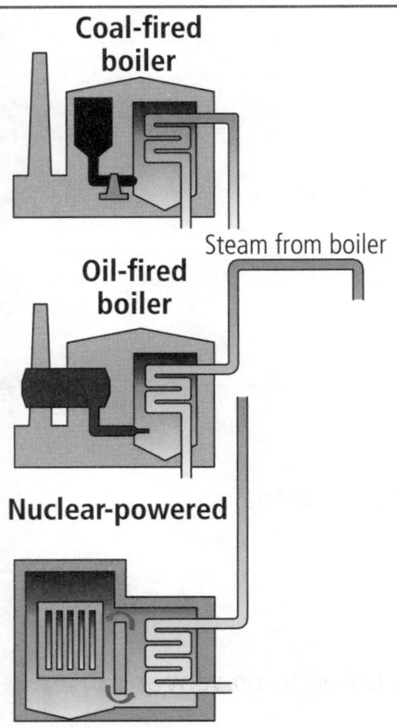

Coal-fired boiler

Steam from boiler

Oil-fired boiler

Nuclear-powered

How electricity is generated in a typical thermal power station

HYDROELECTRIC STATIONS

12. (a) Hydroelectric stations use the power of ________________ in ________________ to rotate a turbine.

(b) A ________________ of ________________ enters the station via a ________________.

(c) The ________________ of the rushing ________________ turns the ________________, which powers the ________________.

(d) The ________________ then joins back up with the ________________ of the ________________.

(e) The electricity is then connected to the ________________ for ________________.

13. Sketch the set-up of a typical hydroelectric power station.

WIND POWER STATIONS

14. (a) Wind turbines use ________________ to drive the ________________.

(b) The ________________ drive the ________________.

(c) A set of ________________ step up the ________________ to the ________________.

(d) This shaft turns the ________________ to create the ________________.

(e) Each turbine has a ________________ which detects ________________.

(f) This sends a signal to an on-board ________________.

(g) This controller operates a ________________, which turns the turbine to ________________.

(h) An on-board ________________ also measures ________________.

(i) If the winds are ________________, a ________________ is applied to prevent any ________________ to the turbine.

15. Label the typical wind turbine components.

1. ______________________ 7. ______________________
2. ______________________ 8. ______________________
3. ______________________ 9. ______________________
4. ______________________ 10. ______________________
5. ______________________ 11. ______________________
6. ______________________

Wind turbine components

ELECTRICITY DISTRIBUTION

16. Using notes and neat freehand sketches, describe how electricity is distributed throughout the country.

17. (a) Electricity is transmitted at low currents and high voltages, such as ______________, ______________ and ______________.

(b) Once the electricity has reached the ______________________________, the voltage is ______________ (to ____________, ____________ and ____________).

(c) The electricity is then transmitted to a ______________________________ or to ______________________________ located on poles.

(d) Before entering a home, it is stepped down a final time to ____________.

18. Complete the schematic of the national grid.

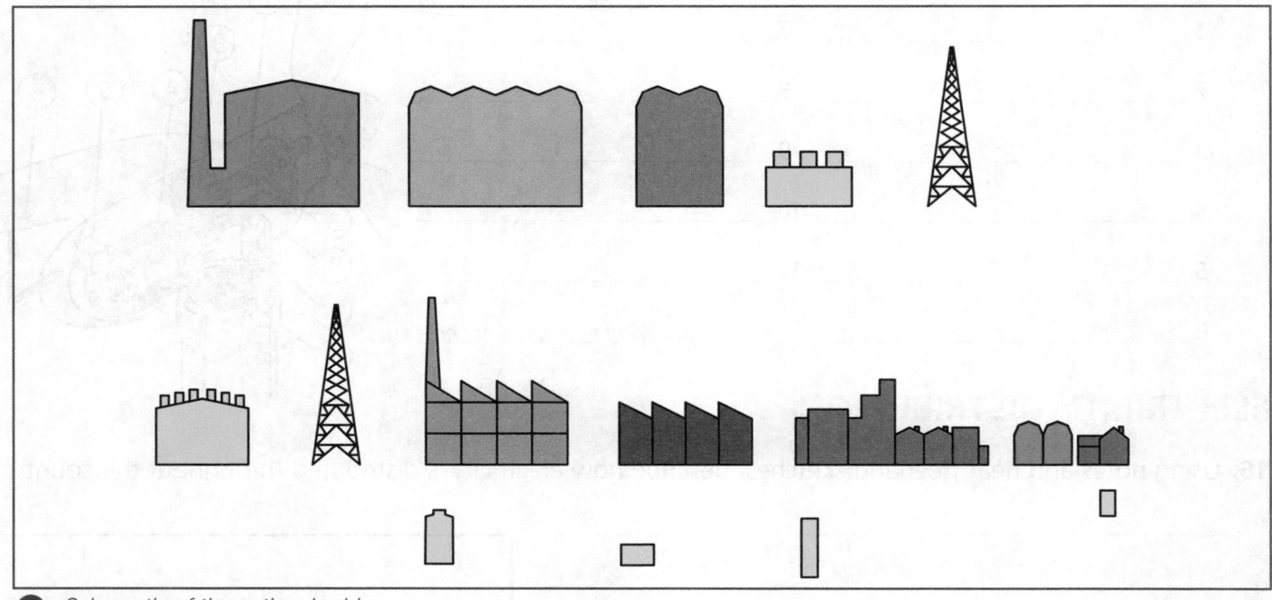

Schematic of the national grid

PHOTOVOLTAIC SOLAR PANELS

19. Increasing numbers of people are now generating their own electricity using photovoltaic solar panels. These panels are made up of two layers of material, a P-layer and an N-layer, separated by a junction material. Describe how a photovoltaic solar panel creates electricity.

20. Label the components of a typical photovoltaic solar panel.

1. __________
2. __________
3. __________
4. __________
5. __________
6. __________

Typical photovoltaic panel components

CONNECTING SOLAR PANELS TO THE GRID

21. (a) To use electricity generated by solar panels in a house, the electricity must be converted from

_______________ (________), to _______________ (________).

(b) This is done using an _______________.

(c) For safety, it is important that the electricity can be _______________ and

_______________ the _______________.

(d) The electricity is then connected to the _______________.

(e) This determines whether there is an _______________ of _______________ to sell back to the grid or whether _______________ is required from the _______________.

(f) Both the _______________ and _______________ electricity is metered using _______________ meters, or a combined _______________ meter.

22. Label the connecting to the grid diagram.

1. _______________
2. _______________
3. _______________
4. _______________
5. _______________
6. _______________
7. _______________

Connecting to the grid

CONNECTING OFF THE GRID

23. (a) It is also possible to generate enough electricity for a house not to have to rely on the national grid. This is known as being _______________.

(b) This will require the generated electricity to be stored in _______________ for use when needed.

(c) Additional electricity can be generated using a _______________ or a

_______________.

24. Label the components of the off-the-grid system.

1. ______________________________
2. ______________________________
3. ______________________________
4. ______________________________
5. ______________________________
6. ______________________________
7. ______________________________

Connecting off the grid

DOMESTIC INTAKE OF ELECTRICITY

25. What are the design features of a domestic electricity supply?

____

____

____

____

____

____

____

SUPPLY TO THE HOUSE

26. (a) The electricity supply entering a house is ____________.

(b) This supply is connected to a ______________.

(c) Usually, the meter is housed in a ________________ located on an ________________________.

(d) From the meter box, the electricity supply is fed to the ____________________________ (commonly known as the ________________).

27. Complete the sectional diagram showing the electrical supply entering a dwelling.
Show the following components:

1. Incoming service cable in plastic
2. 600 x 400 mm meter box
3. Stepped damp-proof course
4. Vertical damp-proof course behind meter box
5. Consumer unit

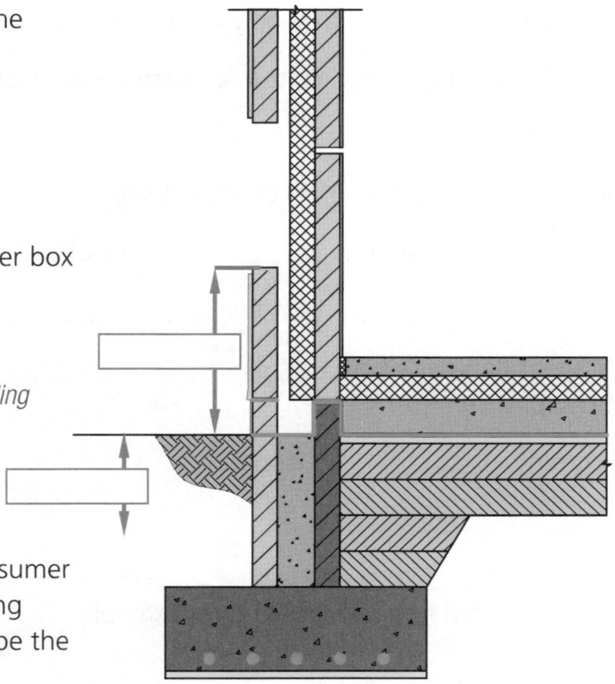

Electrical supply entering a dwelling

CONSUMER UNIT

28. From the meter, electricity is fed to the consumer unit. The consumer unit contains an isolating switch and multiple circuit breakers. Describe the function of each safety feature.

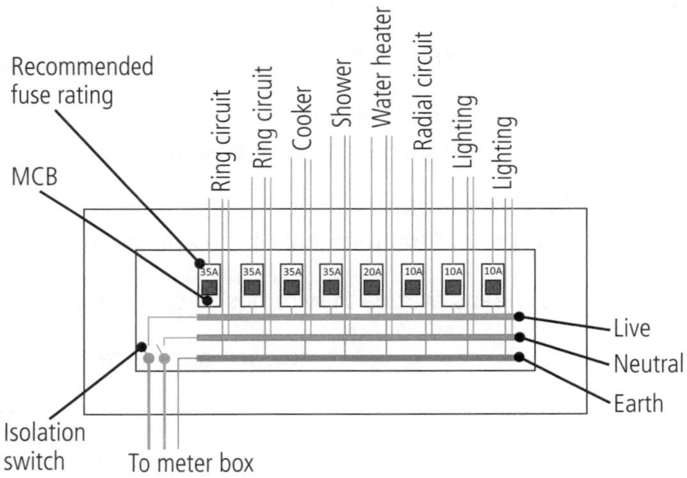

Consumer unit

☐ CIRCUIT TYPES

29. There are two types of circuit used to distribute electricity around the house. A house will have several radial circuits, each serving a different function. List the four radial circuits you would expect to find in a typical house.

30. (a) A ring main circuit is used to supply electricity to __________ (__________).

(b) The number of ring main circuits in a house depends on the __________ of the house.

RADIAL CIRCUIT

31. (a) A radial circuit is a circuit in which the cabling

__________ at an __________, or at the

__________ in the __________.

(b) The current flows along a __________ to the appliance.

(c) The current __________ along a

__________.

(d) __________ appliance can be connected to a radial circuit, for example,

__________.

Cooker control unit

Cooker

Consumer unit

Meter board

Radial circuit

RING MAIN CIRCUIT

32. (a) A ring main circuit is a circuit in which the __________

is connected back to the __________.

(b) The current flows along __________ to the live terminal of the appliance.

(c) The current returns along __________ from the neutral terminal of the appliance.

(d) This means that each wire has to carry only

__________ to each appliance.

(e) This allows __________ to be used

for the circuit, which __________.

Consumer unit

Meter board

Ring main circuit

RADIAL CIRCUIT

33. (a) Lights are wired as part of a __________.

(b) The last light in the series is __________ to the consumer unit.

(c) Each light is wired __________ with the next light in the circuit.

(d) This is known as __________.

(e) A maximum of __________ per radial circuit is recommended. Any more than this would risk __________.

(f) This is why the __________ and __________ are marked as separate on a consumer unit.

(g) Each light must have the ability to __________ and __________; therefore each light is connected to a __________.

(h) The light switch will either __________ or __________ the electrical connection to the light.

34. An electrician is wiring the downstairs lighting circuit shown in the diagram. On the diagram, show the correct wiring for the radial circuit. Use different colour pens/pencils for each wire type.

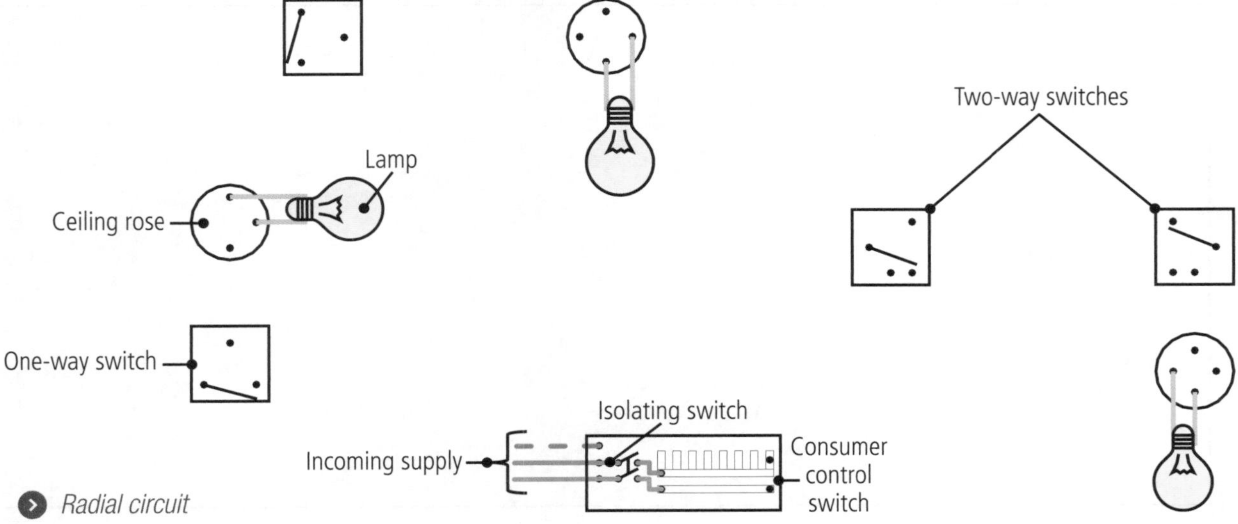

Radial circuit

CEILING ROSE

35. (a) The wiring for the light is typically wired from a ______________________________.

(b) The ceiling rose contains separate ______________________________ for the ______________,

______________ and ____________ cables.

(c) A number of connections can be made from the rose to

______________________________ so a light

can be controlled from ______________________________.

(d) Each ceiling rose will have a cable:

____

____

____

From previous light
To next light
Earth terminal
To switch
Neutral terminal
From switch (live)
Live terminal
Switch terminal (live)
To light

Ceiling rose

TWO-WAY SWITCHING

36. Two-way switching is generally used to control the light fittings in the hallway or the upstairs landing of a house.

(a) This allows the light to be switched __________ or __________ from ____________________________.

(b) Additional wiring is run between __________ switches to allow the current to flow when

________________ switch is thrown.

37. Draw an annotated sketch showing the layout of a typical two-way lighting circuit.

☐ ECONOMICAL USE OF ELECTRICITY IN THE HOME

LIGHTING

38. A family want their use of lighting to be more economical. Discuss some approaches they could take.

RING MAIN CIRCUIT

39. (a) Ring main circuits are used for ______________________.

(b) The circuit forms a ring, because it is connected to the consumer unit at ______________.

(c) Sockets can be installed ______________________ on the ring main circuit.

(d) Additional __________ sockets can be added to the circuit at a later date. They are connected to the ______________ of existing plugs.

40. List the guidelines that prevent overloading in a ring main circuit.

41. An electrician is wiring the downstairs ring main circuit shown in the diagram. On the diagram, show the correct wiring for the ring main circuit. Use different colour pens/pencils for each wire type.

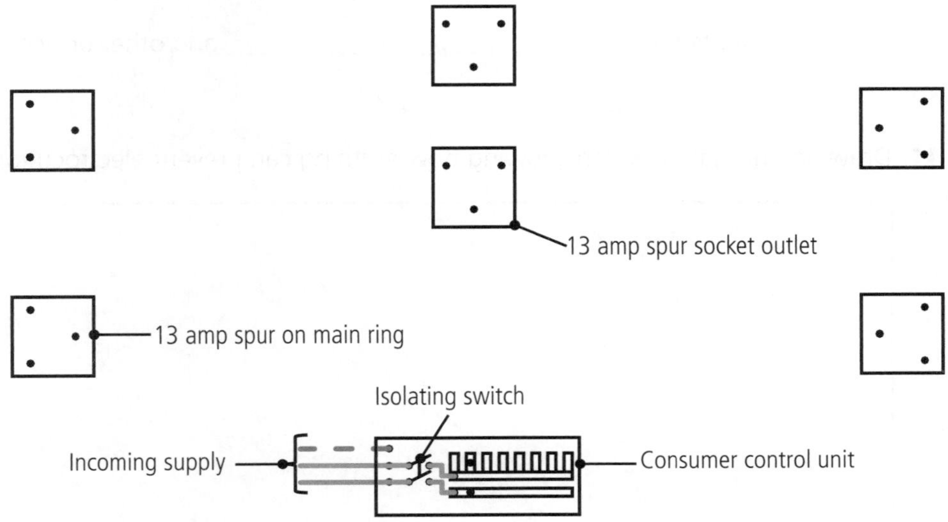

Ring main circuit

☐ ELECTRICAL SAFETY

42. To prevent electric shocks, three design principles must be applied. Explain each design feature.

(a) Earthing:

(b) Isolation devices:

(c) Isolation to live parts:

15

ELECTRICAL SAFETY DESIGN PRINCIPLES

1 EARTHING

43. (a) Earthing is based on the principle that current always takes ______________________________.

(b) In the event of an appliance becoming live, an ______________________________ is provided for the electricity to flow.

(c) This route is called the ______________.

(d) From the consumer unit, a ___________ earth cable is attached to a ______________________ steel bar buried in the ____________ outside the home.

(e) The ______________________________ and ___________________________ are also connected to the earth system.

(f) This prevents the ___________, __________________ and other devices becoming live in the event of a ______________________________.

44. Draw an annotated sketch showing how earthing can prevent electrocution.

2 ISOLATION DEVICES

Miniature circuit breakers (MCBs)

45. (a) Miniature circuit breakers are safety devices located on the ______________________________ that cut off the flow of electricity to an appliance if a ______________________________.

(b) MCBs are built to permit a ______________________________ of electrical current to flow, similar to a ___________.

(c) If a fault occurs in the circuit and ___________________________ of electricity are being drawn from the MCB, the ___________________________.

46. What is the advantage of using an MCB instead of a fuse?

____

____

____

47. What are the two main types of faults that cause an MCB to trip?

____

____

48. (a) What is meant by the term *electrical overload*?

____

____

(b) Give three possible causes of an overload.

____

____

____

____

49. What is a short circuit?

____

____

____

____

____

____

____

Residual current devices (RCDs)

50. (a) A residual current device acts as a ____________________ in the event of a fault.

(b) The RCD __________________ the amount of current flowing in the ____________ and __________________ wires. The current should be ________________ in both.

(c) If a fault occurs, such as a ____________________________, the current will ___________ in one wire. The RCD will register the ____________, and it will ________________ the supply by tripping.

(d) Depending on the specific installation, _________________________ RCDs are used in domestic construction.

3 ISOLATION OF LIVE PARTS

Cables

51. (a) Cables are used to conduct electricity from the consumer unit to ____________, ____________ and ________________.

(b) Cables contain copper wires sheathed in colour-coded PVC.

- Live = __________________
- ______________________ = Blue
- Earth = ________________________________

(c) These sheathed wires are further protected by an ________________, usually ________ in colour.

(d) Therefore the cable is said to be ________________.

(e) Cables are rated in ________. This rating informs the electrician of the ________________ the cable is designed to take without ________________.

Cords

52. (a) A cord is made by winding together numerous ________________.

(b) Cords are sometimes called ________. They much smaller in diameter than a ________, and much more ________ as the PVC sheathing is much lighter.

(c) Cords are ________________.

☐ SOCKETS AND SWITCHES

53. (a) Sockets are sometimes called ________________. They are galvanised steel boxes with a ________________ attached to them.

(b) Modern outlets are fitted with ________ that are lifted as the ________________ of a plug enters the socket.

(c) This prevents the user ________________ the ________________ or ________ terminals.

☐ PLUGS

54. (a) Plugs are used to connect ________ to ________, which connects them to the ________ circuit.

(b) For safety, plugs have an ________________ and a ________________.

(c) A fuse is designed to ________ if electricity beyond the ________________ of the appliance flows through it.

(d) This prevents the appliance ________________.

REMEMBER!

Remember the correct wiring layout of a plug:

- b**R**own (live): **R**ight terminal
- b**L**ue (neutral) : **L**eft terminal
- s**T**riped green and yellow (earth): **T**op terminal)

A plug

55. Label the parts of the plug.

1. ________________
2. ________________
3. ________________
4. ________________
5. ________________
6 ________________

CALCULATING THE FUSE NEEDED

56. Given a microwave with a power rating of 800 W, and a domestic power supply of 230 V, calculate the fuse required for the microwave to operate safely.

THEORY QUESTIONS

1. In our modern energy dependent society, generating electricity using clean environmentally friendly sources is becoming ever more important. Describe how electricity can be generated using a renewable source of your choice. In your answer, you must refer to how the electricity is generated and how it is distributed from the power station to the home.

2. Describe how photovoltaic solar cells can be used to supplement the energy consumption of a standard dwelling which has previously been solely supplied using power from the national grid. In your answer describe:

(a) how the photovoltaic solar panel generates the electricity.

(b) how the house can be wired to ensure that, in times of peak demand, the house can draw electricity form the national grid and how, in times of peak production, it can sell electricity back to the national grid.

HIGHER LEVEL

3. (a) Show, using notes and freehand sketches, the correct wiring layout for two electrical sockets in a ring mains circuit for a domestic electrical installation. Indicate on your sketch the sizes and the colour coding of all electrical cables used in the circuit.

(b) Show, using notes and freehand sketches, **two** safety features that should be incorporated into the design of the above circuit to ensure that the circuit is safe for all users.

(c) Discuss in detail **two** strategies that would ensure the economical use of electricity in the home.

2012 Higher Level Q8

4. (a) Using notes and freehand sketches, show the electrical wiring layout for **two** lights and **two** switches in a radial circuit of a dwelling house.

Indicate on the sketch the typical sizes and colour coding of the electric cables.

(b) Using notes and freehand sketches, show **two** safety features in the design of the lighting circuit that ensure that it is safe for all users.

(c) Using notes and freehand sketches, show **two** features that should be incorporated into the design of the lighting system of a dwelling house to ensure the economical use of electricity.

2008 Higher Level Q9

☐ HYDROLOGICAL CYCLE

1. The hydrological cycle describes the continuous movement of water on, above and under the earth. It consists of a number of key stages.

(a) Evaporation: Firstly, water in the sea, rivers and lakes is heated by the sun and evaporates as a vapour.

(b) Transpiration: Secondly, trees soak up ground-based water through their roots, and release water vapour through their leaves.

(c) Condensation: Next, water vapour rises into the atmosphere, and the air temperature cools and condenses to form clouds.

(d) Precipitation: When a cloud can no longer hold the weight of its water droplets, the droplets fall as rain, snow, hail or sleet.

(e) Percolation: The fallen water soaks into the soil and flows into an underground water source, where it returns to the sea.

(f) Run-off: surface water will also run into nearby streams and rivers and flow back to the sea.

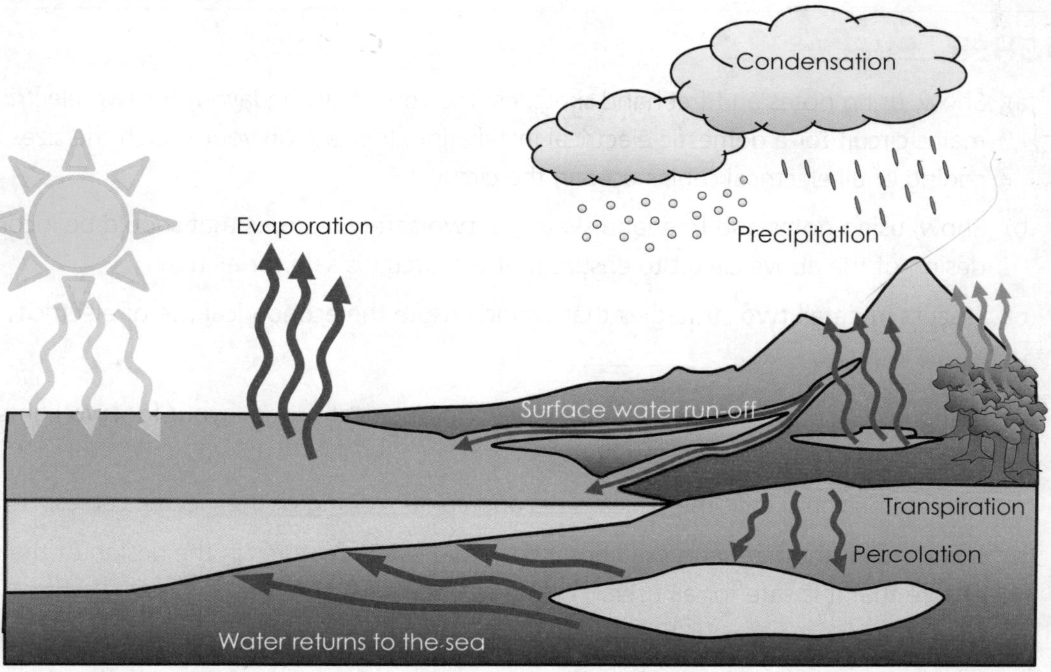

Hydrological cycle

☐ INTRODUCTION TO DRAINAGE

2. Drainage is the term given to the natural or artifical removal of unwanted foul water from a building for safe treatment and release back into the natural environment.

3. Complete the following table:

Term	Meaning
waste water	Dirty water from appliances and showers
Soil water	Dirty water from ____________
foul water	A combination of wastewater and soil water
Surface water	Rain run-off from roads, yards and paved areas

☐ FUNCTIONS AND FEATURES

4. What is the function of an above ground domestic drainage system?

To hygienically dispose of foul and surface water from the building

5. What are the design features of a domestic drainage system?

- Minimise the risk of blockage or leakage
- Prevent foul air from entering the building.
- To be durable and require low maintenance
- To prevent the build-up of gases
- Be accessible for clearing blockages

☐ ABOVE GROUND DRAINAGE

6. Water above ground is drained in a pipe called a stack.

SINGLE-STACK AND TWO-STACK SYSTEMS

7. In a two-stack system, all soil appliances are connected to an individual stack. All waste appliances are also connected to an individual stack. Label the diagram of a two-stack system.

1. Vent
2. Soil stack
3. Gully
4. Waste pipe

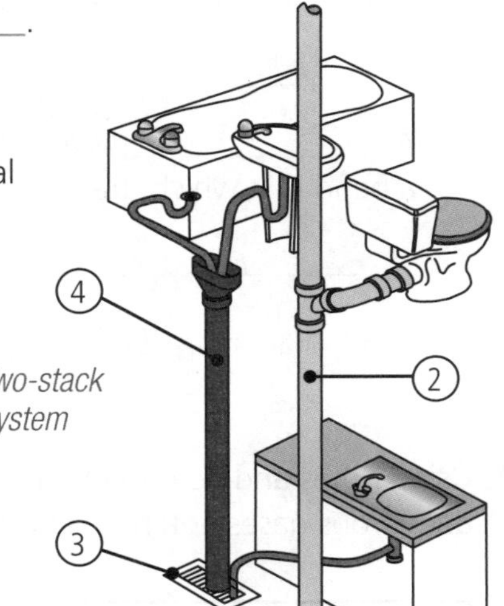

Two-stack system

8. What are the advantages and disadvantages of a two-stack system?

Advantages	Disadvantages
• a reduced risk of siphonage taking place. • greater flexibility when laying out your appliances • the separation of wastewater and soil water add flexibility in treatment i.e wastewater can be recycled.	• It is more expensive to install (twice the pipework). • It has a higher visual impact on the building

9. In a single-stack system, all waste and soil appliances are connected to one combined stack. It is the most widely used system in modern houses. Label the diagram of the single-stack system.

1. Vent
2. Single soil and waste stack

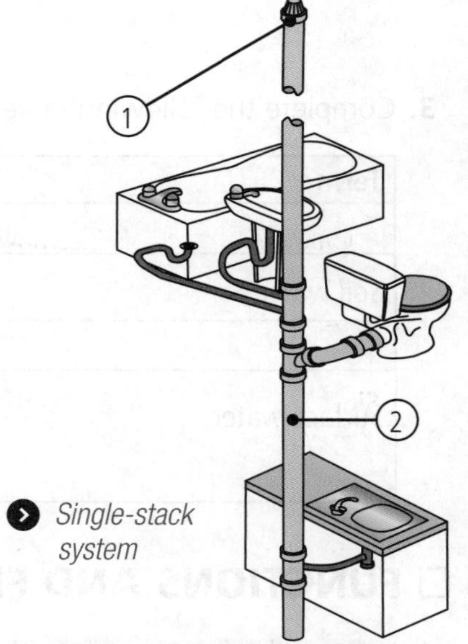

Single-stack system

10. What are the advantages and disadvantages of a single-stack system?

Advantages	Disadvantages
• It is cheaper and easier to install than a two-stack system. • It has a lower visual impact on the building	• there is a greater risk of siphonage occuring • all appliances must be located near the main stack. • Wastewater and soil water are both treated the same.

☐ TRAPS

11. (a) Wastewater systems must be designed to prevent any harmful gases and odurs from entering the house.

(b) One way of doing this is to use a sealing trap at each appliance (sink, toilet and bath).

(c) A trap is a section of pipe that has a bend in it which 'traps' water, creating an airtight seal to prevent any gas from entering the home.

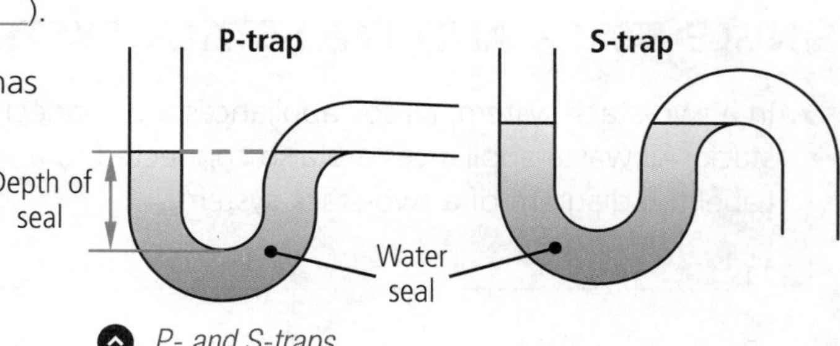

P- and S-traps

12. Using notes and neat freehand sketches, show how a typical trap seals against unpleasant odours and dangerous gases entering a house.

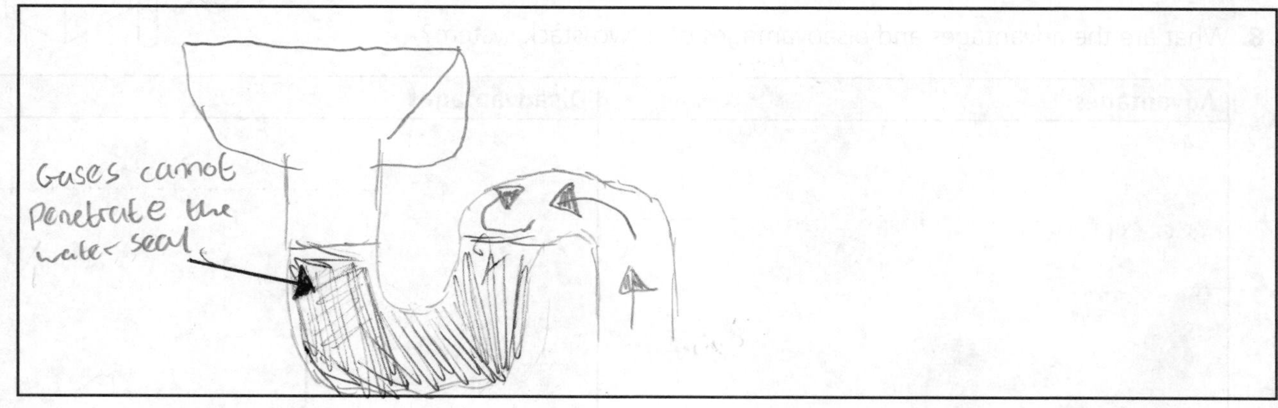

13. Complete the table about standard trap seals for appliances.

Standard trap seals for appliances				
Appliance	Internal Ø size	Length	Depth of seal	Slope
WHB Sink	32 Ø 38 Ø	1700 mm 2300 mm	75 mm	1:25
Bath	38 Ø 50 Ø	2300 mm 4000 mm	75 mm	1:25
WC (toilet)	100 Ø	1500 mm	50 mm	1:25

14. If the water level in a trap falls lower than the trap bend, gas can enter the house and the trap is said to have failed. Give three reasons why a trap might fail.

- back pressure building up in the trap
- Siphonage
- Capillary action

☐ BACK PRESSURE

15. (a) Back pressure typically occurs where there is a sudden change of direction in a pipe, usually at the base of the stack where the vertical pipe enters the ground pipe.

(b) It can be easily prevented by adding a large radius bend at the base of the main stack.

16. Using notes and neat freehand sketches, explain how back pressure causes a seal to break.

- When a large volume of water flows down the stack and is suddenly slowed down or stopped, a rapid change in air pressure in the stack occurs which causes the air to rush back up the pipe, forcing the water out of the trap

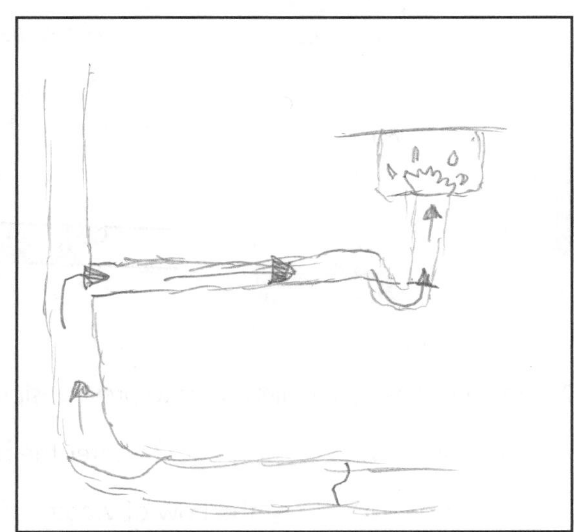

☐ SIPHONAGE

17. There are two types of siphonage:

(a) induced siphonage (b) Self siphonage

16

INDUCED SIPHONAGE

18. Full-bore flow is the term given to when a liquid fills the entire section of a pipe. Using notes and neat freehand sketches, explain how full-bore flow breaks the seal in a trap.

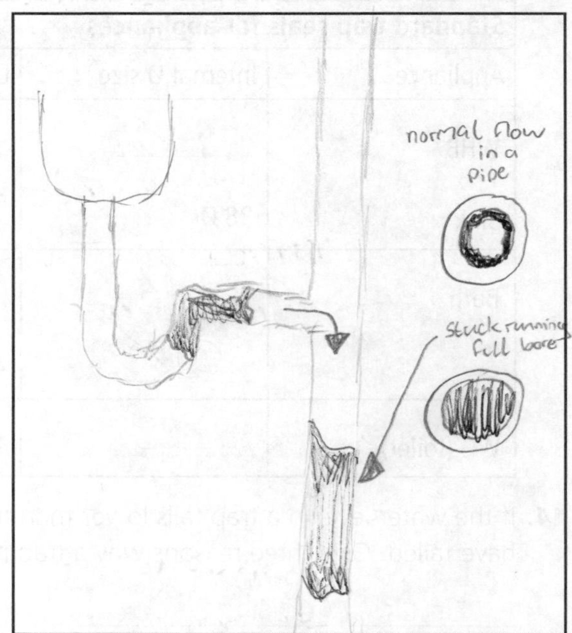

- The water pulls the air behind it, causing low pressure in the pipe behind.
- This low pressure creates a vaccum behind the water.
- This vaccum can be strong enough to suck the water out of the trap and break the seal

19. Capillary action is the ability of water to climb up closely spaced surfaces that contain voids.

20. If strands of hair are caught in a trap, water will travel up the hairs and out of the trap, thereby breaking the seal. On the diagram, illustrate this example of capillary action.

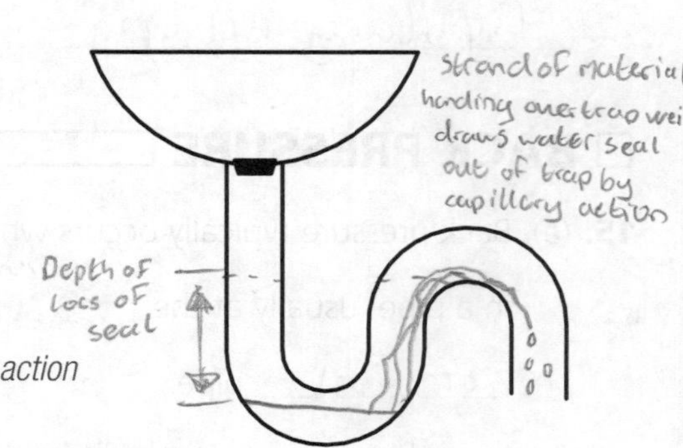

Capillary action

SELF-SIPHONAGE

21. Self-siphonage takes place when induced siphonage occurs in the smaller branch pipes, as shown in the diagram.

Atmospheric pressure

Self-siphonage

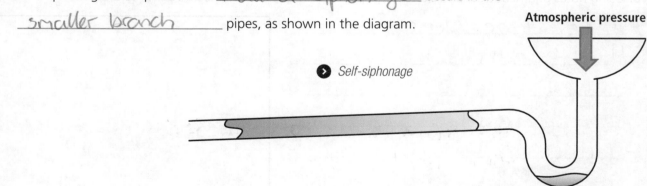

22. (a) The most convenient way to prevent siphonage is by venting the pipework.

(b) This allows air to enter the pipe and prevents a vaccum forming behind the flow of water.

(c) However, an open vent around appliances will allow foul odors to enter into the building.

(d) For this reason, vent pipes or an air admittance valve are attached to each appliance.

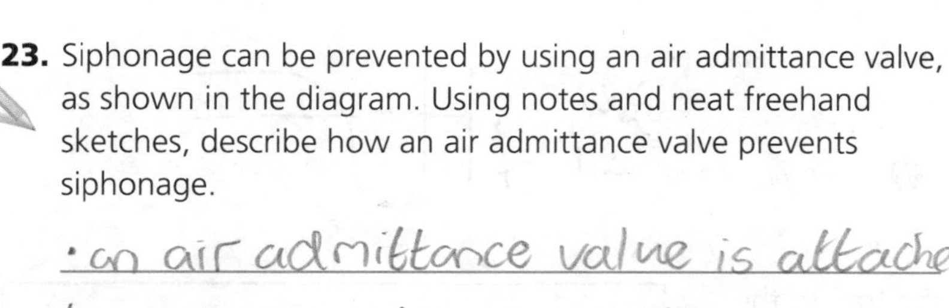

23. Siphonage can be prevented by using an air admittance valve, as shown in the diagram. Using notes and neat freehand sketches, describe how an air admittance valve prevents siphonage.

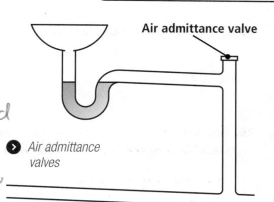

Air admittance valves

· an air admittance valve is attached to the pipes at each appliance.
· If a vacuum is created in the pipe, the vacuum opens a small rubber disk in the valve, allowing air into the pipe
· When the vacuum stops, the rubber disk closes, preventing foul odours entering the home.

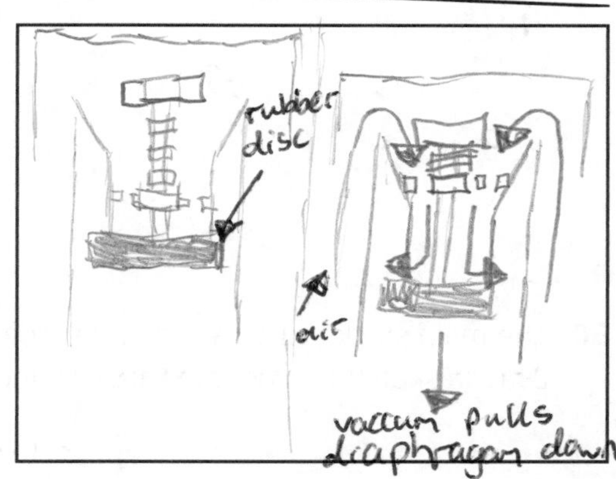

24. (a) Vent pipes are the traditional method of preventing siphonage in a single stack system in a domestic building.

(b) A vent pipe relies on taking air from farther up on the stack, where there is no vacuum.

(c) This approach requires a lot of additional pipework and can be quite costly for larger houses.

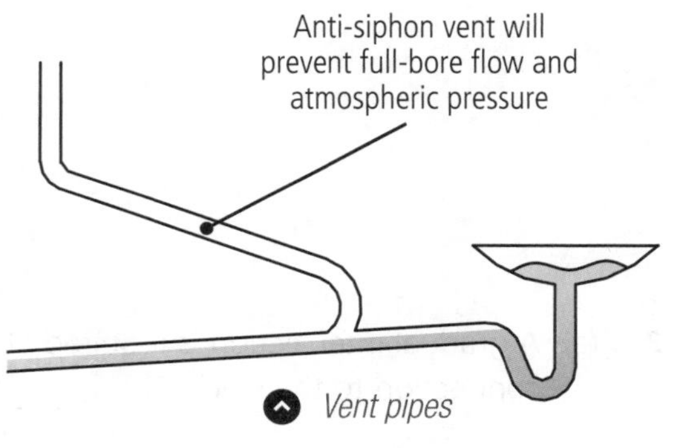

Vent pipes

☐ DESIGN OF THE SINGLE-STACK SYSTEM

25. Eliminating siphonage and back pressure in the main stack is the greatest design challenge in a single-stack system. List three design features that can help to avoid this.

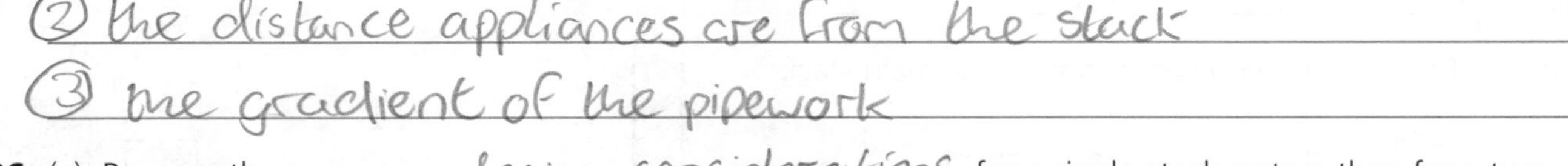

① the placement of branch pipes.
② the distance appliances are from the stack
③ the gradient of the pipework

26. (a) Because there are more design considerations for a single-stack system than for a two-stack system, the choices for placement of appliances can be somewhat limited.

(b) Rooms with toilets and sinks must be located near the main stack.

REGULATIONS GOVERNING THE SINGLE-STACK SYSTEM

27. (a) Deep seal traps must be used on all appliances.

(b) The trap on all sinks must be greater than or equal to 75mm.

(c) The trap on all WCs (toilets) must be greater than or equal to 50mm.

28. On the diagram, indicate how the depth of seal is measured.

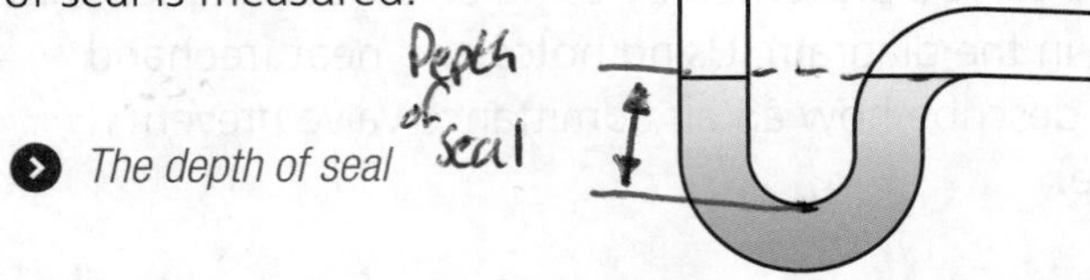

The depth of seal

29. Pipework must have a gradual fall from the trap to the stack. Draw a sketch to illustrate this building regulation.

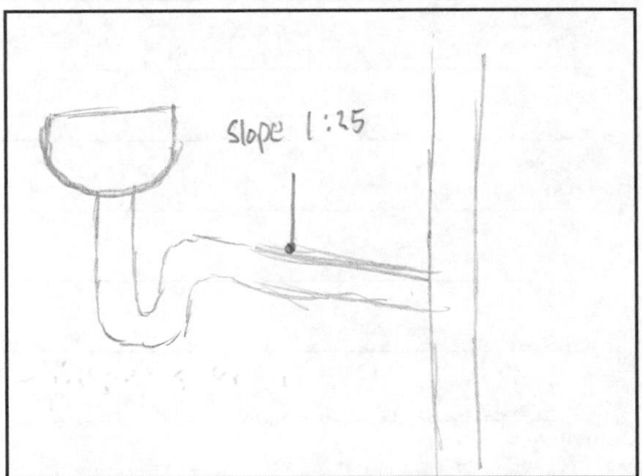

30. The main stack must have a large radius bend at the base. Draw a sketch to illustrate this building regulation.

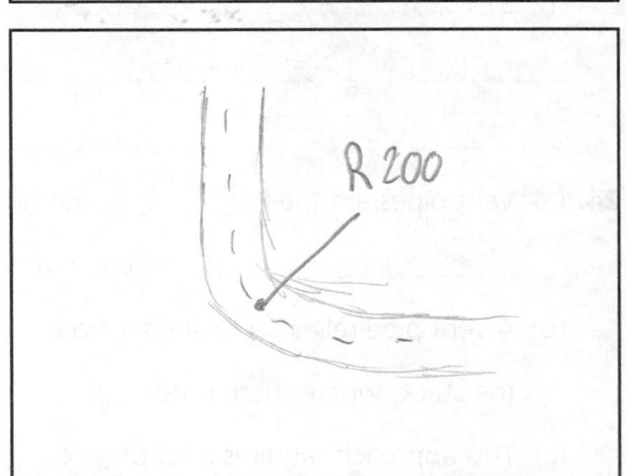

31. (a) A gradual intersection is required at the base of the WC connection to the stack. This is achieved using

prefabricated T-Junction

(b) Label the diagram showing how a WC is connected to a stack.

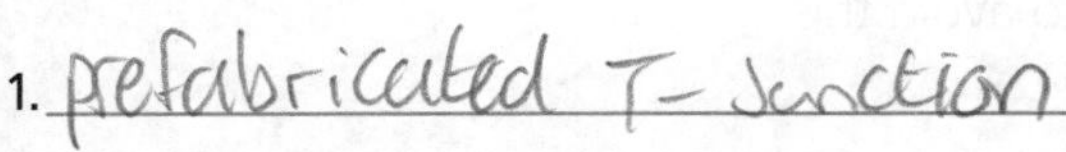

1. prefabricated T-Junction
2. R50 mm bend

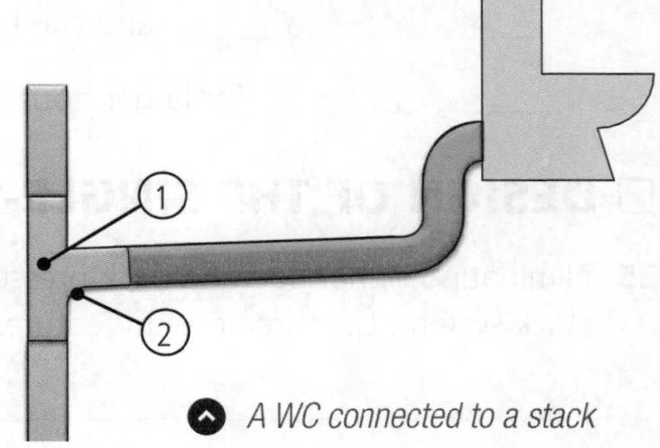

A WC connected to a stack

32. (a) There must be no connection to the main stack within 200 mm below and 200mm above the centre line of the WC branch connection.

(b) Fill in suitable measurements on the diagram of a WC branch connection.

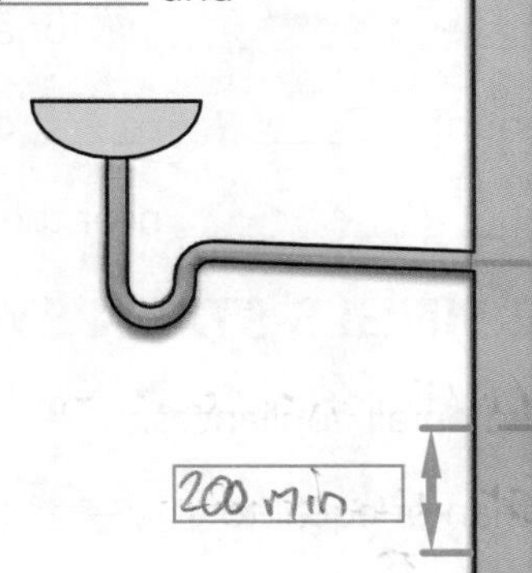

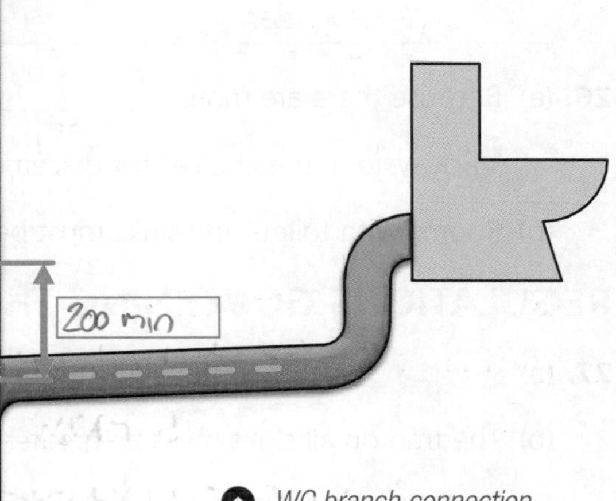

WC branch connection

33. (a) The top of the main stack must project 1m above the highest window and 4m above a house vent. It must also be covered with mesh.

(b) Label these building regulations on the diagram.

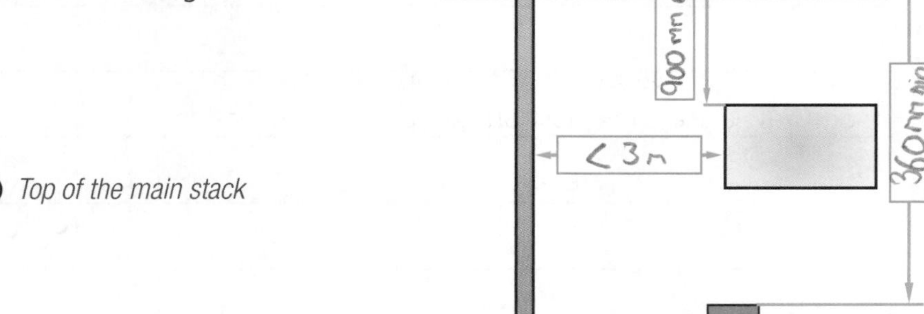

Top of the main stack

34. (a) All ground floor waste appliances must be connected to a gully outside the house, and then to the sewer.

(b) All ground floor soil appliances must be connected directly to the sewer.

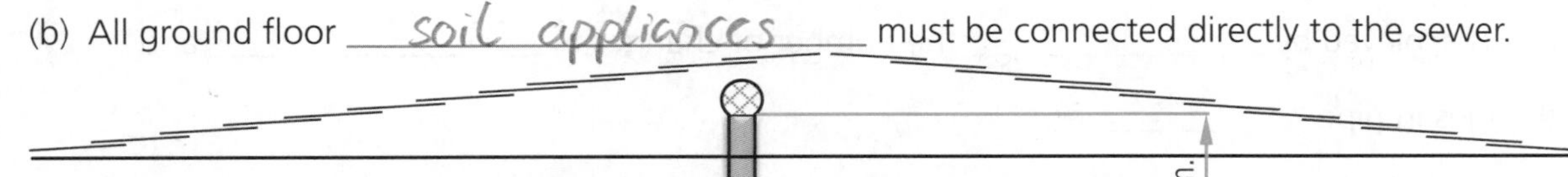

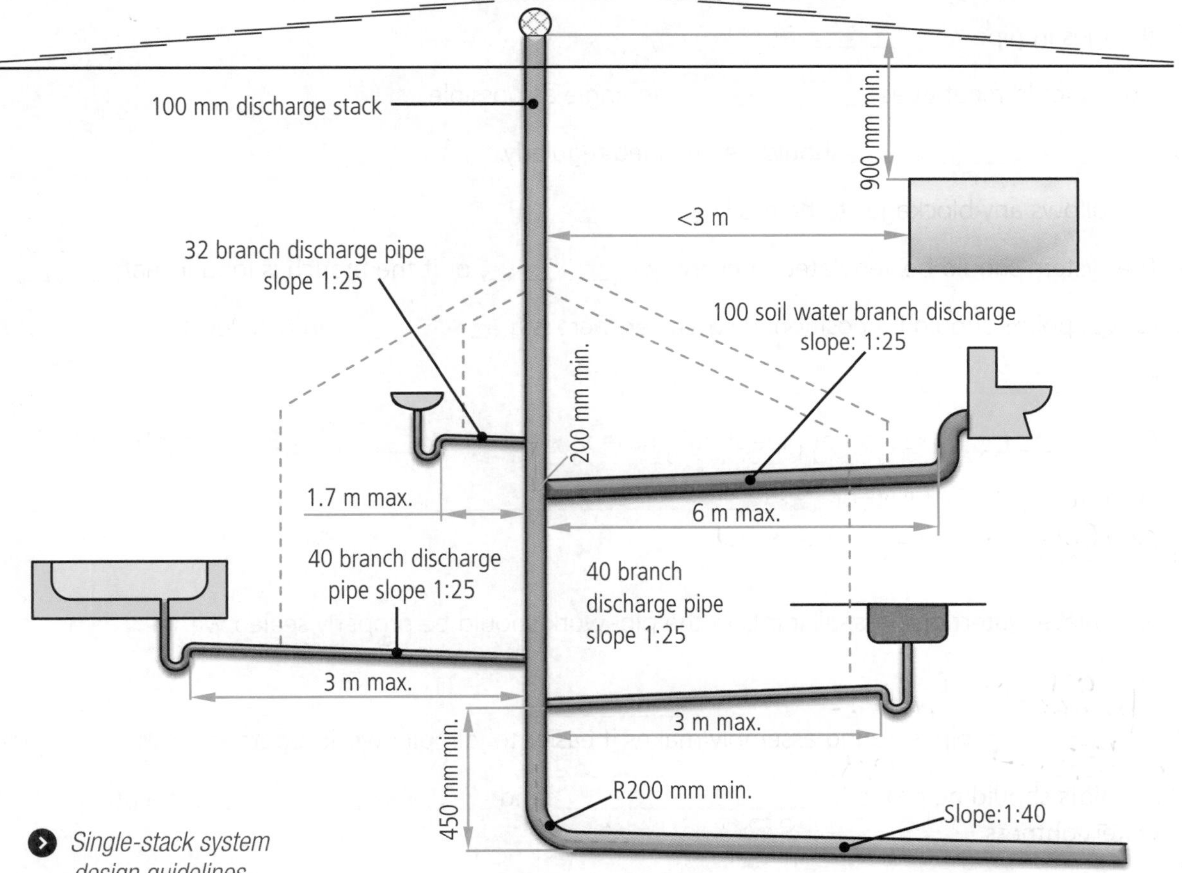

Single-stack system design guidelines

BELOW GROUND DRAINAGE

FUNCTIONS AND FEATURES

35. What are the functions of a below ground drainage system?

- To transport foul water from the home to the point of treatment.
- As most of the pipes are buried underground, the system should be as maintenance free as possible.

36. What are the design features of a below ground drainage system?

- Drain layout and installation
- Watertightness
- Durability
- Resistance to blockage
- Ease of maintenence and access

DESIGN FEATURES

1 Drain layout and installation

37. (a) A drain layout should avoid complicated pipe arrangements.

(b) This is achieved by minimising the number of changes in direction and changes in pipe slope.

(c) Pipes should meet at as shallow an angle as possible.

(d) Access points should be provided regularly.

(e) This allows any blockages to be easily cleared.

(f) The system should be ventilated at every house, or if the branch is longer than 6m.

(g) Access points should be positioned wherever there is a drop in pipe level (invert level).

(h) A curved section of pipe should have as large a radius as possible to prevent blockage or back pressure.

2 Watertightness

38. (a) To achieve watertightness, all joints in the pipework should be properly sealed with a rubber 'O' ring

(b) Greasing pipes during assembly makes it easier to join pipework together.

(c) All joints should be properly aligned and square to maintain watertightness.

39. Draw a sketch to illustrate the consequences of incorrectly aligned pipework.

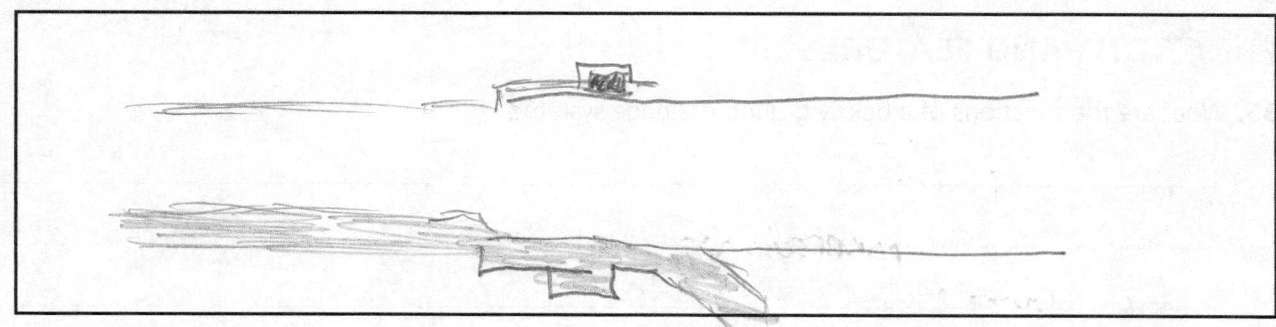

3 Durability

40. List the factors upon which the durability of a treatment system depends.

• the lifespan of the materials
• the amount of soil movement around the pipes due to settlement.
• the effect of chemical attack from effluent and soil on the pipes and joints

4 Resistance to blockages

41. Blockages can be avoided by:

(a) selecting the correct sizing for the drain diameter.

(b) ensuring the correct gradient/fall for the drain.

(c) ensuring nothing projects into the pipes.

(d) avoiding joints or fittings that could cause an obstruction.

(e) ensuring the joints are properly aligned.

(f) keeping the inside surface of the pipe smooth to allow waste to flow easily.

(g) maintaining a constant pipe diameter along any given length of pipe.

5 Ease of maintenance

42. (a) As pipes are buried underground, access points must be provided to ensure that each section of pipe can be inspected and cleared of any blockages.

(b) Access points should be located at any junction where there is:

• a change in direction
• a change in invert level
• a number of pipes joining together

(c) The pipe layout should be a simple as possible (with as few changes in direction as possible) to facilitate clearing of any blockages.

16

☐ PIPE MATERIAL

43. uPVC is a popular material for drainage pipes because uPVC pipes are:

(a) easily cut and assembled, which means they are fast and easy to install.

(b) strong and flexible.

(c) resistant to chemical attack.

(d) stable at high temperatures.

(e) easily stored on site.

☐ DRAIN LAYOUT

44. A builder on site is laying pipework that will connect to a wastewater treatment system. Using notes and a neat freehand sketch, describe the stages involved.

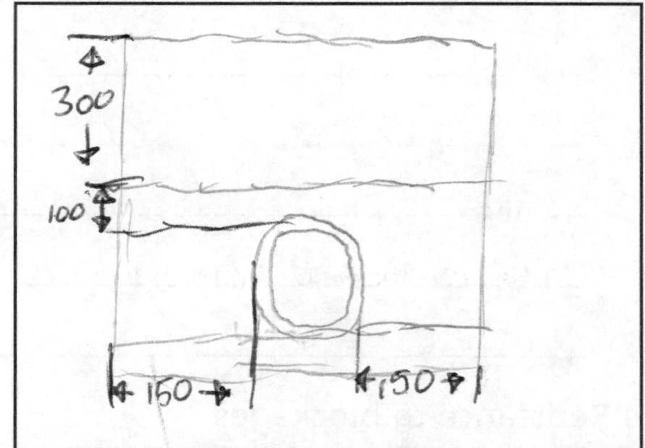

① A trench is excavated at the appropriate gradient in which to place the drain. ② the pipe is laid on a bed of 100mm minium aggregate. ③ the bedding cradle and side fill should consist of non-sharp granular material. ④ 150mm minium of granular fill is placed to the side of the pipe. ⑤ a minium of 100mm cover of granular fill is placed above the pipe. ⑥ Excavated material is then used to fill in the trench.

45. Label the diagram showing the recommended gradients for pipe layout.

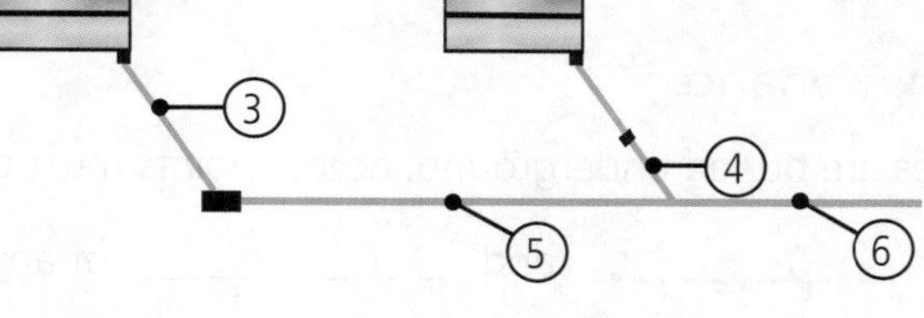

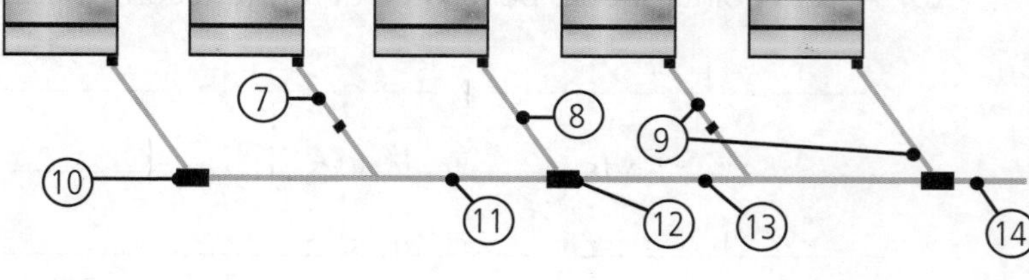

Recommended gradients for pipe layout

1. 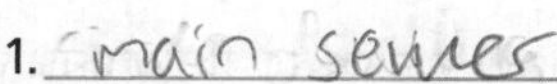 main sewer discharge
2. Ø 100mm slope 1:60
3. Ø 100mm slope 1:40
4. Ø 100mm slope 1:40
5. Ø 100mm slope 1:40
6. Ø 100mm slope 1:40
7. Ø 100mm slope 1:40
8. Ø 100mm slope 1:40
9. Ø 100mm slope 1:40
10.  Access Junction
11. Ø 100mm 1:80
12. inspection chamber
13. Ø 150mm slope 1:80
14. Ø 150mm slope 1:80

☐ ACCESS POINTS

46. Access points are used to inspect and clear a drain of any blockages.

47. List the various types of access points.

gully gate | inspection chambers
rodding point | manhole
access Junction | backdrop manhole

ACCESS TYPES

1 GULLY GRATES

Ø40 wastewater discharge pipe

Gully grate

48. (a) Gully grates allows access from a vertical discharge pipe into a drain.

(b) Beneath the gully grate is a gully seal, which prevents foul air rising up through the gully grate.

Gully grate

2 RODDING POINTS

49. (a) Rodding points are placed to allow the pipes to be cleaned using a rodding brush.

(b) Rodding points are placed along long stretches of pipe.

(c) They are very convenient and do not require much space.

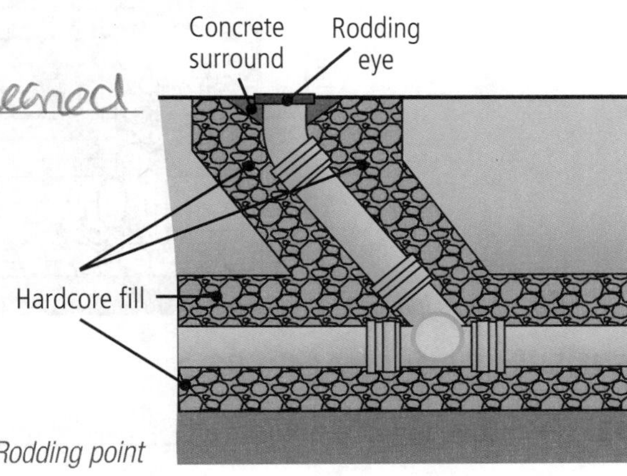

Rodding point

3 MANHOLES

50. (a) Manholes are used to gain access to drains that are buried deep under the ground (deeper than one metre).

(b) As the surrounding soil will exert great pressure, manholes are constructed of concrete with an inbuilt ladder for access.

(c) Manholes will often have their own foundations

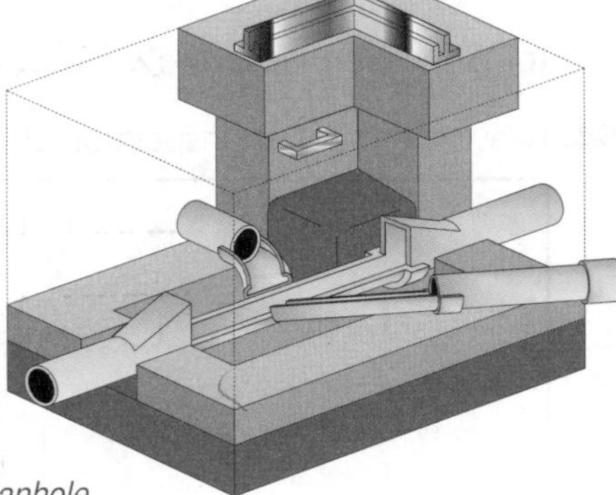

Manhole

51. Draw a sketch of a typical manhole section.

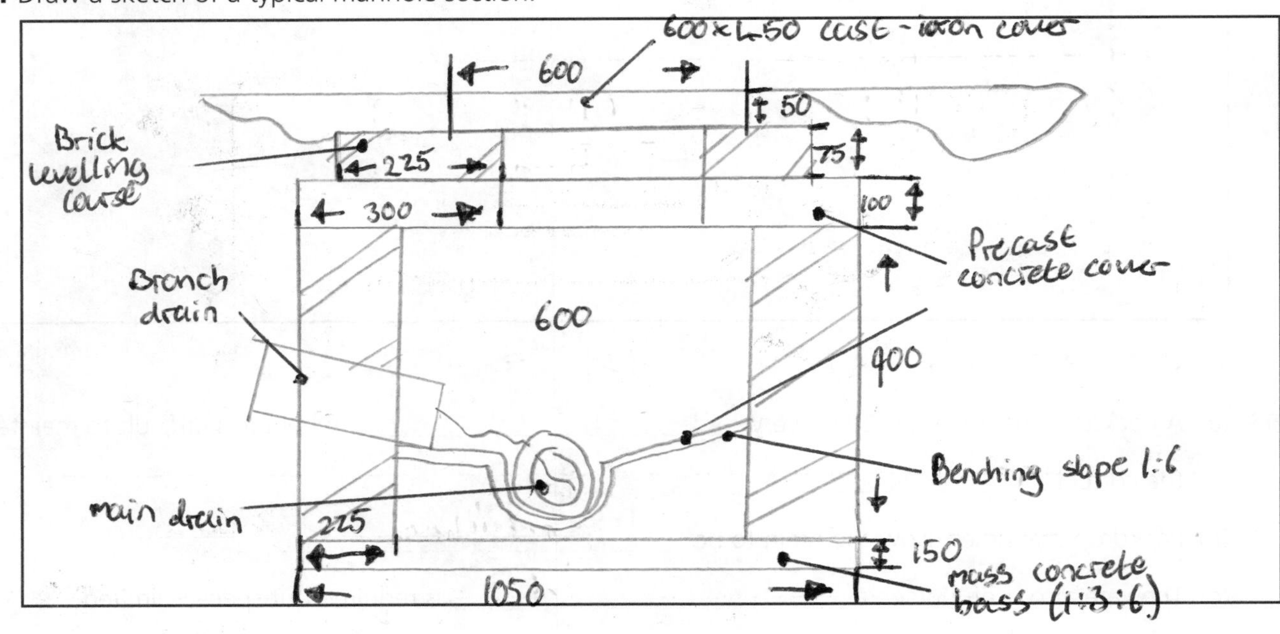

4 ACCESS JUNCTIONS

52. (a) Access junctions are small prefabricated tubes that allow a person to look into pipework and to clear any blockages.

(b) They are used for pipes near the surface.

(c) They are placed at a maximum depth of 600mm.

(d) They are usually located anywhere a blockage is likely to occur, such as at Junctions, turns in direction and changes in gradient level.

600 mm max.

Pipes to meet at shallow angle

Access junction

5 INSPECTION CHAMBERS

53. (a) Inspection chambers are essentially larger access Junctions.

(b) They allow more space than an access Junction, which makes it easier to clear any blockages.

(c) They are placed at a maximum depth of one metre

54. Draw sketch of an inspection chamber section.

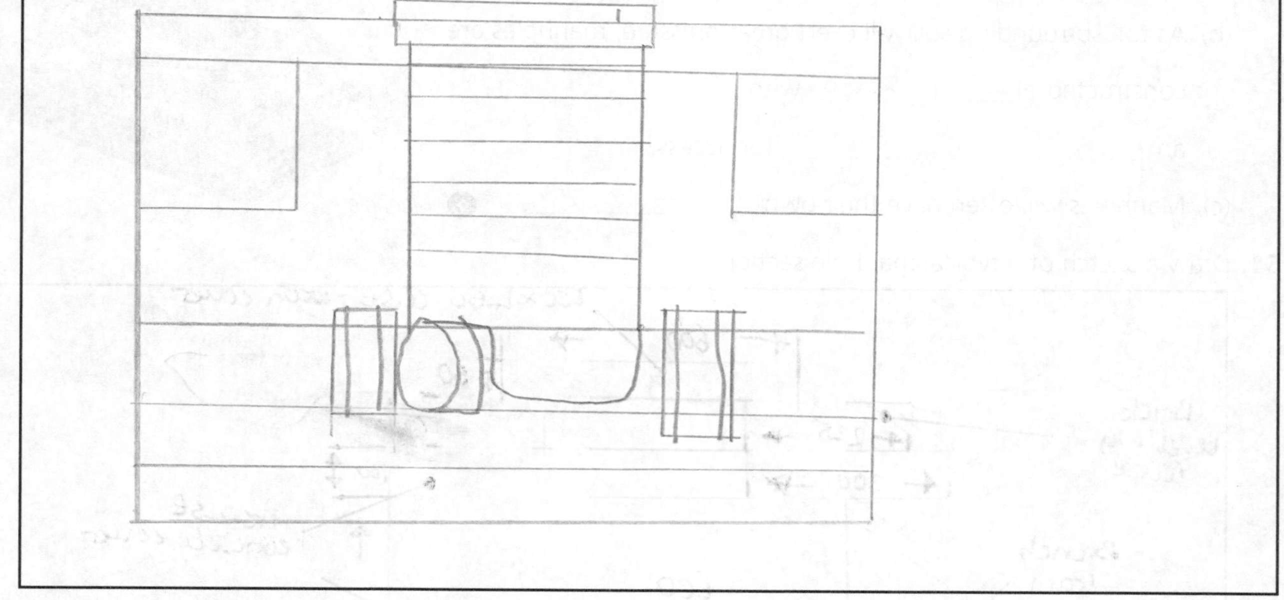

6 BACKDROP MANHOLE

55. (a) A backdrop manhole is used on very steep slopes where it is difficult to maintain the correct gradient for the drain.

(b) Backdrop manholes allow the drain to be dropped/stepped.

(c) They are also useful when a change of level is required but space is limited.

56. Label the components of a typical backdrop manhole.

1. Cast-iron cover
2. Access cap
3. precast concrete chamber sections
4. precast concrete base

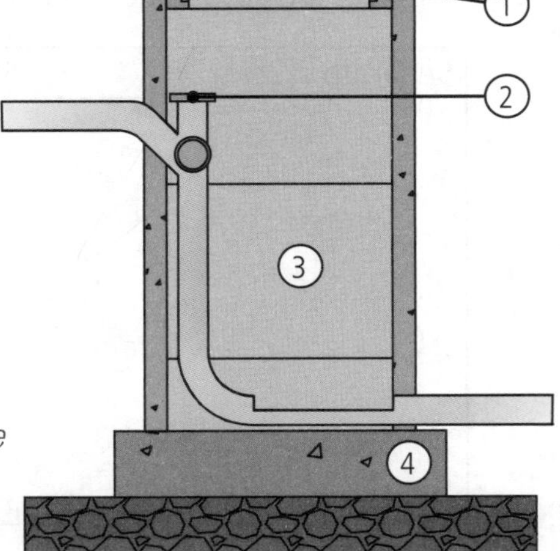

A typical backdrop manhole

☐ SURFACE WATER

57. (a) Surface water is water run-off from paved areas and roofs.

(b) It has not been contaminated with sewage and does not need to be treated in the same way as foul water.

58. A couple are planning to build a home and have yet to decide on a system to treat surface water. Briefly outline the operation of the combined system and the separate system. Insert the pipework on the diagram to support your answer.

The combined system: surface water and foul water both flow into the same drains and are both sent to the same water treatement centre.

The separate system

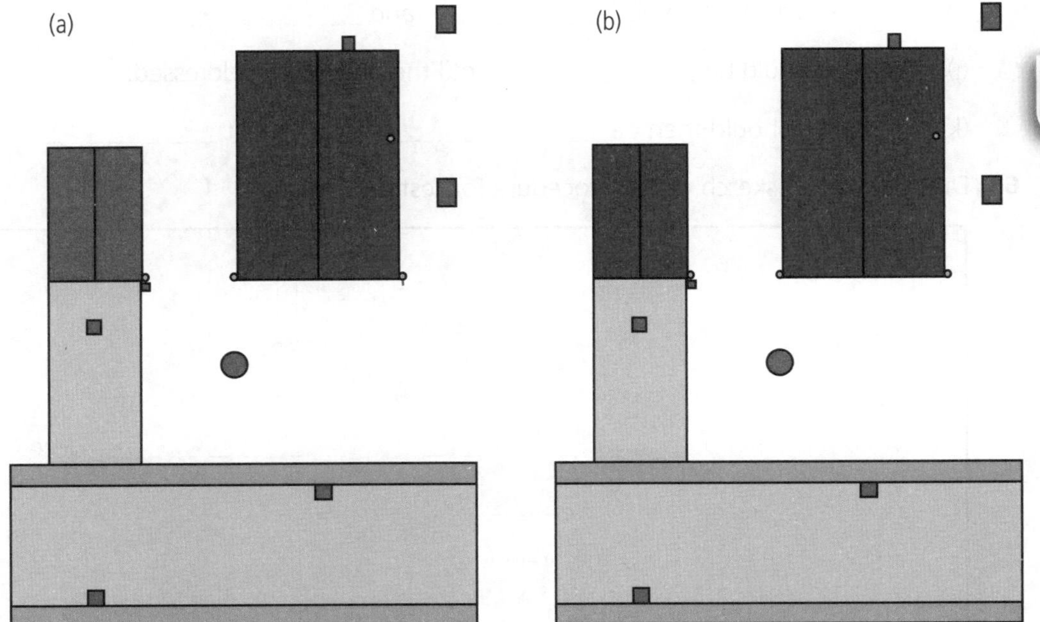

Pipework for (a) separate and (b) and combined systems

59. Compare the advantages and disadvantages of a separate system and a combined system.

Separate system	Combined system

☐ DRAIN TESTING

60. It is vital that all drains are tested for watertightness before being covered over. This can be done by blocking one end of a run of pipes and testing to see if they will allow water to leak out.

(a) One end of the pipe is _______________ with a special ___________________________.

(b) A section of pipe, called an _______________, is attached to the other end and filled with water to a height of _______________.

(c) The water is left for ________________ to allow any ___________________________ to settle.

(d) Any drop in the water level at this stage is ________________________ to the starting water level of ________________________.

(e) After allowing the water to _______________, the water then is left for a further ______________.

(f) Any drop in the water level is ________________________ and ________________________.

(g) If more than _______________ is lost for each ________________ run of ________________ pipe, then the drain is said to have ______________ the test.

(h) This means there are _____________ in the pipe.

(i) The leaks will need to be ________________ and ______________.

(j) The test should be ________________ until the problem is addressed.

(k) The trench should then be __________________ and the test ________________.

61. Draw a labelled sketch of the procedure for testing a drain.

☐ DOMESTIC WASTEWATER TREATMENT SYSTEMS

62. (a) The safe treatment of ____________________ is vital for public safety.

(b) If water is not correctly treated, there is a risk that it may enter the ____________________ and result in the ______________ of ______________ and ____________.

(c) If ________________ water enters the water supply system, it may cause ________________ and even the ______________ of consumers.

(d) Almost all cities, towns and villages have a centralised ______________________________ that ________________ and ______________ foul sewage.

(e) In rural areas, houses may have to treat their own sewage on site using a traditional ____________ system or a modern alternative.

(f) Unlike foul water, surface water is not ____________________ so it does not have to undergo any form of ________________.

(g) Instead, it can be allowed to drain away in a nearby ______________, ______________ or ________________.

(h) A ____________________ is a hole in the ground that is filled with ____________ and allows water to ____________________ into the ______________.

Soakage pit

A soakage pit

63. What factors affect the selection of a septic tank system?

____

____

64. A couple intend to seek full planning permission for a proposed building. Before seeking planning permission, a representative from the local county council must carry out a percolation test to determine whether the site is suitable for a traditional septic tank system. Using notes and neat freehand sketches, describe the percolation test.

Percolation test procedure: Day 1 ____

____

____

____

____

____

____

____

____

____

____

Continued

Percolation test procedure: Day 2 ______________________________

____

____

____

____

____

____

____

____

____

____

____

Layout for a percolation test

65. If a site fails a percolation test, an ______________ must be used to ______________ the wastewater before ______________ into the ______________.

SEPTIC TANK SYSTEMS

66. Septic tanks are the most commonly used wastewater treatment system in rural Ireland. A wastewater treatment system should:

(a) collect all wastewater from the house.

(b) separate suspended solid waste from waste water, and promote the decomposition of solids.

(c) prevent any human & health hazard.

(d) be of adequate capacity for the dwelling.

(e) prevent pollution by direct dischange of untreated wastewater into local ground and surface water.

(f) prevent the build-up of foul gases.

(g) allow access for cleaning and servicing.

(h) minimise the risk of blockage and leakage.

(i) operate with minimal maintenance, but allow access for cleaning and servicing.

(j) have a long lifespan.

SEPTIC TANK OPERATION

67. (a) Treatment of foul/soil water in a septic tank is known as primary treatment.

(b) To prevent the build-up of gases, the tank should be vented.

68. A family have been informed that their site is suitable for a traditional septic tank. Describe how a septic tank separates the liquid water from the solids, and how it begins the breakdown of contaminants.

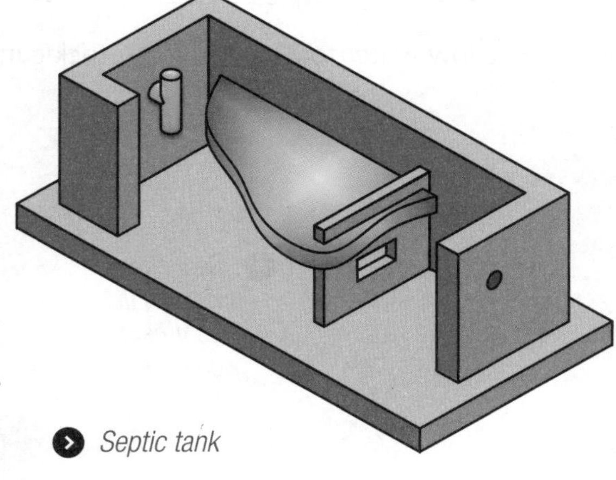

Septic tank

• once entered into the tank, solid waste sinks to the bottom of the tank, forming a layer of sludge.
• less dense liquids, such as cooking oils and grease, form an airtight ~~scum~~ scum on top.

69. Draw an annotated sketch of a septic tank system.

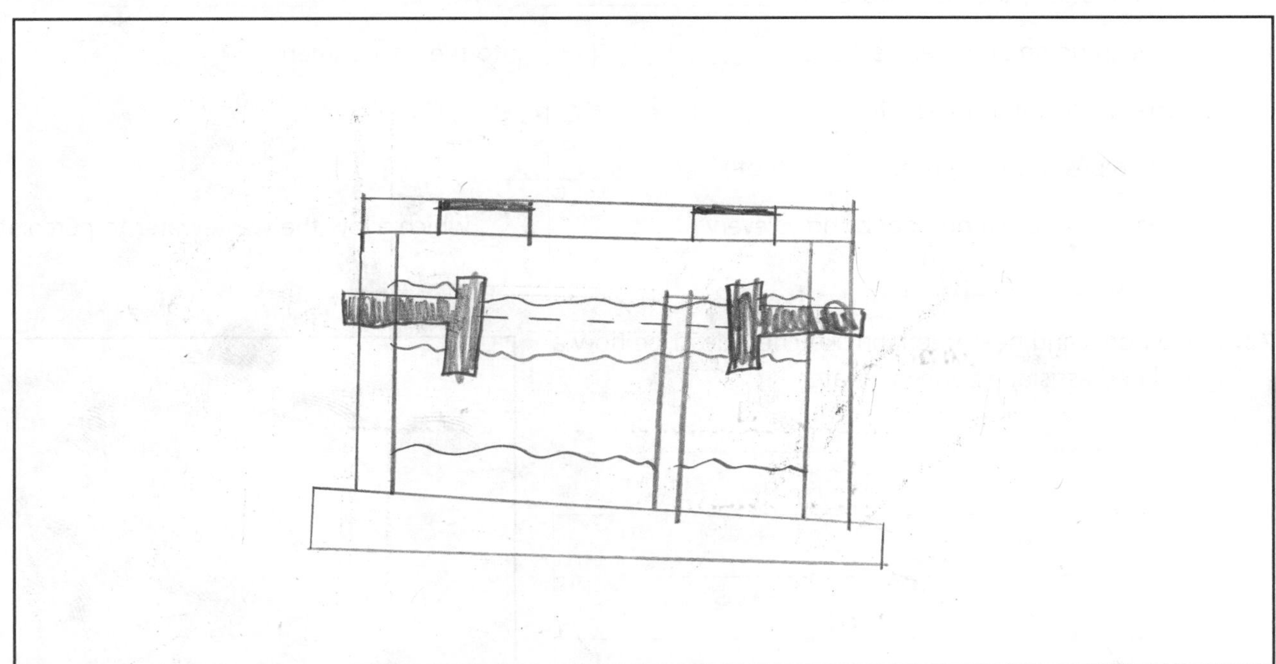

DISTRIBUTION BOX

70. (a) The separated and partially treated wastewater flows from the septic tank to a distribution box.

(b) A distribution box directs and distributes the flow of wastewater to a number of disposal pipes.

(c) The distribution box must:

- be alright and prevent gases or odurs leaking out.
- be solidly built with an appropriate Filled base.
- have a protective cover.
- allow water to slowly trickle into the percolation pipes.

Septic tank wastewater treatment process

PERCOLATION AREA

71. (a) The partially treated wastewater flows from the distribution box into the percolation area for ______________________.

(b) The percolation area is also referred to as a ______________________.

(c) At this stage, the wastewater is ______________________, with all ______________________ broken down and made safe for ______________________ into the environment.

(d) The wastewater flows into ______________________ pipes.

(e) The pipes have a maximum length of ______________________.

(f) The pipes have a number of holes every ______________________, which allow the wastewater to percolate into a ______________________.

72. Using notes and neat freehand sketches, describe how a gravel bed assists in purifying water.

LAYOUT OF A PERCOLATION DRAIN

73. Complete the standard layout (plan and elevation) of a percolation area. It is important to show key dimensions in your sketch.

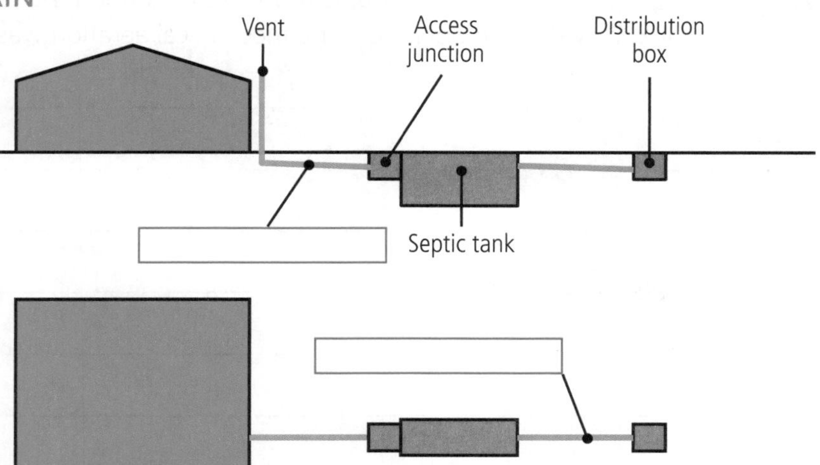

Standard layout of a percolation area

74. (a) A percolation drain should be laid on a ______________________________ washed gravel bed.

(b) The __________________ allows the wastewater to percolate through.

(c) The __________ and _________ of the pipe are filled in with _____________________________.

(d) Topsoil is backfilled over the stones to a ________________ depth of _____________.

75. Add appropriate measurements to the sectional diagram of a percolation drain.

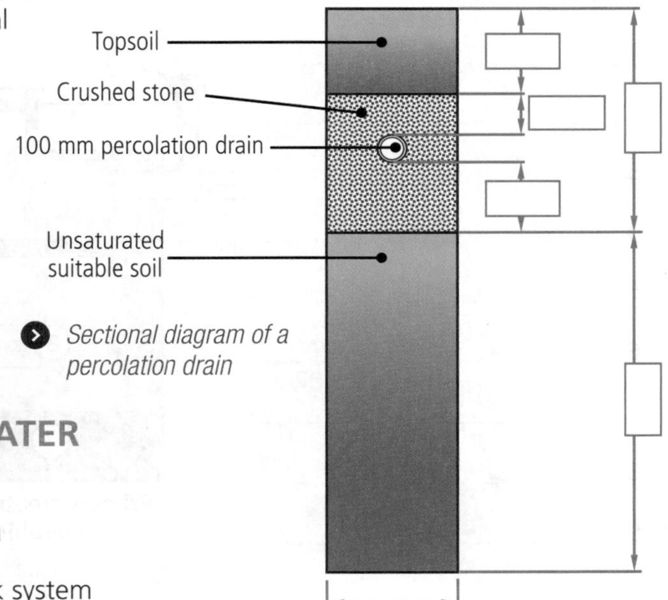

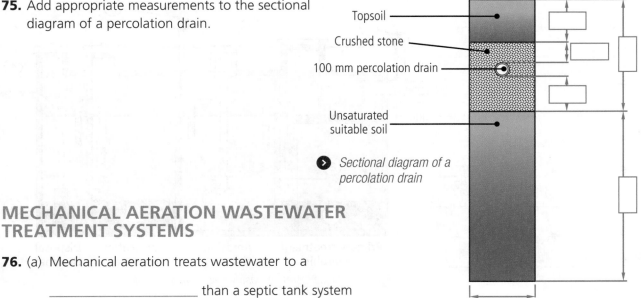

Sectional diagram of a percolation drain

MECHANICAL AERATION WASTEWATER TREATMENT SYSTEMS

76. (a) Mechanical aeration treats wastewater to a

___________________ than a septic tank system

so that the effluent entering the percolation system is

______________________________ and ______________.

(b) Most systems operate in ______________ stages.

(c) Each stage has its own ________________ in the tank.

(d) The wastewater is passed by ________________ through each chamber.

(e) The stages include:

_____________________________ _____________________________

_____________________________ _____________________________

16

77. Following a percolation test, a couple have been informed that their site is not suitable for a traditional septic tank. Describe the operation of a mechanical aeration wastewater treatment system.

____

____

____

____

____

____

____

____

____

____

____

____

78. Label the components of the mechanical aeration wastewater treatment system.

1. ____________________
2. ____________________
3. ____________________
4. ____________________
5. ____________________
6. ____________________
7. ____________________
8. ____________________
9. ____________________

Mechanical aeration wastewater treatment system

SUPPLEMENTARY FILTER SYSTEMS

79. (a) If the percolation of a site is ____________________, or if there is a likely ____________________, wastewater may require further treatment before it can be ____________ into the ____________.

(b) A supplementary filter system acts as a ____________________, removing all ____________________ from the ____________ treated wastewater.

(c) There are two main types of filter systems:

____________________ ____________________

WETLAND WASTEWATER TREATMENT SYSTEMS

80. (a) Wetland systems are also known as a ______________________.

(b) This system does not have a traditional ______________________. Instead, the wastewater flows through a sealed ______________ tank.

(c) The ________ of the reeds release ______________ into the soil.

(d) As the wastewater flows through the reed bed, ______________ feed off the ______________ until only ______________ (often drinkable) water is left.

81. Label the components of the wetland wastewater treatment system.

1. ______________________
2. ______________________
3. ______________________
4. ______________________
5. ______________________

Wetland wastewater treatment system

INTERMITTENT FILTER SYSTEM

82. (a) An intermittent filter system consists of a tank filled with a ______________________ (usually ________ or ________).

(b) The partially treated wastewater is pumped into the tank ______________ during the day, and allowed to ________ through the ______________________ and ____________ in the bottom of the tank.

(c) Like the gravel in the percolation area, ______________________ build up on the ______________________ and break down the ______________ in the wastewater as it flows through.

(d) The now-treated water drains into the ________ through ________ in the bottom of the tank and into the ______________.

16

83. Draw a sketch showing the layout of an intermittent filter system.

PURAFLO

84. Due to the particularly poor soil on a site, a couple are required to install an intermittent treatment system to further assist their wastewater treatment system. They have decided to use a Puraflo system. Puraflo is a type of intermittent treatment system that uses peat as a filter material. Describe the operation of the Puraflo system.

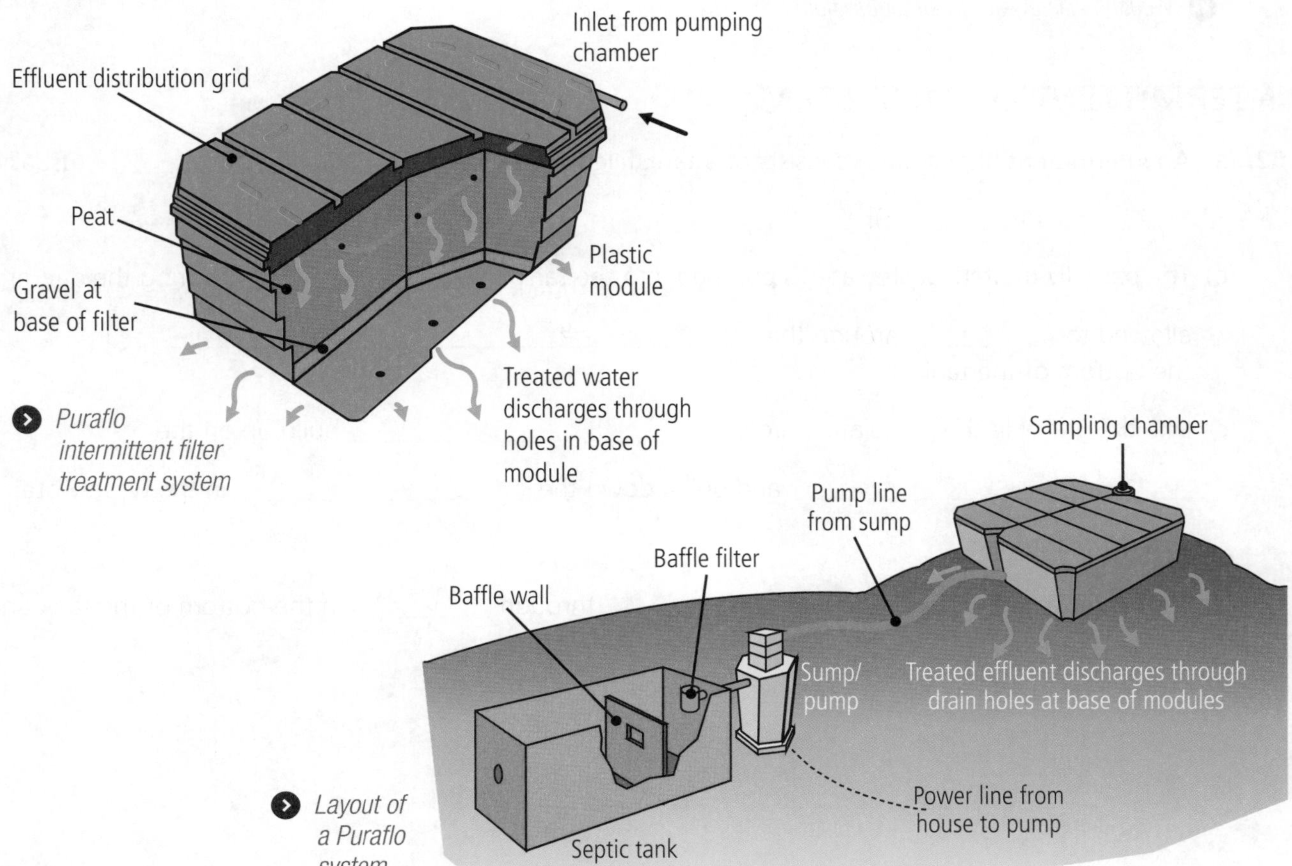

Puraflo intermittent filter treatment system

Layout of a Puraflo system

THEORY QUESTIONS

1. Prior to buying a site, it is often advisable to carry out a percolation test on the soil.
   (a) Why might this be a good idea for potential developers?
   (b) Describe, using notes and freehand sketches, the process involved in carrying out the percolation test.
   (c) Following a percolation test, it was found that the soil on a site has poor drainage capacity and would not be able to accommodate a traditional septic tank and percolation area. Describe two alternative methods that can be used to ensure the safe removal of household waste from the proposed dwelling.

2. (a) Describe the key design features of a single-stack system for a typical domestic dwelling. Discuss the advantages and disadvantages of this system compared to a double-stack system.
   (b) Preventing sealing trap failure is a major concern in the design of a modern single-stack drainage system. Describe the function of a sealing trap in a drainage system and indicate three methods of how the seal may be broken.
   (c) Describe, using notes and freehand sketches, how careful adherence to design guidelines can prevent trap failure.

HIGHER LEVEL

3. The typical layout of an on-site wastewater treatment system suitable for a single house is shown in the accompanying drawing.

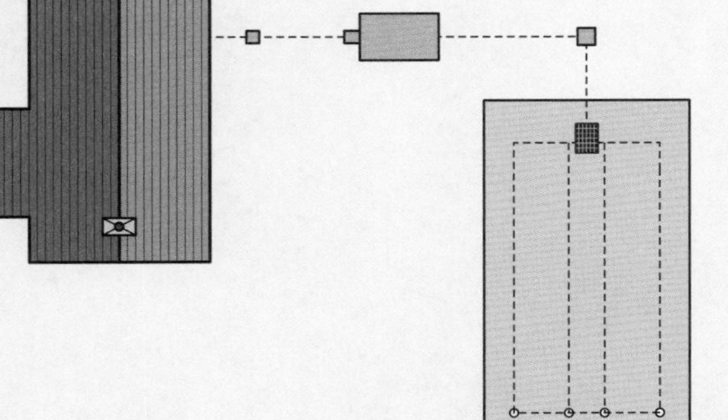

   (a) Describe in detail, using notes and freehand sketches, the operating principles of a conventional septic tank system.
   (b) Show, using notes and freehand sketches, the typical design detailing for the percolation area to ensure the safe treatment of waste from the septic tank. Include dimensions as appropriate.
   (c) Discuss in detail **three** reasons why a proposed site for a dwelling house may be unsuitable for a conventional septic tank wastewater treatment system.

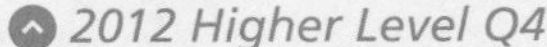
2012 Higher Level Q4

4. (a) Discuss, using notes and freehand sketches, **three** functional requirements of a below ground drainage system to ensure the safe removal of sewage from a domestic dwelling.
   (b) The accompanying sketch shows the location of a manhole at the intersection of a branch drain and a main drain in a below ground drainage system for a domestic dwelling. Using notes and freehand sketches, show the typical construction details through the manhole from the foundation to the manhole cover. Indicate on the sketch the typical dimensions.

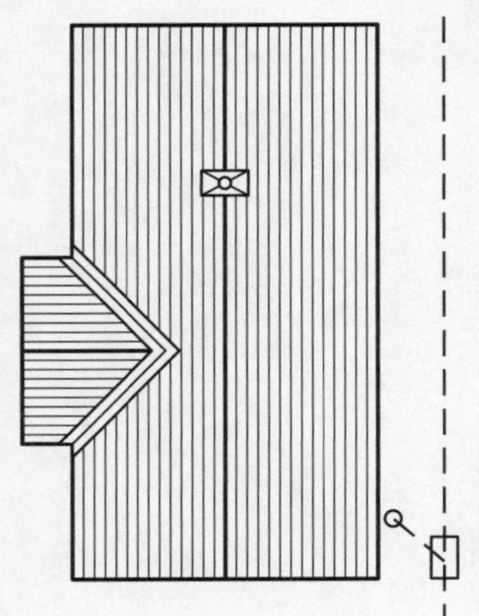

   (c) Using notes and freehand sketches, describe in detail **one** test that may be carried out to ensure that the below ground drainage system is watertight.

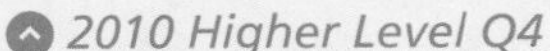
2010 Higher Level Q4

5. A main bathroom, as shown in the sketch, is located on the first floor of a dwelling house.

(a) Using notes and freehand sketches, show **two** design considerations that should be taken into account when locating the bathroom on the first floor of a dwelling house.

(b) Using notes and freehand sketches, show the above-ground pipework necessary for the safe discharge of waste from the following fittings: wash hand basin, bath.

Include in your sketch typical sizes of the waste pipe for each fitting.

(c) Using notes and freehand sketches, show the design detailing necessary to prevent the penetration of sewer gases into the bathroom at the WC.

2009 Higher Level Q4

HEAT

CONSTRUCTION STUDIES

☐ HEAT IN DOMESTIC DWELLINGS

1. (a) The unwanted loss of heat is often a major problem in many modern homes. Heat loss results in:

- an increase in the ___________ of heating the home.
- an increase in the ____. This gas is a major contributor to climate change.
- an ____________________________ of comfort in the home as the living temperature is constantly ______________________.

(b) The correct ____________________________ at the design stage and the correct ____________________________ will have a huge impact on reducing the overall loss of heat from the home.

INSULATION

2. Complete the table on the types of thermal insulation.

Types of thermal insulation		
Type	**Example**	**Used**
Flexible insulation	Quilted mineral wool, fibreglass	
	Foiled back polystyrene	Between cavity walls, under solid floors, between timber joists/rafters/studs
Loose fill insulation		Attic spaces and between timber floors/ internal walls
Reflective insulation		Dry-lining external walls, internal stud wall and ceilings
	Thermal blocks, insulating plaster	As part of structural elements of the building

3. In Ireland, it is becoming more commonplace to add extra insulation to an existing home. This is due to:

____

____

____

____

4. Three of the most popular insulation methods are:

(a) ____________________________ space with insulation fill.

(b) adding extra insulation to the ______________________ of a house.

(c) adding extra insulation to the ______________________ of the house.

PUMPED CAVITY FILL

5. Pumped cavity fill is a very popular method for insulation cavity walls. List the two types of pumped cavity fill.

______________________ ______________________

6. Using notes and neat freehand sketches, describe the process of adding pumped insulation to an existing cavity wall.

____
____
____
____
____
____
____
____
____
____
____

7. Complete the table outlining the advantages and disadvantages of pumping the cavity in a wall.

Advantages	Disadvantages
The ________ of the building envelope is increased when the cavity is pumped.	The cavity is ________ across the insulation and the wall ties.
This ________ both ________ and ________.	________ may travel across the filled cavity.
There is no need to remove ________ or ________ when inserting the insulation.	After filling the ________ made from drilling the wall, the marks may ________.
The ________ of the house remains unchanged.	The beads may not fill the cavity completely, which results in ________.
It is an ________ and ________ method of improving insulation of an existing wall.	

INTERNAL INSULATION

8. (a) Internal insulation, often called ____________________, is a process in which ____________________ ________________, ____________________ and a ____________________ are attached to the inner leaf of a building.

(b) When internal insulation is applied, the cavity can also be ________________ with insulation to further insulate the building.

(c) Special composite plasterboards can be used. These are plasterboard slabs (12.5 mm) with insulation (80 mm minimum) and a ____________________ attached.

9. A family want to add dry lining to an existing garage space. As their architect, you must describe the process for two methods of attaching the dry lining to the existing wall. Illustrate your answer by completing the diagrams below.

Method 1

Dry lining a wall: method 1

Method 2

Dry lining a wall: method 2

10. Complete the table below outlining the advantages and disadvantages of dry lining.

Advantages	Disadvantages
The U-value of the wall is ______ by adding internal insulation	The ______ of the rooms is reduced.
This reduces both ______ and ______.	The installation process is ______, ______ and ______.
Internal insulation is ______ to install, and can be carried out by local tradespeople.	It is ______.
As ______ are not altered, ______ is not required.	The plasterboard may be easily ______.
As this method does not interfere with the ______ of the house, the ______ can be maintained.	______, ______ and ______ need to be repositioned.
There is no loss of ______ such as window-cills, which is ______ associated with replacing these items.	
Internal rooms ______ as the inner leaf is not absorbing the heat from the room.	
It can improve the ______ of some interior walls.	

EXTERNAL INSULATION

11. (a) External insulation consists of ______ fixed to the outer surface of the external walls.

(b) External insulation is made up of ______ layers of ______, ______ and ______.

(c) These materials are attached to the existing wall using ______ and ______.

12. Two materials are commonly used for external insulation.

(a) Expanded polystyrene (EPS)

- A minimum thickness of ______ is needed to achieve a U-value of 0.25 W/m^2 K, but ______ is typically used.
- Detailing around ______ and ______ requires particular attention to ensure the insulation has a ______.

(b) Phenolic foam

- This insulation has good __________________ strength and a low thermal conductivity.
- A minimum thickness of ______________ is needed to achieve a U-value of 0.25 W/m^2 K, however ______________ typically used.

13. The following stages are required to attach external insulation:

(a) The external walls are ________________ and ________________.

(b) A base coat of ________________ is applied over the existing external render or brickwork.

(c) The ________________ is attached to the wall using the base coat adhesive.

(d) ________________________________ are applied to securely fix the insulation to the wall.

(e) A ________________________________ is overlaid onto the insulation.

(f) Two ________________ of ________________ specialist external ________________ are applied over the mesh.

(g) ____________________________________ are required for the external corners and plinth.

(h) A _______________-type ________________ is used at the soffit and doors and around window frames.

14. Label the components of external insulation.

1. ____
2. ____
3. ____
4. ____
5. ____

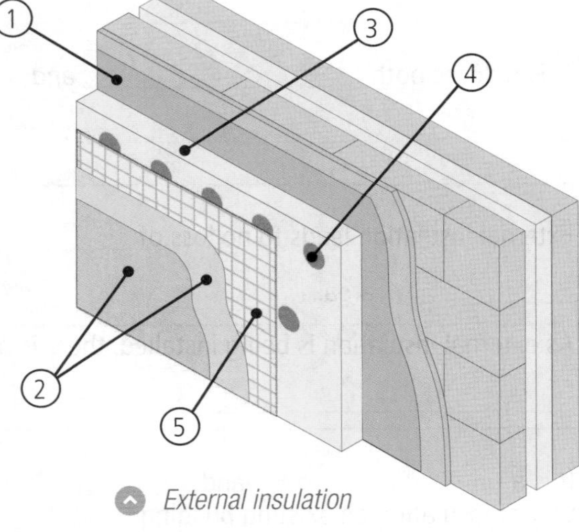

External insulation

15. Complete the given detail, showing how an external wall is retrofitted with external insulation.

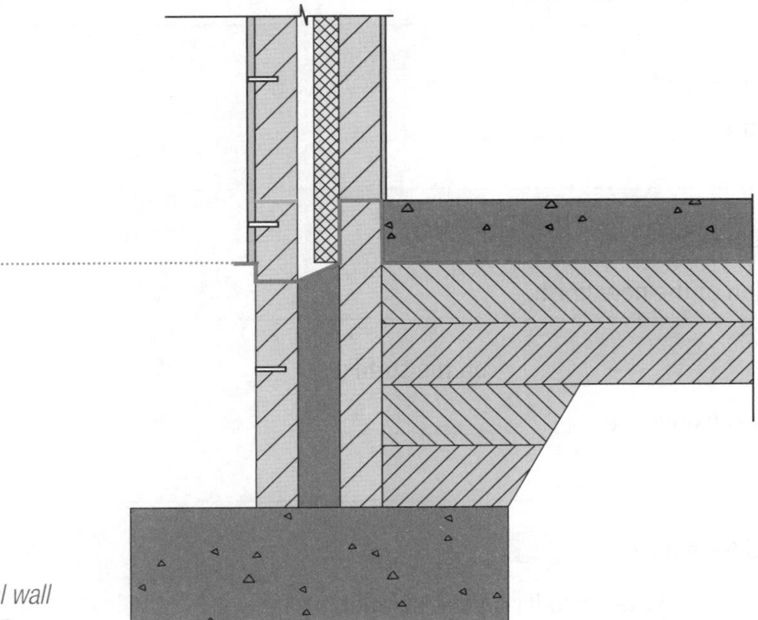
Retrofitting an external wall with external insulation

16. Explain the process involved in retrofitting a window detail with external insulation. As part of your answer, complete the given detail of a typical retrofitted window-cill and head detail.

Window-cill and head detail

____

____

____

____

____

____

____

17. Complete the table, outlining the advantages and disadvantages of external insulation.

Advantages	Disadvantages
External wall insulation reduces ________________ from the building.	External insulation is ________________ to buy and ________________.
This reduces both ________________ and ________________.	External insulation should only be installed by a ________________, which adds to the ________________ of installation.
External insulation leads to no loss of ________________ area.	External insulation can be easily ________________ by a ________________.
As external insulation is being installed, there is no ________________.	
It is a ________________ and ________________ way of insulating an existing building.	
The external walls become a ________________, capitalising on the ________________ of the building.	
The surface of the external wall may be ________________ by the application of the new finish.	
It leaves no ________________ on the surface as the mechanical fixings are ________________ behind the ________________.	
There is no need to remove ________________ or ________________ when installing the insulation.	

☐ METHODS OF HEAT TRANSFER

18. Using notes and a neat freehand sketch, explain the three methods of heat transfer.

(a) Method 1: ______________________________

____

____

____

____

____

(b) Method 2: ______________________________

____

____

____

(c) Method 3: ______________________________

____

____

____

☐ HEAT TERMS

THERMAL CONDUCTIVITY

19. (a) Thermal conductivity is the measurement of the ____________ at which heat is ______________ through a particular material under specific conditions.

(b) It can be simply defined as the ______________________________ (no movement of molecules) through a material.

(c) It is the amount of heat conducted through ____________ of 1 m thick material in ______________.

(d) It is measured in watts per metre degrees ______________ (W/m K or W/m °C). Its symbol is

________ or ________.

(e) ______________ (K) is an SI unit for temperature.

THERMAL RESISTIVITY

20. (a) Thermal resistivity is a measure of the ______________ to heat ______________ offered by a particular ______________ in a building element.

(b) It can be simply defined as the rate at which heat is ______________ by a material.

(c) It is the ______________ (opposite) of conductivity. This means that r = ____________.

(d) It is measured in ______________. Its symbol is ____________ or ____________.

RESISTANCE

21. (a) Resistance is the ability of a material to ________________ the passage of heat through it.

(b) It is calculated by multiplying thermal resistivity by the ________________ of a material ($r \times T$).

(c) It can also be calculated by ________________ the thickness of a material by its thermal ________________ ($T \div k$).

(d) It is measured in ________________. Its symbol is ____________.

(e) The total resistance of a building section, e.g. a wall, is the ____________ of the resistance of all its elements (bricks, blocks, etc.) added together: $R_t = R_1 + R_2 + R_3 \ldots R_n$.

THERMAL CONDUCTANCE

22. (a) Thermal conductance is the ability of a material to ________________ heat.

(b) It is measured in ______________ or ______________. Its symbol is ____________.

(c) Thermal conductance ($C = \frac{1}{R}$) is the ____________________ of resistance.

(d) The thermal conductance value obtained (C) is for ____________________________ of ____________________________ elements (bricks, blocks, insulation, etc.) and not the total conductance (C_t) of the building section, which is known as thermal transmittance.

THERMAL TRANSMITTANCE (U-VALUE)

23. (a) Thermal transmittance (the U-value) is a measure of the ________________ rate of heat transfer/loss through a particular ________________ of construction.

(b) It is the total conductance of all the building elements combined (C_t).

(c) Alternatively, it is calculated by dividing 1 by the total resistance ($\frac{1}{R_t}$).

(d) To meet building regulations, all elements of the house (walls, roof, etc.) must meet a ________________ U-value.

(e) The ________________ the U-value the better insulated the section.

Standard minimum U-values	
Fabric element	**Maximum elemental U-value (W/m^2 K)**
Pitched roofs	0.016
Walls	0.21
Ground floors	0.25
Other exposed floors	0.21
External doors, windows and roof lights	1.60

THICKNESS

24. (a) The thickness of a building material has an impact on its ________________ to the passage of heat.

(b) Thickness is measured in ____________. Its symbol is ____________.

(c) In your calculations, all mm measurements should be converted to ________________. For example, a 100 mm block wall = 100 ÷ ____________ = ____________ m.

SURFACE RESISTANCE

25. Using notes and neat freehand sketches, explain what is meant by the term *surface resistance*.

____

____

____

____

____

____

____

____

____

CAVITY RESISTANCE

26. (a) Trapped air inside a cavity space can offer ________________ to heat passing through it.

(b) There is no conductivity value given for this as heat travels by ________________ instead of conduction.

(c) For calculation purposes, a ________________ value is given to account for heat transferred across the cavity.

STEPS FOR CALCULATING U-VALUES

27. (a) Make a quick cross-sectional sketch of the element (e.g. a wall).

(b) Label each layer.

- Don't forget to indicate the internal and external surface resistance.
- This can be done by marking a red line on the inside and outside surface of the sketch.

(c) Metres are the standard measurement, so all material thickness given in mm must be converted into metres (e.g. 19 mm = 0.019 m).

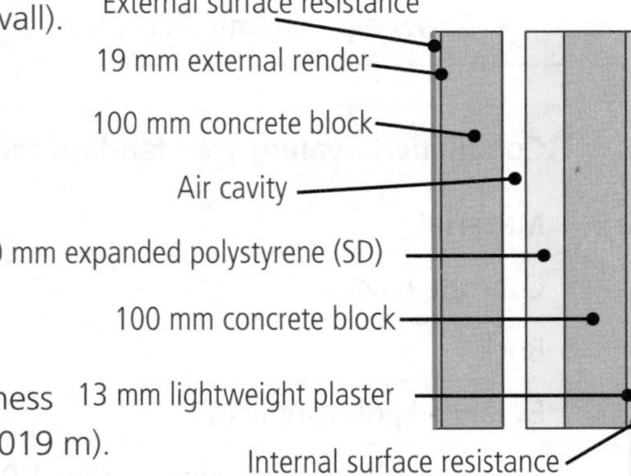

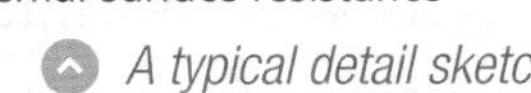
A typical detail sketch

(d) Draw a table and insert all information given in the question.

NOTE!

Sometimes the conductivity of the material is given and sometimes the resistivity is given.

(e) Convert all resistivity values to conductivity using the formula $\frac{1}{\text{Resistivity}}$ = Conductivity.

(f) Calculate the resistance of each layer by dividing the thickness of the component by its conductivity (i.e. $\frac{\text{Thickness}}{\text{Conductivity}}$).

(g) Calculate the total resistance by adding up the layer/surface resistances.

(h) Calculate the reciprocal of the total resistance (1 divided by the total resistance to get the U-value).

NOTE!

All figures should be rounded to three decimal places (i.e. 0.000) until the U-value is determined (which can be rounded to two).

Typical layout for a U-value question

Layer/surface (name)	Thickness (m)	Resistivity (mK/W) $r = \frac{1}{k}$	Conductivity (W/m K) $k = \frac{1}{r}$	Resistance (m^2 K/W) $R = r \times T$ $R = \frac{T}{k}$
External surface				0.04
External render	0.019		0.57	0.033
Concrete block	0.100		1.33	0.075
Air cavity				0.18
Expanded polystyrene board (standard density; SD)	0.060		0.037	1.621
Concrete block	0.100		1.33	0.075
Plaster (lightweight)	0.013	5.55	0.18	0.072
Internal surface				0.130
Total resistance				2.226

U-value = $\frac{1}{2.226}$ = 0.449 W/m^2 K

IMPORTANT THINGS TO CONSIDER WHEN SOLVING U-VALUE QUESTIONS

- Remember the internal and external resistance values.
- Remember to add the resistance of the cavity air space.
- Do not confuse the resistivity of the material with the conductivity.
- Show all calculations on the page in a neat and orderly fashion.

Conductivity values for standard materials

Material	**Conductivity**
Concrete block	1.33
Brick	0.770
Expanded polystyrene (SD)	0.037
Expanded polystyrene (high density; HD)	0.031
External render	0.57
Plaster (lightweight)	0.18
Plasterboard slab	0.25
Phenolic foam	0.025
Polyurethane board	0.025
Glass fibre insulation	0.04
Timber (softwood)	0.13
Timber plywood sheeting	0.13

SAMPLE EXERCISES

ADJUSTED CAVITY WALL

28. A 150 mm cavity wall contains 100 mm high density expanded polystyrene rigid insulation. The wall consists of a 100 mm block inner and outer leaf. The inner surface is plastered with 13 mm lightweight plaster with a resistivity value of 5.55 mK/W. The outer surface is rendered with 19 mm external render. Calculate the U-value for this wall.

NOTE!

Use the conductivity values for each material given above.

- external surface resistance = 0.04
- internal surface resistance = 0.13
- cavity resistance = 0.18

Layer/surface (name)	Thickness (m)	Resistivity (mK/W) $r = \frac{1}{k}$	Conductivity (W/m K) $k = \frac{1}{r}$	Resistance (m^2 K/W) $R = r \times T$ $R = \frac{T}{k}$
Total resistance				
U-value = $\frac{1}{\square}$ = ____ W/ ____				

ADDITION OF INSULATED PLASTER BACKED SLAB TO INNER WALL

29. A family want to increase the insulation value of a cavity wall by dry lining the inside leaf of the wall with a 75 mm polyurethane board on a 13 mm plasterboard slab.

Calculate the improved U-value for the renovated wall if the original wall consists of 19 mm external render on 100 mm concrete block external wall. 60 mm expanded polystyrene insulation (SD), with a resistivity value of 27.027 mK/W is fixed to a 100 mm concrete block inner leaf. The inside of the house is finished with 13 mm lightweight plaster.

- External surface resistance = 0.04 m^2 K/W
- Internal surface resistance = 0.13 m^2 K/W
- Cavity resistance = 0.18

NOTE!

Use the conductivity values for each material given opposite.

Layer/surface (name)	Thickness (m)	Resistivity (mK/W) $r = \frac{1}{k}$	Conductivity (W/m K) $k = \frac{1}{r}$	Resistance (m^2 K/W) $R = r \times T$ $R = \frac{T}{k}$
U-value = $\frac{1}{\square}$ = ______ W/ ______				

PUMPED CAVITY WALL

30. It is becoming more popular for builders to build the cavity wall first and pump the cavity space with full-fill insulation after the wall has been erected. A wall is constructed of 19 mm external render on a 100 mm concrete block external wall. The inside of the house is finished with 13 mm lightweight plaster on 100 mm block inner leaf.

(a) Calculate the U-value across the cavity space before and after the cavity has been pumped with phenolic foam insulation.

Fill in their calculations on the next page 

NOTE!

Use the conductivity values for each material given above.

- external surface resistance = 0.04 m^2 K/W
- internal surface resistance = 0.13 m^2 K/W
- air cavity resistance = 0.18

Continued

Layer/surface (name)	Thickness (m)	Resistivity (mK/W) $r = \frac{1}{k}$	Conductivity (W/m K) $k = \frac{1}{r}$	Resistance (m^2 K/W) $R = r \times T$ $R = \frac{T}{k}$
Total resistance				

U-value = $\frac{1}{\square}$ = _____ W/ _____

Layer/surface (name)	Thickness (m)	Resistivity (mK/W) $r = \frac{1}{k}$	Conductivity (W/m K) $k = \frac{1}{r}$	Resistance (m^2 K/W) $R = r \times T$ $R = \frac{T}{k}$
Total resistance				

U-value = $\frac{1}{\square}$ = _____ W/ _____

(b) Determine the percentage increase in thermal resistance from before and after the insulation was added.

ADJUSTING U-VALUES

31. An uninsulated cavity wall has a U-value of 0.91 W/m² K. If insulation board of thermal conductance of 0.025 W/m K is added, what thickness of insulation board is required to achieve a U-value of 0.35 W/m² K? Use the table below for your calculations.

Step	Calculation	Answer
Target U-value	U_2	
Calculate target total resistance	$R_2 = \frac{1}{U_2}$ $\frac{1}{\square}$	
Existing U-value	U_1	
Calculate existing total resistance	$R_1 = \frac{1}{U_1}$ $\frac{1}{\square}$	
Extra resistance required	$R_2 - R_2$ ______ – ______	
Conductivity value of proposed material		
Resistance = $\frac{T}{k}$	So $T = k \times R$ ______ x ______	

☐ CALCULATING THE RATE OF HEAT LOSS

32. (a) The rate of heat loss is the amount of heat energy lost from a building or building component, given a ______________________________ between the outside of the building and the inside.

(b) The rate of heat loss is measured in __________ (W) or ___________ per second (J/sec).

Note: _________ = 1 J/sec.

> **NOTE!**
>
> Heat loss is calculated using the formula: $T \times T_d \times A$, where:
> - T = thermal transmittance (U-value)
> - T_d = difference in temperature between outside and inside
> - A = area of the component

SAMPLE EXERCISES

33. Calculate the rate of heat loss for a wall 8 m x 2.5 m. The U-value of the wall is 2.56 W/m² K. The external temperature 11 °C and the desired internal temperature is 22 °C.

A = _______ x _______ = _______ m²   T = _______ W/m² K

T_d = _______ – _______ = _______   _____ x _____ x _____ = _____ W

34. A double-glazed window in a living room is 1.5 m high by 4 m wide. The glass is 5 mm thick and its conductivity value is 1.02 W/m.

The resistance for the external surface is 0.08 m² °C/W and the resistance for the internal surface is 0.12m² °C/W. The resistance of the air space between the panes is 0.15 m² °C/W.

(a) Complete the table to calculate the U-value for the window.

Layer/surface (name)	Thickness (m)	Conductivity (W/m K) $k = \frac{1}{r}$	Resistance (m² K/W) $R = \frac{T}{k}$
External surface			
Glass			
Air space			
Internal surface			
R_t			

(b) Calculate the rate of heat loss through the window when there is a difference of 11 °C between inside and outside temperatures.

U-value $\frac{1}{R_t} = \frac{1}{\square}$

U-value = ____________

Area of window = __________ x __________ = __________ m²

Rate of heat loss = __________ x __________ x __________

= ____________ W

☐ CALCULATING HEATING COSTS

NOTE!

The cost to heat a building is calculated using the formula:

$$\frac{PRATT_d}{1000C}$$

where:

- P = price of heating fuel
- R = thermal Transmittance (U-value)
- A = area
- T = time
- T_d = thermal difference from outside to inside
- C = calorific value of the heating fuel

SAMPLE EXERCISES

35. An external wall of area 145 m² and U-value 1.828 W/m² K is to be heated for 10 hours a day for 42 weeks. Calculate how much it would cost if the price of oil is €0.68 per litre with a calorific value of 37 350 kJ/litre. The average external temperature is 5 °C and the average internal temperature is 18 °C.

NOTE!

Make sure to use the appropriate units for each value, e.g. time must be given in seconds.

T = 10 hours for 42 weeks

T = _____ sec x _____ min x _____ hrs x _____ days x _____ weeks

T = ______________________ sec

R = ______

A = ______

P = ______

T_d = ____________

C = ____________ = ____________________ J

= (____________ x ________ x ________ x ________ x ________) ÷ (________ x ________)

= (____________________) ÷ (____________________) = __________

36. Calculate the cost of heat loss through the external wall of a timber-framed house, if the house is heated for 12 hours a day for 40 weeks.

- The U-value of the wall is 0.21 W/m^2 K covering an area of 125 m^2.
- The price of oil is €0.65 per litre with a calorific value of 37 350 kJ/litre.
- The internal temperature is 18 °C and the external temperature is 6 °C.

37. It is proposed to replace the existing 4 mm single-glazing in a house with a double-glazed unit made up of two 4 mm panes with a 12 mm air space.

(a) Using the data in the table, calculate, the U-value for both the single- and double-glazed units.

Thickness of glass	4 mm
Conductivity of glass	1.02 W/m °C
Resistance of air space	0.17 m^2 °C/W
Internal surface resistance	0.12 m^2 °C/W
External surface resistance	0.08 m^2 °C/W

Single-glazed unit			
Layer/surface (name)	**Thickness (m)**	**Conductivity (W/m K) $k = \frac{1}{r}$**	**Resistance (m² K/W) $R = \frac{T}{k}$**
Total resistance			

U-value = $\frac{1}{\square}$ = ____ W/ ____

Double-glazed unit			
Layer/surface (name)	**Thickness (m)**	**Conductivity (W/m K) $k = \frac{1}{r}$**	**Resistance (m² K/W) $R = \frac{T}{k}$**
Total resistance			

U-value = $\frac{1}{\square}$ = ____ W/ ____

(b) The house has a window area of 20 m² and the average air temperature difference across the windows is 8 °C. The calorific value of oil is 37 350 at a cost of €0.40 per litre. Calculate the daily savings in fuel costs resulting from the installation of the double-glazing.

THEORY QUESTIONS

ORDINARY LEVEL

1. A dwelling house, as shown in the sketch, has a 300 mm external block wall with 50 mm expanded polystyrene insulation in the cavity. The wall has a smooth external render finish. It is proposed to improve the insulation properties of the wall by adding an external system of insulation.

(a) Using notes and neat freehand sketches, show **one** suitable method of applying an external insulation system to the wall. Specify the insulation material used, indicate its typical thickness and include details of the external surface finish to the insulation.

(b) List **two** advantages of applying an external system of insulation to the walls of an existing house.

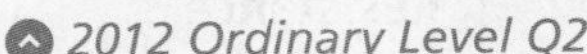
2012 Ordinary Level Q2

2. A dwelling house built 40 years ago, as shown in the sketch, has a 300 mm external concrete block wall with a 100 mm uninsulated cavity. The owner intends to refurbish the house to improve the thermal insulation levels of the external walls by:

- injecting insulation into the cavity of the external walls and
- fixing an internal insulation system to the external walls.

(a) For each insulation system listed above, show using notes and neat freehand sketches the procedures to be followed when applying the insulation system. For each system, specify the insulation material used.

(b) Discuss **one** advantage and **one** disadvantage of each system of insulation.

2011 Ordinary Level Q2

HIGHER LEVEL

3. A section through a triple-glazed, high performance wooden window is shown at A. The frame is a thermally broken, insulated frame as shown. Two of the panes of glass have a low-emissivity (low-e) coating and the spaces between the panes are filled with argon gas. A section through a traditional single-glazed solid wooden window is shown at B.

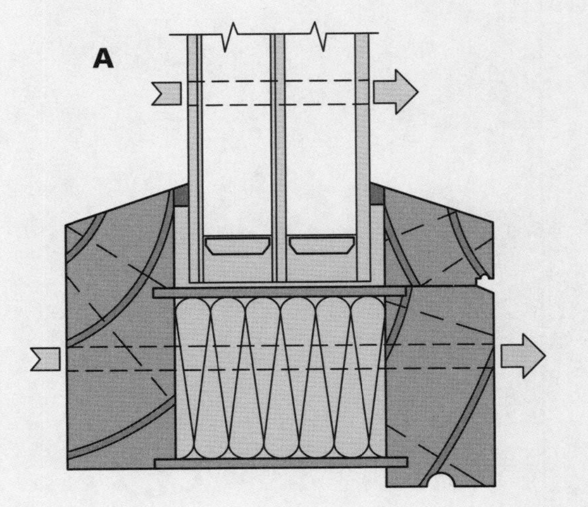

(a) For window A, using the given data, calculate the U-value of each of the following:

- the thermally broken wooden frame and
- the triple glazed argon-filled glazing unit.

Glass	thickness	4 mm
Space between panes of glass	each space	20 mm
Wood in thermally broken frame	each piece	30 mm
Rigid urethane insulation in frame	thickness	60 mm

Data for thermally broken wooden frame:

Conductivity of wood	(k) 0.150 W/m	°C
Conductivity of rigid urethane insulation	(k) 0.021 W/m	°C
Resistance of external surface of frame	(R) 0.950 m²	°C/W
Resistance of internal surface of frame	(R) 1.400 m²	°C/W

Data for triple-glazed unit:

Conductivity of glass	(k) 1.050 W/m	°C
Conductivity of argon gas	(k) 0.160 W/m	°C
Resistance of external surface of glass	(R) 0.075 m²	°C/W
Resistance of internal surface of glass	(R) 0.110 m²	°C/W
Total resistance of the low-e panes of glass	(R) 3.400 m²	°C/W

(b) The traditional single-glazed solid wooden window shown at B has the following U-values:

- U-value of the solid wooden frame 0.317 W/m² °C
- U-value of the single glazing 5.300 W/m² °C

Using the U-values of the high performance window frame and glazing unit obtained at (a) and the U-values of the traditional single-glazed wooden window given at (b) above, discuss the performance of both windows under the following headings:

- thermal properties
- environmental considerations

(c) Using notes and freehand sketches, show the design detailing of a window which is fixed in a 350 mm concrete block wall with an insulated cavity, to ensure minimum heat loss.

Note: Show design details at the window head only.

2013 Higher Level Q5

4. A house built in the 1970s has an uninsulated solid concrete ground floor with a sand/cement fine screed finish.

(a) Calculate the U-value of the concrete ground floor given the following data:

Sand/cement fine screed	thickness	60 mm
Concrete floor slab	thickness	100 mm
Damp-proof membrane (DPM)	thickness	0.25 mm
Sand-blinding	thickness	50 mm
Hardcore	thickness	225 mm
Subsoil	thickness	300 mm

Thermal data of concrete ground floor:

Resistance of internal surface	(R) 0.104 m^2	°C/W
Resistivity of fine screed	(r) 0.710 m	°C/W
Conductivity of concrete floor slab	(k) 0.160 W/m	°C
Conductivity of DPM	(k) 0.250 W/m	°C
Conductivity of sand blinding	(k) 0.160 W/m	°C
Conductivity of hardcore	(k) 1.330 W/m	°C
Conductivity of subsoil	(k) 1.800 W/m	°C

(b) Using the U-value of the concrete ground floor obtained at (a) above and the following data, calculate the cost of heat lost annually through the uninsulated concrete floor slab:

Dimensions of floor	9.0 metres × 7.0 metres
Average internal temperature	20 °C
Average external temperature of subsoil	5° C
Heating period	12 hours per day for 40 weeks per annum
Cost of oil	85 cent per litre
Calorific value of oil	37 350 kJ per litre 1000 Watts 1 kJ per second.

(c) An insulated concrete ground floor is designed to prevent the penetration of radon gas through the floor and to meet the Passive House standard. Using notes and freehand sketches, show the typical design detailing for such a floor.

2012 Higher Level Q5

5. In a dwelling house it is proposed to replace the existing 4 mm single glazing with double-glazed units. The double-glazed units consist of two 4 mm panes of glass with a 12 mm air space.

(a) Using the data given below calculate:

(i) the U-value of the single glazing.

(ii) the U-value of the double-glazing.

Data:

Thickness of glass	4 mm
Conductivity of glass	1.02 W/m °C
Resistance of 12 mm air space	0.17m^2 °C/W
Internal surface resistance	0.12m^2 °C/W
External surface resistance	0.08m^2 °C/W

(iii) If the dwelling house has 20 m^2 window area and the average air temperature difference across the windows is 8 °C, calculate the daily savings in fuel costs resulting from the installation of double-glazing, given the following:

Calorific value of oil	37 350 kj per litre
Cost of oil	4c per litre

(b) Discuss in detail the merits of installing double-glazing in a dwelling house.

2001 Higher Level Q7

☐ WHAT IS LIGHT?

1. (a) Light is energy in the form of ______________________________ radiation.

(b) Light travels as a __________________ form similar to how ocean waves travel.

(c) Light does not need ____________________ to travel and can travel through a ___________________.

(d) Light travels in ____________________________.

☐ PROPERTIES OF LIGHT

2. Describe the following properties of light:

(a) transmission (b) diffuse reflection (c) specular reflection (d) refraction

Draw neat sketches to support your answer.

____

____

____

____

____

____

____

____

(a)

(b)

(c)

(d)

☐ BUILDING REGULATIONS AND NATURAL LIGHT

3. To maximise natural light in a building, it is important that the design does not block the light with unnecessary obstructions. Using annotated sketches, outline two building regulations that aim to maximise light in a typical domestic dwelling.

DESIGNING FOR NATURAL LIGHT

4. Natural light is essential for human comfort and well-being. The benefits of natural light include:

(a) better conditions for ________________ and ________________.

(b) saving money on ________________________________.

(c) reducing heat-associated ________________________________.

(d) creating a ____________________ indoor environment.

(e) creating a more ________________ living space.

(f) conserving the ________________________________.

APPLYING THE GUIDELINES

5. Using notes and neat freehand sketches, describe any two design guidelines for accommodating natural light in the home. Explain how these guidelines can be applied to a typical domestic dwelling.

Continued ➜

SUN SPACES

6. Due to planning permission constraints, a couple building a new home have found that they cannot orientate their building as they would like to capture the sun's south-facing thermal gain. Using notes and neat freehand sketches, describe what a sun space is and how it can work to overcome the couple's thermal gain problem.

7. Well-designed sun spaces should:

(a) be located on the __________ side of the house.

(b) not be excessively __________ by __________ or __________.

(c) have the maximum amount of __________ possible in the walls.

(d) have a well-insulated __________.

(e) have connecting walls of a high __________ mass.

(f) have a __________ roof.

8. Draw a sketch showing the correct design and use of a sun space.

☐ CONTROLLING SUNLIGHT

9. Excessive exposure to sunlight has the following disadvantages:

   (a) ____________ cast by sunlight can make it difficult to see objects.

   (b) Excessive sunlight will result in ________________.

   (c) Heat and light can be harmful to materials and cause them to ____________________.
   For example, paintings and furniture can fade.

   (d) Excessive sunlight can cause ________________.

10. There are two types of glare.

    (a) ________________ glare lessens the ability to see detail, without necessarily causing visual discomfort.
    An example is glare when driving into the sunset.

    (b) __________________ glare causes visual discomfort, without necessarily lessening the ability to see
    detail. An example is staring at a computer screen for long periods of time.

11. Knowing how to control the entry of natural light into a house can greatly help to maximise the building's use of light and minimise the disadvantages of excessive glare. Using notes and neat freehand sketches, describe four design methods that can be used to control the entry of light into a building.

Continued

Method 1

Method 2

Method 3

Method 4

12. Other ways to control sunlight and solar heat gain include:

(a) using an ______________________ to allow light to reach as far into the building as possible.

(b) using __________________________ and ________________________ floor finishings to _________ light around the room.

(c) selecting the correct colour paint: _______________ colours reflect light while _________ colours absorb light.

(d) correct __________________ and __________________ of the building on the site to maximise the amount of available light.

(e) the height of buildings: in winter ____________ buildings cast more of a shadow. This is important if building extensions or garden sheds.

(f) the _________________ and _________________ of rooms in the dwelling.

(g) the use of devices such as _________________, _________________ and ___________________.

☐ RETROFITTING FOR ADDITIONAL LIGHT

13. Additional light can created in an existing building by adding either a Velux window or a light tube through the roof space. Using annotated freehand sketches, describe how a light tube allows light into a building.

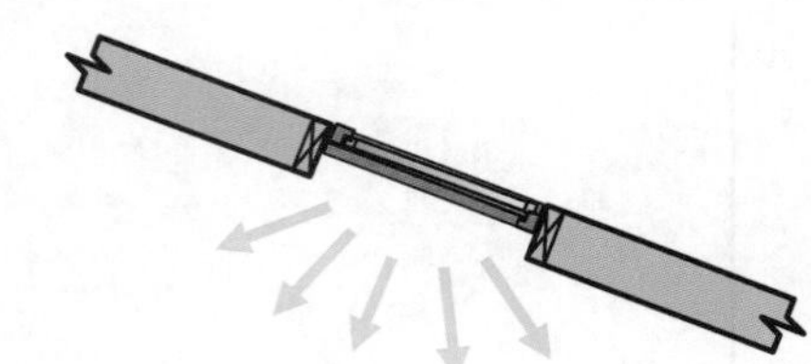

A Velux window

PRACTICAL APPLICATION

14. The diagram shows the proposed plan and elevation of a small two-bedroom bungalow. Analyse the proposed layout of the bungalow in terms of maximising the use of light in the building. Sketch at least two improvements that can be made to the original building design.

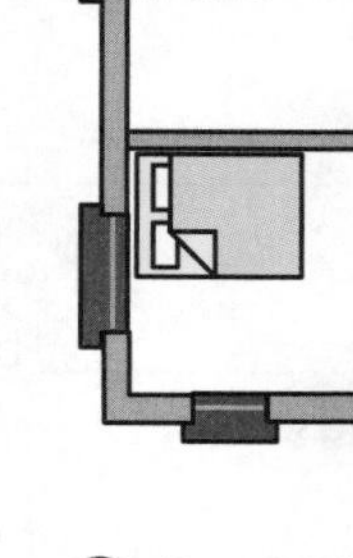

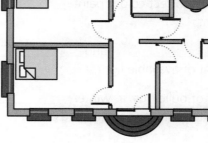

Proposed house layout

Continued

☐ CALCULATING LIGHT IN BUILDINGS

15. Explain each of the following terms relating to the various components of light:

(a) Sunlight: ______________________________

(b) Skylight: ______________________________

____

(c) Daylight: ______________________________

(d) Luminance:

- Luminance is the ______________ of light shining from a light source.
- It is measured in ______________.

(e) Luminance flux:

- Luminance flux is the rate of ______________ of light energy.
- It is measured in ______________.

(f) Illumination:

- Illumination is the ______________ of luminance falling (shining) on a ______________, i.e. how bright the surface is.
- It is measured in ______________.

16. Label the diagram showing the components of light.

1. ______________________ 4. ______________________

2. ______________________ 5. ______________________

3. ______________________ 6. ______________________

Components of light

DAYLIGHT FACTOR

17. The daylight factor is the ratio between the ______________________________ at a point inside a room and the ______________________________ from an unobstructed sky.

> **NOTE!**
>
> $$\text{Daylight factor} = \frac{\text{Actual luminance}}{\text{Possible luminance}}$$
>
> If the luminance in a kitchen table is 1500 lux and the total luminance possible from an unobstructed sky is 5000 lux, the daylight factor is $\frac{1500}{5000} = 30\%$.

18. Draw a sketch to show possible and actual luminance.

RECOMMENDED DAYLIGHT FACTORS

19. As different jobs and situations require different amounts of light, different levels of luminance are acceptable in different rooms. Generally, any room in which ______________________ work is carried out will require a higher ______________________________ than a room used for general use.

DAYLIGHT FACTOR COMPONENTS

20. Light that arrives at the work plane level in a room can be made up of three different components. Describe each of these components.

(a) Internally reflected component (IRC): ______________________________

(b) Externally reflected component (ERC): ______________________________

____

____

(c) Internally reflected component (IRC): ______________________________

____

21. The daylight factor component is made up of all the individual components combined.

Daylight factor component = ________ + ________ + ________.

22. On the diagram, indicate and label the three daylight factor components.

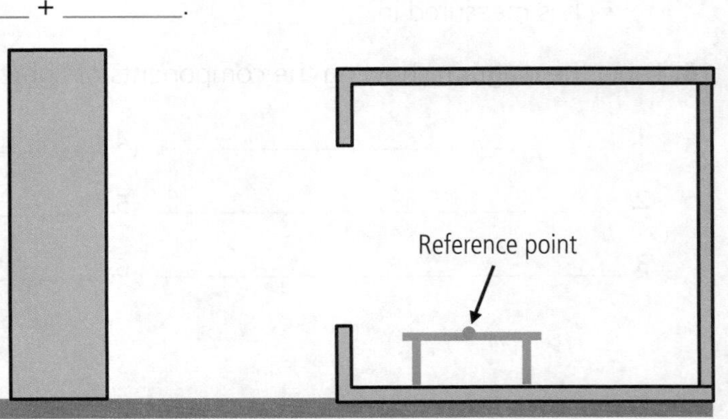

Three daylight factor components

☐ CALCULATING WINDOW SIZE

23. Because the amount of light from the sky (luminance) varies, we have to assume an average value for the luminance from the sky. To calculate window size, we need to determine a standard overcast sky.

(a) The ________________________________ (CIE) came up with a figure of __________ __________ as being the constant luminance.

(b) The symbol for the standard overcast sky is __________.

WINDOW FACTOR

24. (a) Most windows are positioned __________.

(b) Due to this, only _____% of all the available light from a standard overcast sky is available to shine through the window.

(c) The other __________% is reflected off the window.

(d) This is called the window factor. Its symbol is __________.

(e) The window factor is generally taken to be 50% or 0.5.

- A standard overcast sky, E_a, is __________ lux.
- Because of the window factor, only 2500 lux is available to shine in the window.
- 5000 x 0.5 = __________

ENERGY COEFFICIENT

25. (a) Because of __________ on windows, only _____% (_____) of the light passes through the glass.

(b) This is called the energy coefficient. The symbol for the energy coefficient is __________.

WINDOW AREA

26. (a) The number of windows in the room determines the amount of light __________ to the room.

(b) The __________ of these windows also determines the amount of light available.

(c) To calculate the amount of light available, we find the total window area using the formula __________ x __________.

(d) The symbol for window area is __________.

FLOOR AREA

27. (a) To calculate the size of the window area required, we also need to know the total floor area of the room we are __________.

(b) We find the floor area using the formula __________ x __________.

(c) The symbol for floor area is __________.

THE DEGREE OF EFFICIENCY FORMULA

NOTE!
The degree of efficiency formula is used to calculate the luminance inside a building, taking into account all factors affecting light entering the building: $E_a \times f \times n \times \frac{F_f}{F_b}$

28. In the degree of efficiency formula $E_a \times f \times n \times \frac{F_f}{F_b}$:

(a) ____________________ is the luminance outside.

(b) ____________________ is the window factor.

(c) ____________________ is the efficiency coefficent.

(d) ____________________ is the window area.

(e) ____________________ is the floor area.

SAMPLE EXERCISES

29. A 3 m x 4 m room with an unobstructed view requires an average illumination of 100 lux. Using the degree of efficiency method, determine the size of window required to provide this level of illuminance.

Step 1: Record the information given in question.

- Illumination inside = ________ lux
- Illumination outside (E_a) = ________ lux
- Floor size (F_b) = ____ x ____ = ____ m²
- Window factor (f) = ____
- Efficiency coefficient (n) = ____

Step 2: Insert the information into the formula.

______ = (______) × (______) × (______) × ($\frac{\square}{\square}$)

Step 3: Calculate the answer. Make sure to include the correct units in your final answer.

______ = ______ × ($\frac{\square}{\square}$)

______ / ______ = $\frac{\square}{\square}$

______ × ______ = $\frac{\square}{\square}$

______ = ______ m²

30. The average illumination in a room is to be increased from 90 to 150 lux by enlarging an existing window. Using the degree of efficiency method, determine the size of the window required if the room is 3800 mm long x 4800 mm wide.

Step 1: Record the information given in question.

- Illumination inside = ________ lux
- Illumination outside (E_a) = ________ lux

- Floor size (F_b) = _____ x _____ = _____ m^2
- Window factor (f) = _____
- Efficiency coefficient (n)= _____

Step 2: Insert the information into the formula.

_____ = (_____) × (_____) × (_____) × ($\frac{\square}{\square}$)

Step 3: Calculate the answer. Make sure to include the correct units in your final answer.

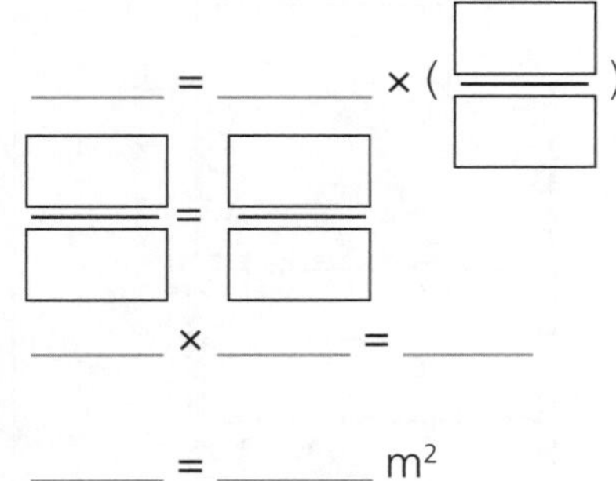

_____ × _____ = _____

_____ = _____ m^2

31. An architect's office requires an average luminance of 750 lux on the working plane. If the drawing office is 28.8 metres long and 7.2 metres wide, calculate the area of window required to illuminate the room to this level. You can assume:

- an unobscured sky.
- a standard sky of 5000 lux.
- 60% of light is reflected or absorbed by the window or dirt on the window.

THEORY QUESTIONS

HIGHER LEVEL

1. The drawing shows the elevation, ground floor plan and portion of the rear garden of a two-storey semi-detached house. The rear wall B-B of the house is south facing.

   The external walls are 350 mm concrete block walls with an insulated cavity.

   All internal walls are of 100 mm solid block construction and the internal wall A-A is load-bearing.

   It is proposed to build a single-storey extension to the rear of the house to:

   - allow increased sunlight into the interior of the house and
   - improve the view to the rear garden.

   (a) Show, using notes and freehand sketches, a proposed design for the extension to the rear of the dwelling house and a revised layout for the ground floor to include the extension.

   (b) For each of the above, discuss in detail the reasons for your proposed design choices.

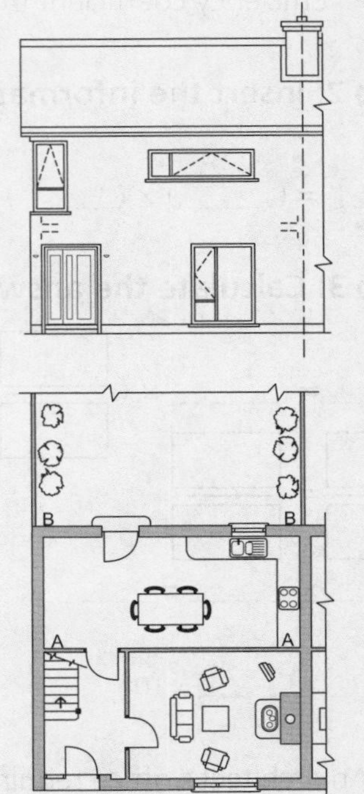

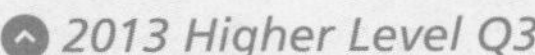
2013 Higher Level Q3

2. The drawing shows the elevation and plan of a semi-detached house with an adjoining storeroom. All external walls are of single leaf 215 mm hollow block construction and all roofs are slated. All internal walls are of solid block construction and the internal wall A-A is load-bearing. The storeroom wall B-B is south facing. It has been decided to convert the storeroom in order to enlarge the living space. In the conversion, you need to give consideration to:

   - redesigning the ground floor layout to allow increased penetration of sunlight to the interior and
   - upgrading the thermal properties of the external walls.

   (a) Show, using notes and freehand sketches, a revised design detailing for the dwelling house.

   (b) For each of the above, discuss in detail the reasons for your proposed design choices.

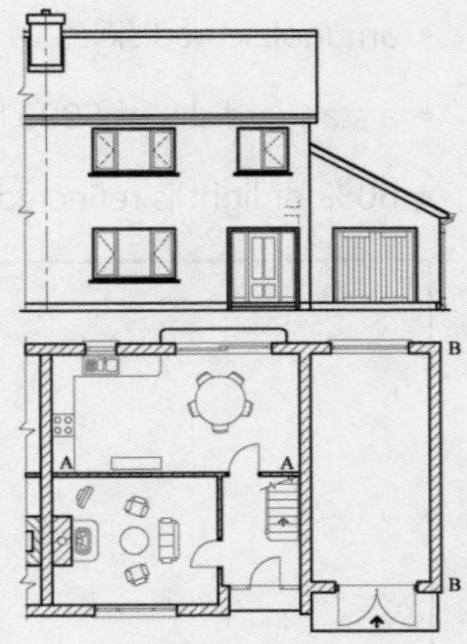

2012 Higher Level Q3

3. (b) The accompanying sketch shows a dwelling house with an attached sunspace. Using notes and freehand sketches, propose a design layout for the rooms adjoining the sunspace that would maximise the passive solar heat gain from the sun space.

   (c) Give **two** reasons for the proposed room layout adjoining the sun space.

2008 Higher Level Q10 (b) and (c)

4. (b) The accompanying sketch shows a terrace of houses with fully glazed façades. Using notes and freehand sketches show the preferred orientation of the houses to maximise passive solar gain. Justify your choice of orientation.

(c) Overheating may occur in summer as a result of glazing the full façade as shown. Using notes and freehand sketches show, for one of the houses, **two** design details that would help prevent such overheating.

2009 Higher Level Q10 (b) and (c)

5. A storm proof casement window made from softwood is located in an external wall and provides natural lighting to a kitchen area.

(a) Describe in detail, using notes and freehand sketches, **two** design details that ensure that the window is weather proof.

(b) Discuss **two** advantages and two disadvantages of using softwood in the manufacture of windows.

(c) An illuminance of 300 lux is required on a working plane in the kitchen. The daylight factor at a point on the working plane in the kitchen is 5%. Show by calculation if the illuminance is sufficient, assuming an unobstructed view and the illuminance of a standard overcast sky to be 5000 lux.

2003 Higher Level Q9

6. (a) Determine by degree of efficiently method, or by any other suitable method, the approximate size of a vertical window suitable for a kitchen 4.80 m long by 3.60 m wide requiring an average illumination of 150 lux on the working plane. Assume an unobstructed view and the illumination of a standard overcast sky to be 5000 lux

(b) Select **two** materials commonly used in the manufacture of window frames and discuss in detail the advantages and disadvantages of each material for window frame manufacture.

2000 Higher Level Q7

WHAT IS SOUND?

1. In your own words, describe what sound is and how it is travels from its source to be heard by a listener. Use a neat freehand sketch to support your answer.

____

____

____

____

____

____

____

____

HOW DO WE HEAR SOUND?

2. (a) Sound is made by air ____________________.

(b) The vibrating air causes a thin layer of skin (__________________) in the ear to vibrate.

(c) The vibration in the ear causes small bones in the inner ear to tug on small ____________________ connected to the brain.

(d) The brain translates this ____________________ into comprehensible __________________.

3. Label the parts of the ear.

1. ______________________________
2. ______________________________
3. ______________________________
4. ______________________________
5. ______________________________
6. ______________________________

The parts of the ear

☐ WHAT DOES SOUND LOOK LIKE?

4. Sound travels as a ________________ similar to how water in the sea moves.

5. There are three main characteristics of a sound wave:

(a) Frequency is the number of ________________ made by a vibrating object in one second. It is measured in________________.

(b) Wavelength is the distance from the ______________ of one wave to the ______________ of another.

(c) The amplitude of a wave is the ________________ of each waveform measured from the ________ of the crest to the ___________________________.

6. Sketch the different characteristics of a sound wave.

7. Sound waves are made up of two main parts. What are they?

______________________________ ______________________________

8. The diagram shows how a sound wave is formed. Describe this process in your own words.

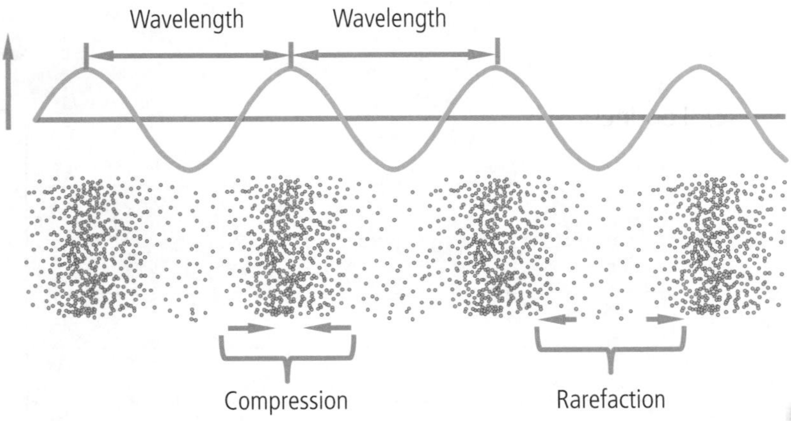

How a sound wave is formed

PRACTICAL CHARACTERISTICS OF SOUND

9. The characteristics of sound can be explained in terms of (a) velocity, (b) pitch and (c) loudness. Using notes and neat freehand sketches, explain each of these terms. Provide examples of where each of the characteristics might be observed in everyday life.

(a) Velocity

Demonstrating the velocity of sound

(b) Pitch

Demonstrating the pitch of sound

(c) Loudness

Demonstrating the loudness of sound

☐ SOUND IN BUILDINGS

10. When sound is produced in a building, three reactions can occur.

(a) The ________________________ come into contact with the walls, floor or ceiling and are ________________________ back into the building.

(b) Some of the sound is ________________________ by these surfaces and/or furnishings.

(c) Upon reaching the walls, floor and ceiling, the sound waves can cause these surfaces to ________________________, and thereby ________________ the sound into the adjacent rooms.

11. Not all sound is created in the same way, and not all sound is transferred from one room to the next in the same way. Discuss the different types of sound and how it can be transferred throughout a building. Indicate each method on the diagram provided.

The different methods of sound transfer

ABSORPTION AND REFLECTION

12. (a) Sound absorption is the reduction in ________________________ as it is ________________ by the ________________ of the room.

(b) Generally, ________________________ surfaces, such as tiles and concrete, ____________ a lot of sound and ____________ surfaces, such as ____________ and ________________________, ________________ sound.

(c) Sound is reflected in a similar way to how light is reflected. The angle of ________________ is equal to the angle of ________________.

19

13. Draw sketches to illustrate (a) sound reflection and (b) sound absorption.

(a)

(b)

RESONANCE

14. (a) Resonance occurs when a vibrating object causes a ________________ object to vibrate at the same ________________.

(b) This happens because the ________________________ being emitted is the same as the ________________________ of the material. An example is shattering a glass using a high-pitched sound.

COINCIDENCE EFFECT

15. (a) When sound bounces off a material, it causes the material to ________________.

(b) The coincidence effect is a reduction in the ________________________ value of the material, due to the material ________________ at the same ________________ as the sound.

(c) At which sound range the coincidence effect occurs will change depending on the material's ________________________.

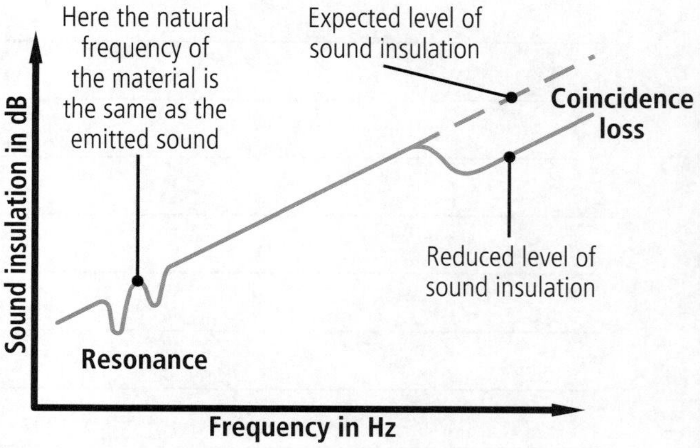

Resonance and the coincidence effect

☐ INSULATING A BUILDING FOR SOUND

16. The overall sound insulation of a structure depends upon its performance in reducing the airborne and impact sound transferred by all direct or indirect sound paths. List the four principles upon which good sound insulation depends.

________________________ ________________________

________________________ ________________________

MASS

17. Discuss how mass can affect the sound insulation of a building. In your answer, make specific reference to everyday examples of where the mass principle is used in a dwelling.

____

____

____

____

____

____

Continued

____

____

____

____

____

____

18. Draw two examples of the mass principle being applied for sound insulation.

19. Complete the detail showing one method of how the mass principle can be used to increase sound insulation performance of an upper floor.

How the mass principle can be used to increase sound insulation

COMPLETENESS

20. (a) The completeness of a structure is also an important factor for sound insulating a building. This involves the elimination of __________ or ____________________.

(b) A hole or crack in a brick wall may only represent 0.1% of the total area but can reduce the sound reduction index (SRI) value from 50 dB to __________ dB.

NOTE!

An air gap of 1% of a structure can decrease the SRI by up to 40%.

(c) ____________________ often exist because of inadequate ____________ around partitions, particularly at the ______________ between ____ ________________________. Doors and windows should be ____________________ when closed.

(d) The principle of __________________ is also important. Doors, windows and other openings should be kept to a ____________________ and those in place should be well __________________.

21. Indicate on the diagram how to apply the principle of completeness to increase sound insulation performance of an upper floor.

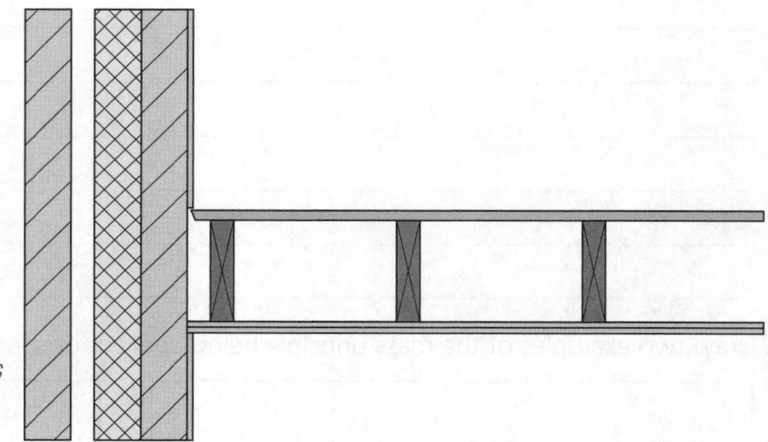

The principle of completeness to increase sound insulation performance

FLEXIBILITY

22. Describe how the use of flexible materials can help reduce sound transferral in a building. In your answer, give examples of typical sound-absorbing materials used in a dwelling.

23. Complete the detail showing three simple ways flexible materials can be used to increase the sound insulation performance of a floor.

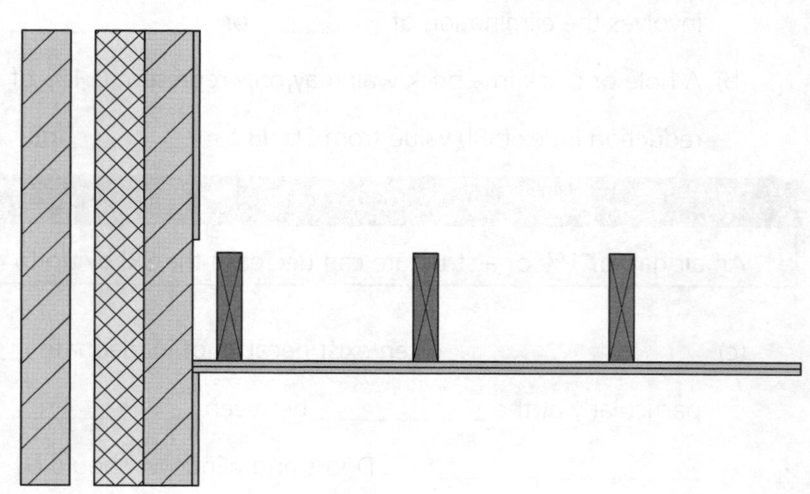

Three simple ways flexible materials can be used to increase sound insulation performance of an upper floor

ISOLATION/DISCONTINUOUS CONSTRUCTION

24. Explain what is meant by *isolation* and *discontinuous construction* in relation to sound insulation in a dwelling. In your answer, draw two examples of where they can be used in a dwelling.

Example 1

Example 2

APPLYING THE PRINCIPLES

1 PARTITION WALLS

25. A family want to create a music room by dividing up an existing room in their house. Design a suitable timber partition wall that will ensure a high level of soundproofing for the new room. In your answer, you must use the principles of mass, isolation and flexibility to achieve the highest level of soundproofing.

sketches, explain how
ꞁn can be applied to a
o buildings.

3 UPPER FLOORS AND SUSPENDED TIMBER FLOORS

27. The diagram shows the construction of a suspended timber floor that has been retrofitted to increase its sound insulation performance. Explain how the techniques used in this construction incorporate the principles of sound insulation.

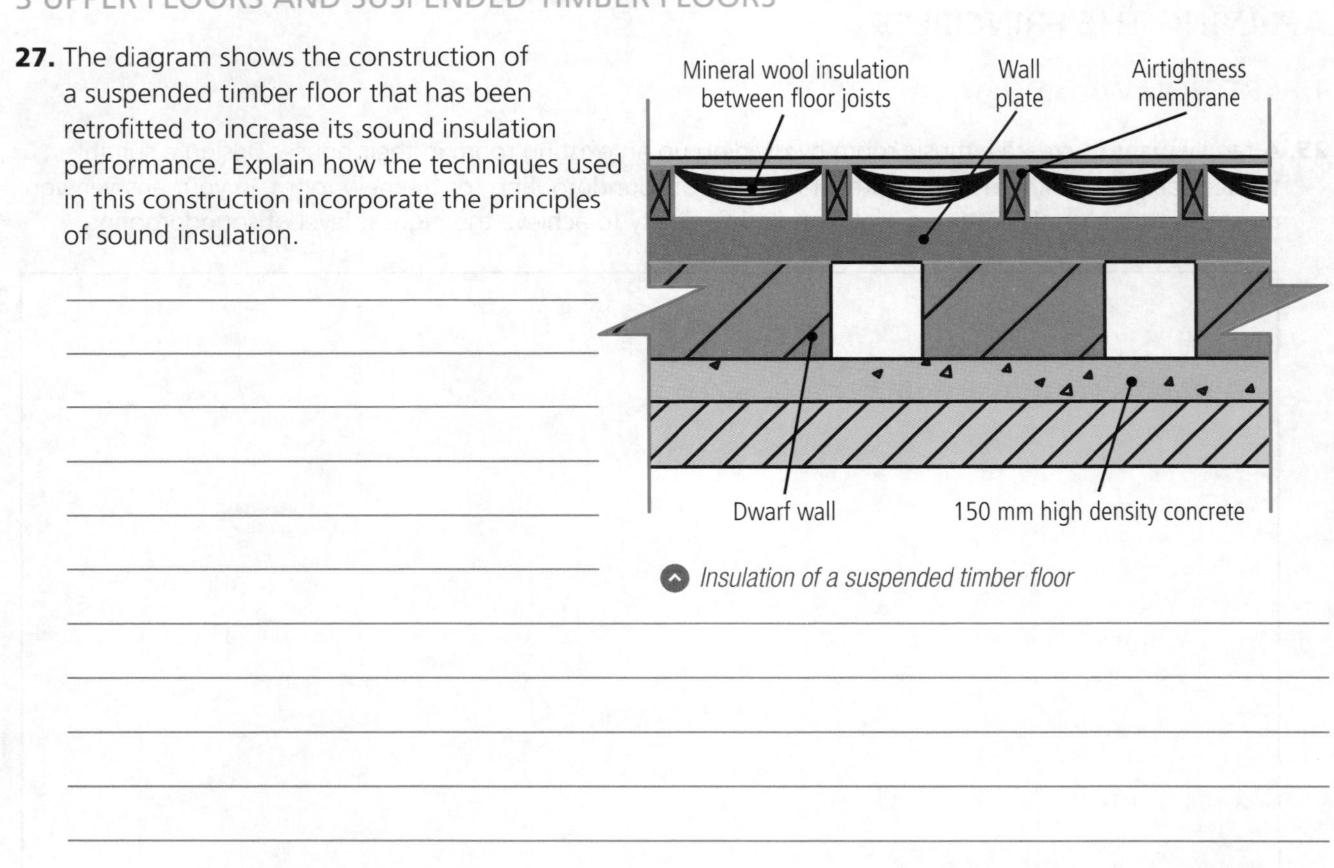

Insulation of a suspended timber floor

☐ REVERBERATION

28. Reverberation can be defined as ______________________________

____

29. Indicate sound reverberation on the diagram of a room.

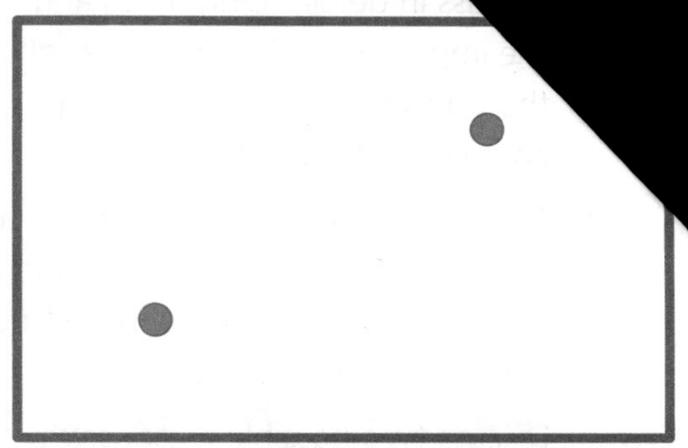

Sound reverberation in a room

REVERBERATION TIME

30. (a) The amount of time it takes for sound to die away is called ______________.

(b) It is the time taken from when ______________, for it to ______________ by ________ dB from its ______________.

(c) The time taken for this decay in a room depends upon the following factors:

- ______________ of exposed surfaces.
- sound ______________ at the surfaces.
- ______________ between the surfaces.
- ______________ of the sound.

31. Draw a sketch to illustrate reverberation time.

INVERSE SQUARE LAW

32. The diagram shows a graphical explanation of the inverse square law. In your own words, explain how the inverse square law applies to sound.

____

____

____

____

____

____

____

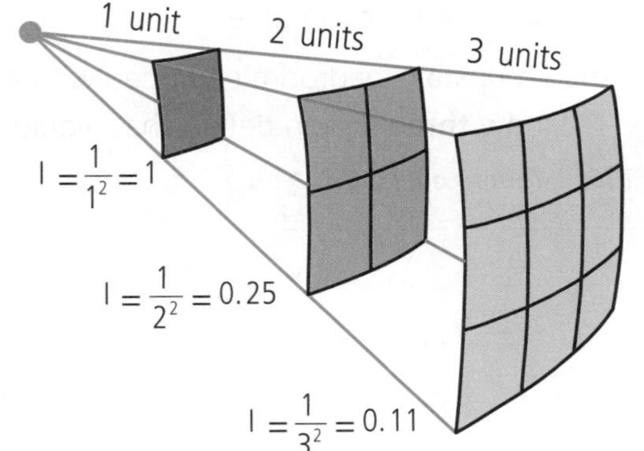

The inverse square law

19

s and freehand sketches, ne following in reducing n a dwelling house: mass,

two semi-detached houses concrete block construction. ouse can hear everyday sounds ouse.

Discuss **two** possible reasons why sound is transmitted between the houses, and using notes and freehand sketches, show the revised design detailing that would improve the sound insulation properties of the party wall between both houses.

2011 Higher Level Q4 (a) and (b)

2. It is proposed to install a music system in the living room of a single-storey dwelling house. The house has a concrete floor and the living room is separated from an adjacent bedroom by a standard stud partition. The walls and ceilings have a smooth hardwall plaster finish. It is proposed to carry out renovations to improve sound insulation.

(a) Using neat freehand sketches, show **two** design details that would increase the sound insulation properties of the stud partition.

(b) Explain in detail **two** sound insulation principles which would influence the design of the stud partition.

(c) Using notes and sketches, suggest **two** modifications which would improve the acoustic properties of the living room.

2004 Higher Level Q9

3. The first floor of a house consists of tongued and grooved softwood flooring on timber joists with a plasterboard ceiling beneath.

Using notes and freehand sketches, show two design details that would increase the sound insulation properties of the first floor in order to minimise the transmittance of sound.

2007 Higher Level Q9 Part B

4. (a) Using notes and sketches, explain the following:

(i) sound absorption.

(ii) sound reflection.

(iii) reverberation time.

(b) An upstairs bedroom equipped with a music system is being renovated. Using notes and sketches, show **three** design details that would improve the sound insulation properties of this room.

2001 Higher Level Q6

20 UNIVERSAL DESIGN

☐ INTRODUCTION

1. Explain what is meant by the *universal design* of a dwelling. Outline the key design criteria that it sets

____

____

____

____

____

____

____

____

____

____

____

____

____

____

☐ APPROACH TO A DWELLING

2. The front entrance to a house should have:

(a) a gentle ________________ (______:______ maximum).

(b) an entrance route with a firm ______________________________.

(c) a maximum threshold ________________ of _______ mm.

(d) a maximum threshold ________________ of ______°.

(e) adequate ______________ for a wheelchair user to manoeuvre out of a car.

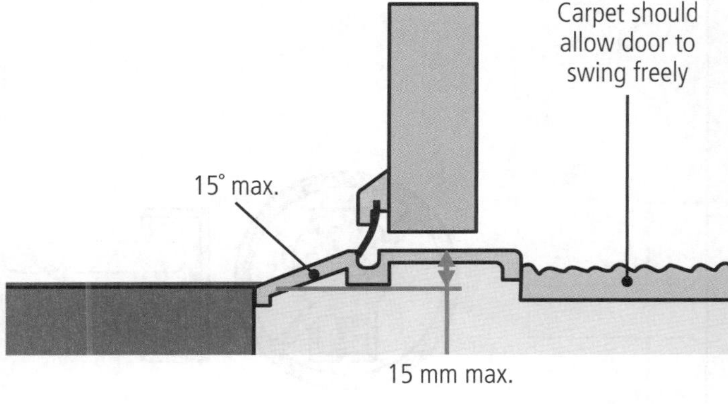

Typical threshold detail

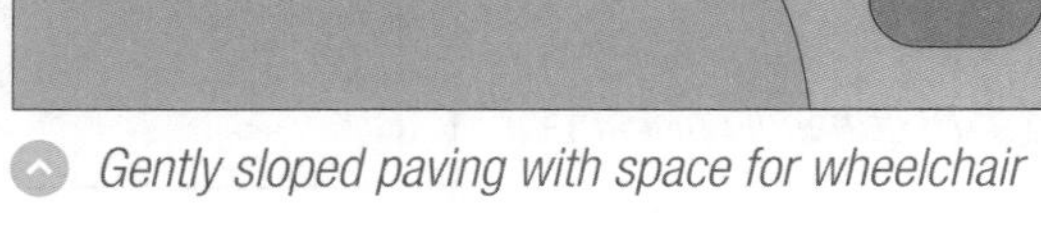

Gently sloped paving with space for wheelchair

20

…d be avoided where possible. If they are unavoidable, their design … as possible. Using notes and neat freehand sketches, explain these

Typical handrail detail

Standard step dimensions

☐ ACCESS TO A DWELLING

4. (a) At least one entry door should have a minimum ______________ width of ______ mm.

(b) Door handles should be located at a height between ______ mm and ______ mm (______ mm is optimum).

(c) Visibility ______________ in the door aids its use.

(d) The handle should be designed so that it does not require ______________ strength.

(e) On the diagram below, insert appropriate measurements for the height of a door handle.

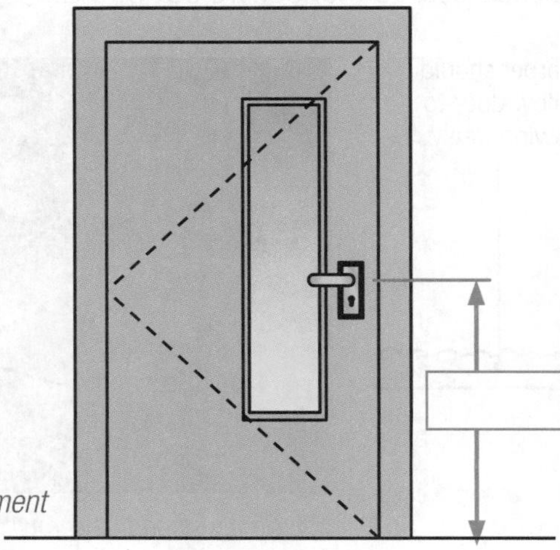

Door handle placement

Correct handle design

☐ CORRIDORS

5. The free and unobstructed passage through corridors and walkways helps make a hom
In your own words, explain the building requirements for corridor design. Support your an
completing the diagrams.

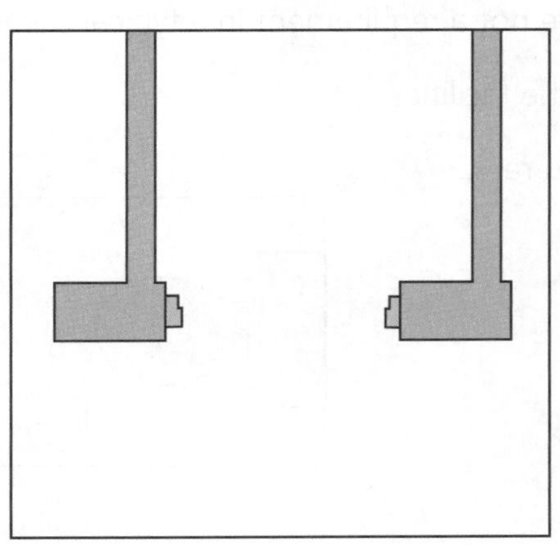

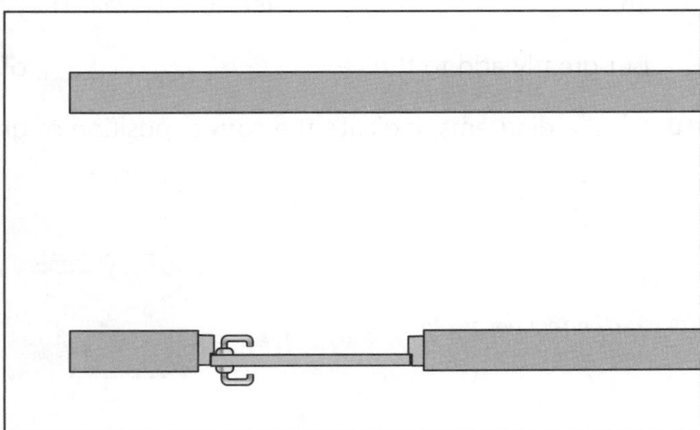

Indicate the relevant regulations governing corridor design

☐ PLACEMENT OF FIXTURES AND FITTINGS

6. Fixtures and fittings should be placed at an appropriate height to be easily used by a person in a wheelchair. Add appropriate measurements to the diagram, showing the correct placement of switches and sockets for a wheelchair user.

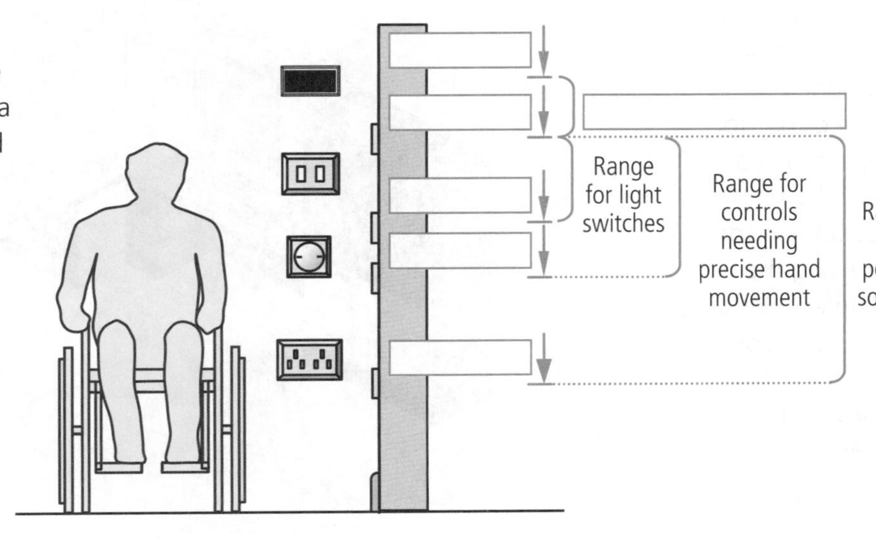

Correct placement of switches and sockets for a wheelchair user

IGN

_______ at entry level should be _______________.

a minimum of _________ mm from any wall to the _________

_______________ space of 1200 x 750 mm to allow a person

The appropriate dimensions for the layout of a WC

GRAB RAILING IN A WC

9. Grab rails offer assistance to the person getting on and off the toilet. They are Ø___ mm steel rails that are _______________ fixed to the wall. They are not a requirement in a typical domestic dwelling but greatly add to the _______________ of the facilities.

10. On the diagrams, indicate the correct position of grab rails.

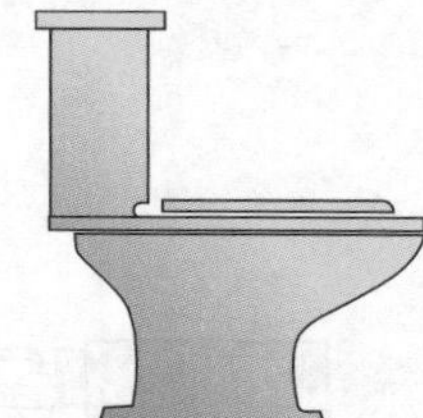

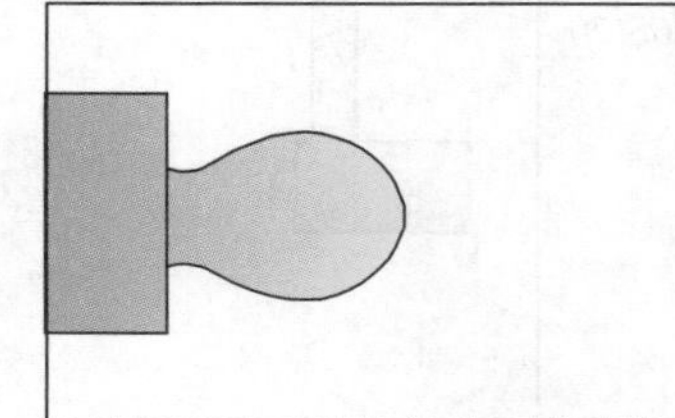

The correct position of grab rails

☐ KITCHEN DESIGN FOR WHEELCHAIR ACCESS

11. The diagram shows a kitchen that has been designed for ease of use for a person in a wheelchair. Identify on the drawing the different design considerations that have been used in this space.

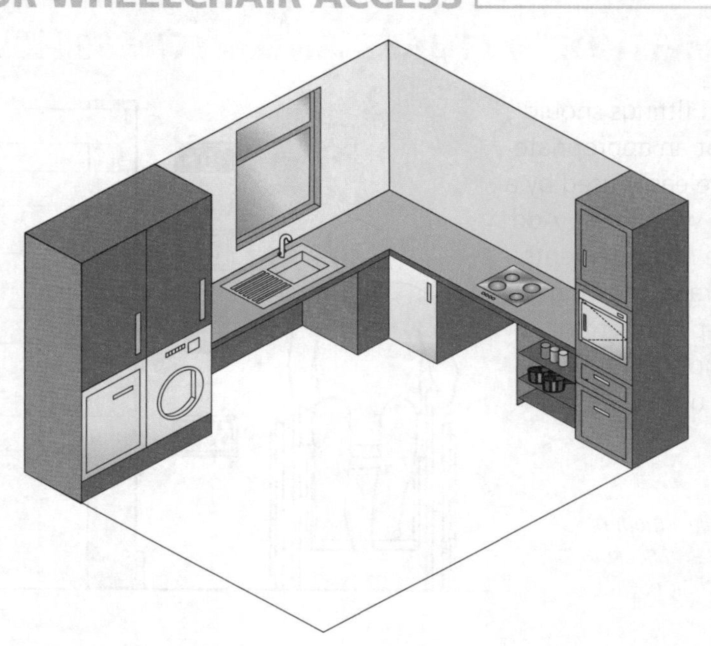

Kitchen design considerations for a wheelchair user

☐ GENERAL DESIGN GUIDELINES

12. (a) ______________________ reduces the number of ______________ and ______

and allows more ______________ into a building.

(b) Each room should have a turning circle of a minimum of ____________ mm.

(c) ______________ should have a larger ____________ mm turning circle.

(d) Corridors should be as ____________ as possible with as ____________ doors as possible.

(e) ______________ on doors, wardrobes and taps should be easy to use and not require excessive strength.

(f) Avoid installing ____________ and changes in ____________ within the building.

(g) Windows should not include a ______________________ which ______________ a wheelchair user's view.

13. An ageing couple living in a two-storey house built in the 1980s want to improve the accessibility and usability of their house. One of the couple has mobility issues and has recently been confined to a wheelchair. On an initial viewing of the first-floor plan of the house, outline three changes the couple could make to improve the usability of their home. Indicate your suggestions on the plan.

____

____

____

____

____

____

____

____

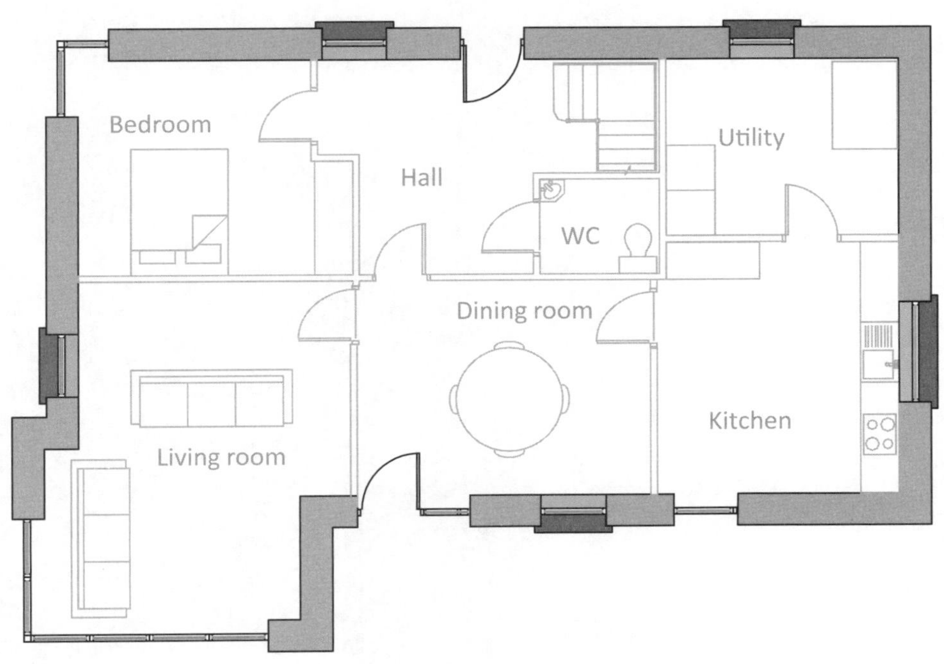

First-floor plan of house requiring accessibility and usability improvements

20

UNIVERSAL DESIGN

and freehand sketches, **two** functional requirements of a dwelling house
fer in particular to the: main entrance and internal corridor layout.

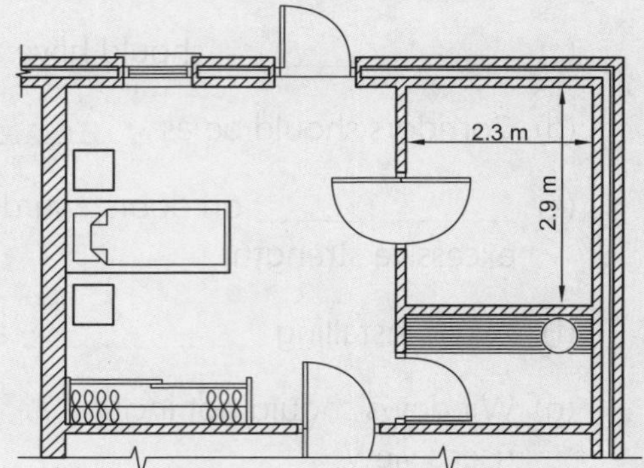

an adjoining bathroom,
wn in the accompanying
shown. Using notes and
referred layout for the
that it is suitable for a person
ndicate in your design sketches the
location of the following: window, shower area, toilet, wash hand basin and grab rails.
Include **three** typical dimensions.

(c) Discuss your preferred location for the bathroom items listed at part (b) above.

2012 Higher Level Q2

2. The accompanying diagram shows an open-plan living, dining and kitchen space suitable for a person in a wheelchair. The floor is an insulated solid concrete ground floor. From the given diagram, select any **two** areas that need specific consideration to ensure suitability for a person in a wheelchair. For each area selected, using notes and freehand sketches, show the specific design detailing that ensures ease of use for a person in a wheelchair. Indicate on your design sketches typical dimensions as appropriate.

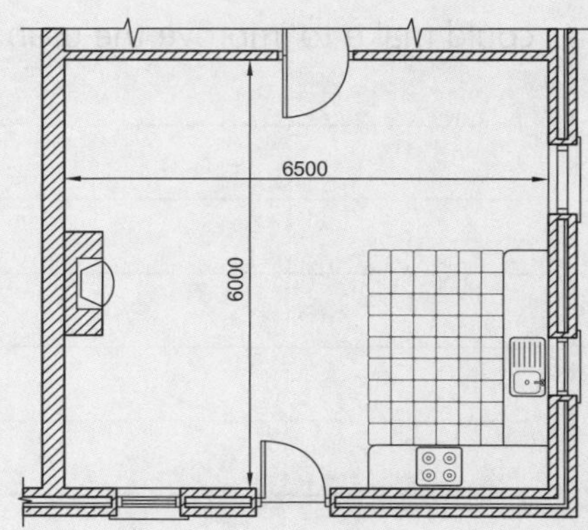

2010 Higher Level Q2 (c)

BUILDING ENERGY RATING (BER)

☐ FUNCTIONS AND FEATURES

1. What is the function of conducting a Building Energy Rating (BER) test? ______________________

____

2. What are the features of a BER test?

____

____

____

____

____

____

____

____

____

____

☐ ENERGY PERFORMANCE

3. (a) All buildings require energy to maintain a ______________________.

(b) Energy is used to ______________ and ______________ the building, and to ______________ for domestic use.

(c) Most energy is used to ______________ a building.

(d) ______________________ houses retain their heat for longer, and maximise their intake and use of ______________________, such as solar gain.

(e) Energy efficient houses are ______________________, which saves the occupants money on their ______________________ bills.

4. The diagram shows an energy inefficient house. Using arrows, indicate some typical heat loss paths, showing how much energy is generally lost through each path.

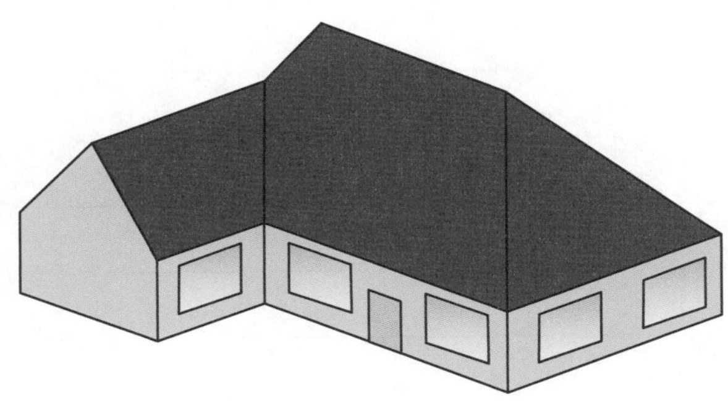

Typical heat loss paths

gs, and any building intended for

______________, must be issued with

te the building's ______________

____

______________.

Building Energy Rating (BER)

BER for the building detailed below is: C1

Name of House, Street Name One, Street Name Two, Town name One, Town Name Two, County name One, County name Two.

BER Number: XXXXXXXXXX
Date of Issue: Day Month Year
Valid Until: Day Month Year
BER Assessor No.: XXXX
Assessor Company No.: XXXX

The Building Energy Rating (BER) is an indication of the energy performance of this dwelling. It covers energy use for space heating, water heating, ventilation and lighting, calculated on the basis of standard occupancy. It is expressed as primary energy use per unit floor area per year (kWh/m²/yr).

'A' rated properties are the most energy efficient and will tend to have the lowest energy bills.

Building Energy Rating kWh/m²/yr
MOST EFFICIENT
LEAST EFFICIENT

Carbon Dioxide (CO_2) Emissions Indicator $kgCO_2/m^2/yr$

IMPORTANT: This BER is calculated on the basis of data provided to and by the BER Assessor, and using the version of the assessment software quoted above. A future BER assigned to this dwelling may be different, as a result of changes to the dwelling or to the assessment software.

Building Energy Rating certificate

6. In what units is a building's energy performance measured?

____

____

____

7. (a) All buildings built since 2011 should achieve ______________.

(b) The process of assessing a building's energy consumption is called ______________

______________. It must be carried out by a ______________.

8. Apart from the BER certificate shown in Q5, the homeowner should receive an advisory report, shown on the right. Describe what this advisory report should contain.

____

____

____

____

____

____

____

____

____

____

____

sei SUSTAINABLE ENERGY IRELAND | Energy Performance of Buildings Directive

Building Energy Rating (BER)
ADVISORY REPORT

Energy use in homes is responsible for more than a quarter of Ireland's total CO_2 emissions. Reducing energy use, especially electricity, will save you money and is good for the environment. This report provides advice on reducing energy costs and energy use in your home.

Report Date: 30/10/2007

Building Fabric - Walls, Roofs and Floors

Insulation
Proper insulation will help retain valuable heat and improve overall comfort levels. If insulation is disturbed or damaged at any time e.g. in attic space, make sure to restore or replace it.

Windows and Doors

Energy-Efficient Glazing
Energy-efficient glazing helps to retain heat within the heated rooms and improves comfort through elimination of cold window surfaces and associated downdraughts and condensation. Use of lined curtains, blinds or shutters can improve heat retention at night and further reduce downdraughts.

Ventilation

Adequate ventilation is required in all houses for the following reasons
- To provide fresh air for occupants
- To provide air for combustion appliances including open fires, fuel effect gas fires and room heaters
- To remove odours
- To remove pollutants e.g. cigarette smoke
- To remove water vapour - persistent condensation can result in mould growth and damage to furnishings and building materials

Draught Proofing
Draught Proofing reduces heat loss and improves comfort. Among actions to consider:
- Doors are a major source of draughts and should be draught proofed as a priority.
- Loft hatches, gaps around pipes, etc. should be sealed to prevent warm moist air entering the roof space, resulting in possible condensation and rot.
- Letter boxes should be fitted with a letter box cover to reduce draughts.

For health and safety reasons it is important to ensure an adequate air supply to combustion appliances e.g. gas fires.

Space Heating

Report

☐ FACTORS INVOLVED IN CALCULATING THE BER

9. The DEAP software used is an Excel spreadsheet, which takes into account all factors that affect a building's energy gains and losses. These factors include:

______________________________ ______________________________

______________________________ ______________________________

______________________________ ______________________________

______________________________ ______________________________

______________________________ ______________________________

______________________________ ______________________________

1 HOUSE DIMENSIONS

10. Why must the internal dimensions of the house be measured?

____

____

2 VENTILATION

11. (a) Vents, fans, chimneys and windows provide ______________________.

(b) Fresh air is required to prevent the build-up of ______________________ and to create a ______________ and ______________ living environment.

(c) However, newly introduced air needs to be ______________.

(d) As such ______________________ of heated air, and the uncontrolled introduction of cold fresh air is undesirable and can be very ______________________.

(e) For this reason, the ______________ and __________ of vents are measured by the DEAP software.

(f) Mechanical heat recovery systems are factored into the DEAP software, and will assist in achieving a ______________________.

3 AIR PERMEABILITY

12. Air can escape through walls, poorly sealed doors and window frames, and many other routes. Indicate on the diagram some typical air leakage routes.

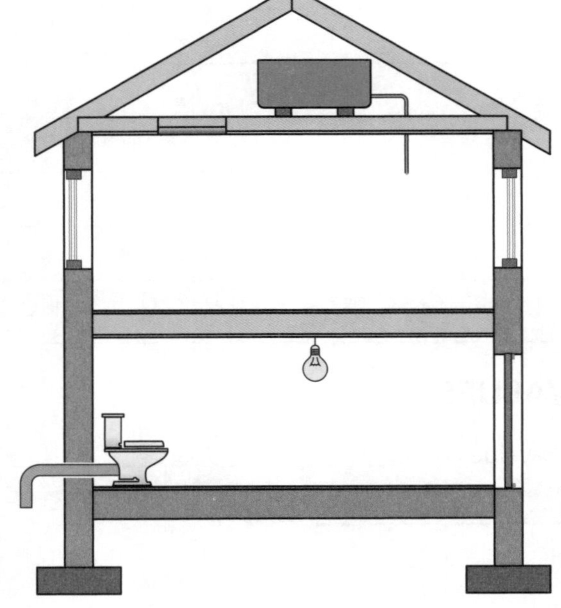

Air leakage routes

21

13. A couple have recently built a house and want to ascertain its energy rating. To assess the extent of air leakage, a 'blower door' test is undertaken. Using notes and neat freehand sketches, describe in detail the stages of conducting an air permeability (blower door) test.

14. Using notes and neat freehand sketches, explain how we can ensure a perfect seal around a door frame during an air permeability test?

4 U-VALUES

15. The U-values of a ____________________ are measured to assess how effective a building is at ____________ its heat.

5 THERMAL BRIDGING

16. (a) ______________________________ is lost through thermal bridging.

(b) Thermal bridging can even occur through ______________________________.

(c) An estimated heat loss figure is assigned to account for thermal bridging across ____________________.

(d) This figure is based on the type of ______________________________ used and the level of prevention achieved in stopping thermal bridging.

(e) An overall figure is also applied to ______________________________ of thermal bridging, for example, ________________ in the wall or ____________ between blocks.

6 GLAZED UNITS

17. Heat can be both gained and lost through a window. What factors must be taken into consideration about windows when running the DEAP software calculations?

____

____

____

____

7 WATER HEATING

18. (a) Hot water is required for many domestic activities such as ________________ and ________________.

(b) Heating water requires a vast amount of ________________.

(c) Due to this, the BER assesses the following:

- if hot water is supplied ____.
- the level of ____________________ on storage cylinders.
- the level of insulation around ______________________.
- if controls for temperature and time are installed on the ______________________________.

8 SPACE HEATING

19. The DEAP software assesses the following:

(a) the ________________________ used.

(b) the __________________________ of the boiler.

(c) whether underground heating or ________________________ are used.

(d) the level of ________________________ around pipework.

(e) whether controls for heating, temperature, time and ______________________________________ are installed on the heating system.

9 CONTRIBUTION OF RENEWABLES

20. As renewable technologies ____________________ the amount of energy required to ________________ or ____________________ a building, their energy contribution is factored in by the DEAP software.

Renewable technologies

21. List the most commonly installed renewable energy technologies in Ireland.

____

____

____

____

____

10 LIGHTING PROVISIONS

22. As artificial lighting is required in all buildings, the DEAP software factors in the ____________________ ______________ of the light fittings.

PASSIVE HOUSE CONSTRUCTION

☐ FUNCTIONS AND FEATURES

1. What is the function of a passive house?

comfortable interior enviroment without a reliance on active heating or cooling systems

2. List the design features of a passive house.

compact form | Super insulation
Solar gain | Airtightness
thermal mass | MVHR
preventing thermal bridging |

☐ PASSIVE HOUSES

3. (a) A passive house maintains year-round comfort without the use of a conventional heating system.

(b) The concept of a passive house is to minimise heat loss and maximise heat gain.

(c) The passive house concept was developed in germany by the passivhaus insitute.

(d) Passive houses are independently assessed using a specialist software package called the pasive house planning package.

(e) Passive house certification is seperate to the BER.

(f) A BER A1-rated house would not necessarily meet passive house Standerds.

4. What is an active house? Use notes and a neat freehand sketch to explain your answer.

Active houses rely on the compsumption of fossil fuels to meet the majority of its heating lighting and electricity needs

- This result in the generation of vast amounts of CO_2
- Sun provids heating for the house.

5. Using notes and neat freehand sketches, briefly describe the features/principles of a passive house.

A passive house is a house that maintains year-round comfort without othe use of a conventional heating system
- Solar gain.

6. The following is a list of criteria a house must meet to qualify as a passive house:

(a) a maximum energy demand of 15 wh/m² per year to heat the building.

(b) a total electrical consumption not exceeding 120 kwh/m² per year.

(c) when a blower door test creates a pressure difference of 50 pascals between the interior of the building and the outside, the air inside the building must not be exchanged more than 0.6 times per hour.

(d) must maintain a comfortable indoor air temperature of 20°C.

(e) the indoor air temperature should not exceed 25c for more than 10% of the hours of the year.

(f) must provide a constant supply of clean fresh air.

(g) must maximise its use of the sun's energy to provide for its heating and lighting needs.

☐ DESIGN FEATURES

1 COMPACT FORM

7. An architect's client wants to build a passive house. The architect has recommended that a passive house have a compact form. Using notes and neat freehand sketches, explain what is meant by compact form.

- A passive house should have a compact form. 0.7 or less
- A compact form is a simple house design that has a minimum of extensions of additions
- As heat is lost through external surfaces the greater the surface area of the house the greater the heat loss
- In a passive house design the goal is to achieve a compactness ratio is the relationship between the surface area of the house and its volume
- A passive house aims to have a large volume enclosed by the smallest possible area.

Continued

2 SOLAR GAIN

8. (a) Much of the heating in a passive house is gained from maximising the ______________________

from the __________.

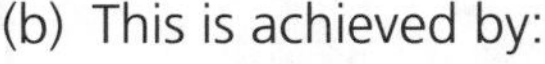

(b) This is achieved by:

- orientating the house __________ off __________.
- placing the majority of the __________ facing __________.
- ensuring high-quality __________-glazed __________ are used.
- appropriate ____________________ of the house (simple ______________ shapes work best).
- ensuring the ______________________ used rooms are __________-facing.

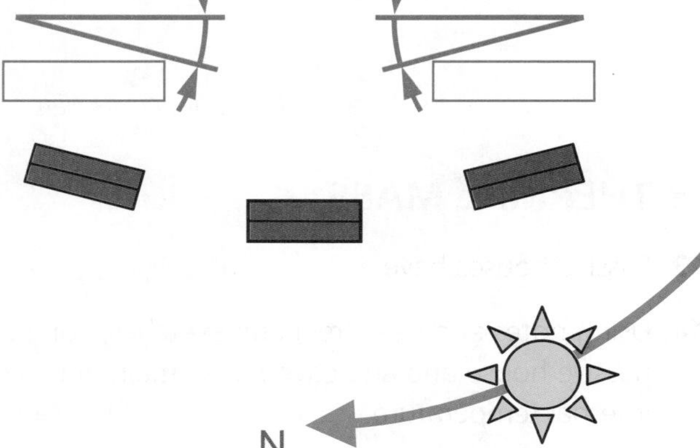

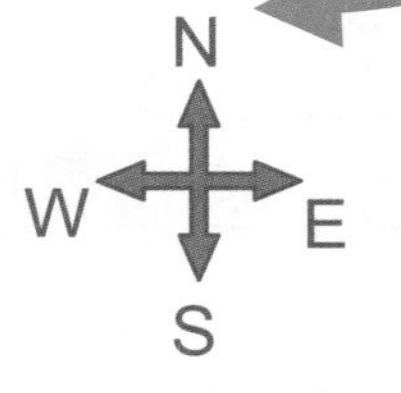

Orientation off south

(c) Add appropriate measurements to the diagram showing orientation off south.

9. The diagram shows a sun path created during the winter months. Draw the summer sun path on the diagram.

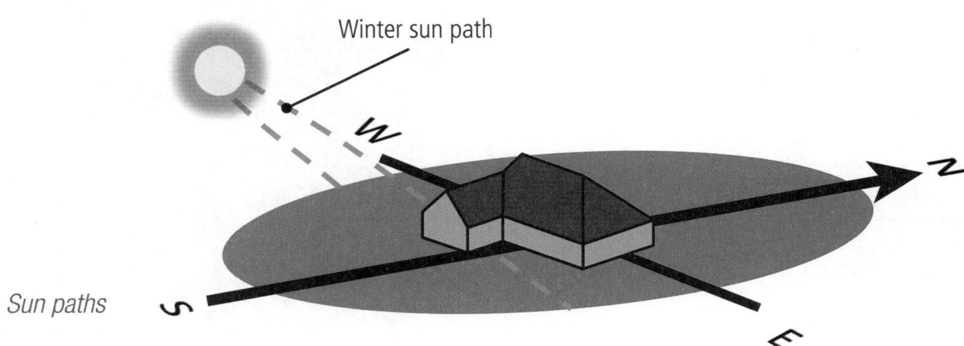

Sun paths

10. (a) During summer months, overheating can be an issue in passive houses.

(b) The overheating problem can be prevented by using sun shades in the building that block high summer sun and allow for the lower winter sun.

11. The three diagrams show a large overhanging roof, a pergola and a light shelf. Using the diagrams, demonstrate how each of these features prevents overheating in the summer.

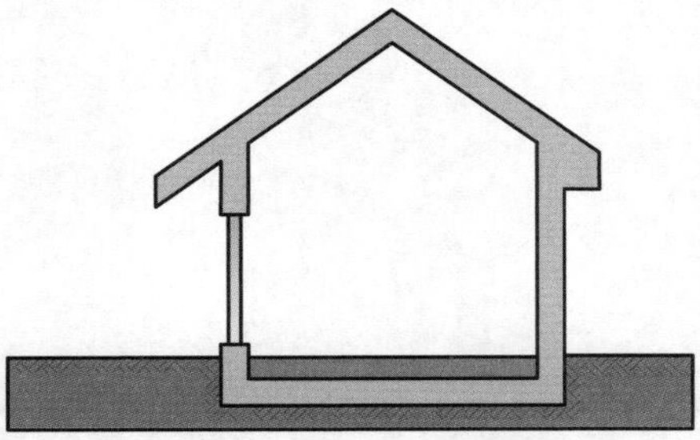

Large overhanging roof

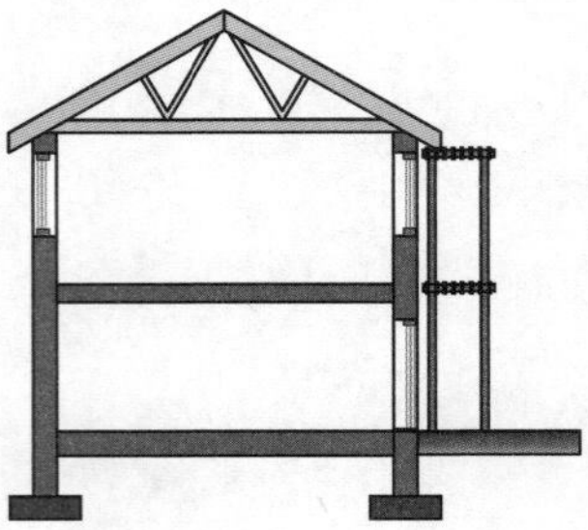

Pergola

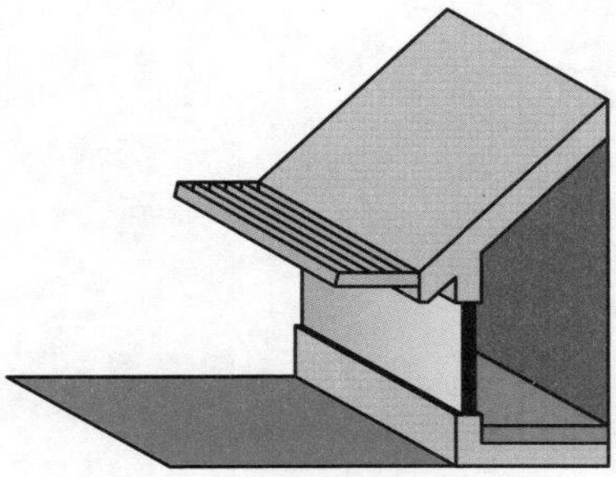

Light shelf

12. The diagram shows the ground floor plan of a passive house. Indicate on the plan the design features that this house uses to maximise solar gain.

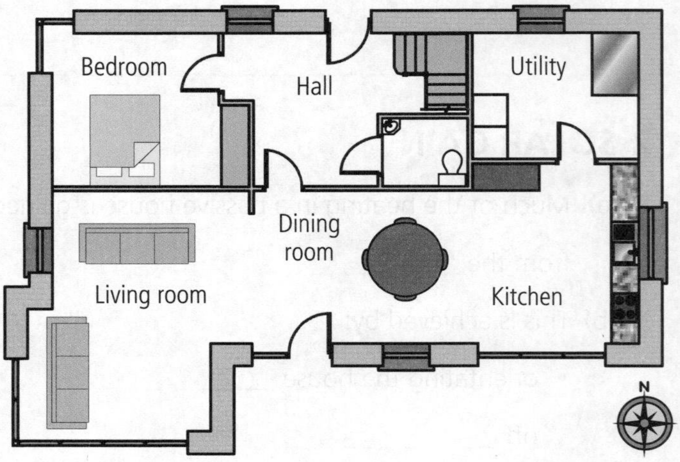

Bedroom
Hall
Utility
Dining room
Living room
Kitchen
N

Passive house plan

3 THERMAL MASS

13. Passive houses have a high thermal mass.

14. Using notes and neat freehand sketches, compare how a passive house and an active house maintain a comfortable internal temperature.

the fabric of the building quickly heats up and rapidly releases its heat.

lack of heating controls and fossil fuels results in an inconsistent temperture

4 REDUCING THERMAL BRIDGING

15. A passive house should have no thermal bridges in the construction

16. Using notes and arrows, indicate on each of the diagrams how thermal bridging was avoided in the construction of the house.

(a) Closing the cavity at the eaves

(b) Around lintel and cills

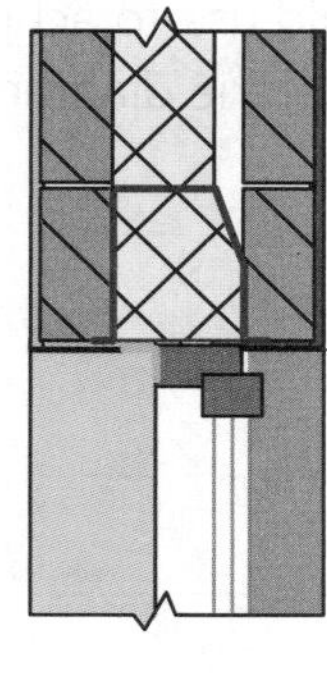

Passive eaves

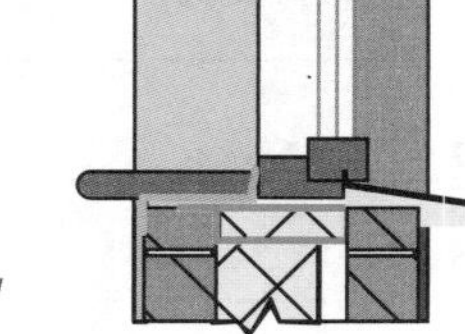

Passive lintel and cill

(c) The rising wall

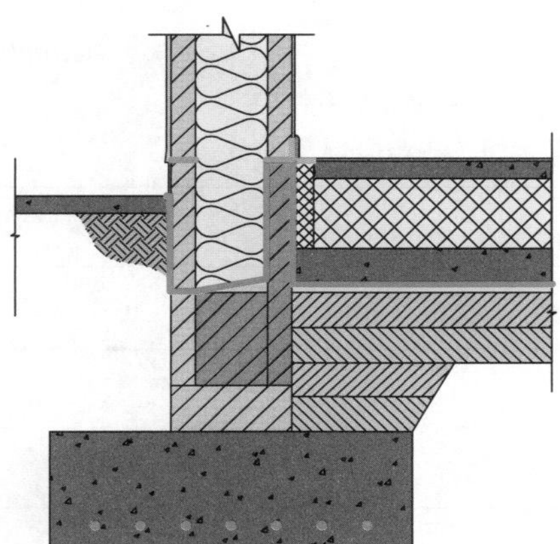

Passive rising wall

5 SUPER INSULATION

17. Passive houses must have the highest standards of insulation. Below are three possible methods. Complete the hatching for each diagram.

(a) Cavity fill

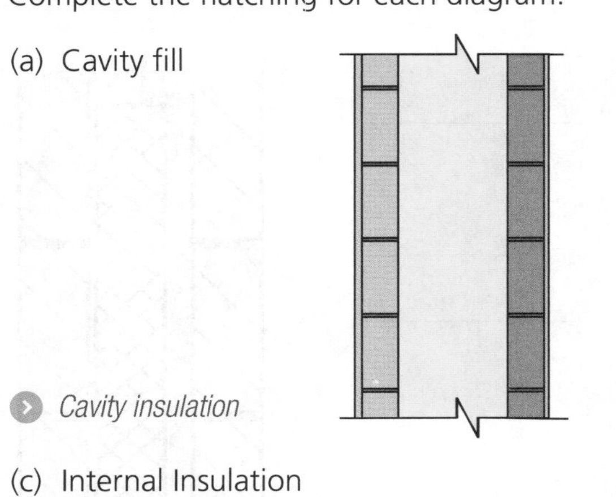

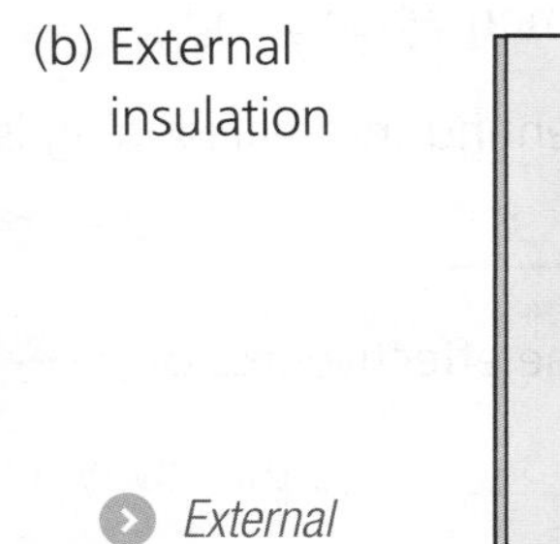

Cavity insulation

(b) External insulation

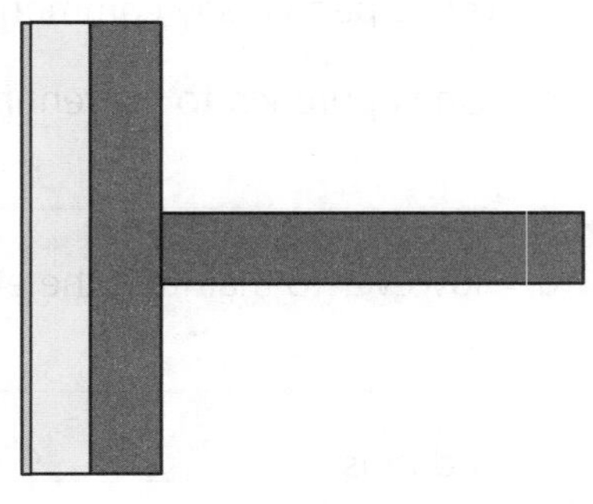

External insulation

(c) Internal Insulation

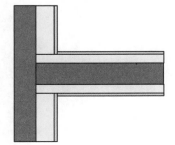

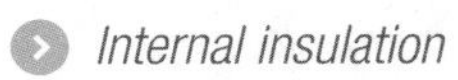

Internal insulation

18. A couple have bought a house and want to retrofit it to meet passive house standards. The diagrams show two possible approaches they could use to achieve passive house standards. Label the diagrams.

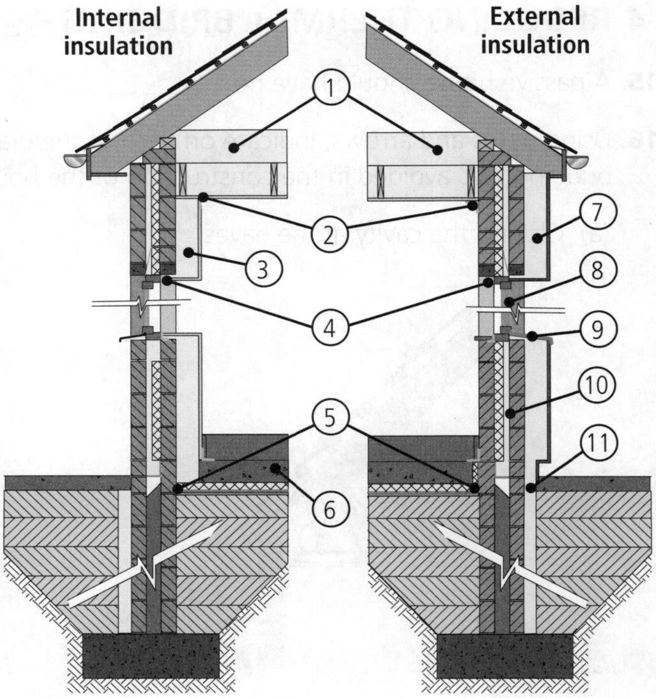

Internal insulation

External insulation

Retrofitting to passive house standards

1. Additional insulation in the attic
2. Airtight tape sealed to the wall
3. Additional internal insulation
4. Airtight tape sealing window
5. Airtight tape sealing floor
6. ________
7. ________
8. ________
9. ________
10. ________
11. ________

19. (a) If a slight gap exists, a convection current called thermal looping will occur.

(b) This is particularly common when using rigid insulation.

(c) One approach to preventing thermal looping is to use quilted insulation.

(d) However to maintain the effectiveness of ~~quilted~~ quilted insulation, the cavity must be airtight, and must be moisture-free.

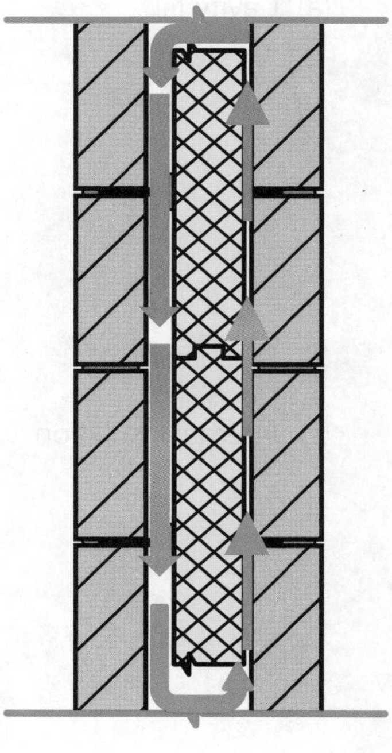

Thermal looping

20. Using notes and neat freehand sketches, demonstrate two approaches for achieving an airtight and moisture-free cavity.

parging, airtightness membranes, service cavities, acrylic renders and high quality workmanship will achieve this

Approach 1

Approach 2

6 AIRTIGHTNESS

21. When a blower door test creates a pressure difference of 50 pascals between the interior and the outside of the building, the air inside the building must not be exchanged more than 0.6 times per hour to be considered airtight.

22. Passive houses must have the highest standards when sealing against unwanted air leakage. To achieve this, a continuous airtight barrier must be created inside the dwelling. Using a neat freehand sketch, illustrate this concept.

roof
window
door

23. List some common areas that should be sealed to ensure airtightness.

floors
ceilings
windows
around electrical and plumbing ~~fixture~~ fixings.
around floor ~~joists~~ joints

7 MECHANICAL HEAT RECOVERY VENTILATION (MHRV)

24. As a passive house is airtight and Super insulated, fresh air needs to be introduced to the building without compromising the building's thermal peformaces. This is achieved by using a heat recovery & ventilation.

25. Heat recovery ventilation (HRV) is a system in which the heat is transferred from stale air exiting a building, over to fresh incoming air, within the mechanical ventilation system. Label the diagram of a mechanical heat recovery system.

1. __________
2. __________
3. __________
4. __________
5. __________
6. __________
7. __________

3 2 1 7 4 5 6

Heat recovery ventilation system

26. Up to 90%. of heat generated can be reused heating the incoming air.

27. (a) HRV consists of a heat transfer unit (usually positioned in the attic space).

(b) fresh cool air enters through a fresh air inlet.

(c) warm stale air enters through a stale air inlet.

(d) The heat is transferred from the ________ to the ________ air in a heat exchange core.

(e) The now ________ air is pumped outside through an exhaust.

(f) The now ________ is circulated around the house through a network of pipes.

28. The diagram shows a sectional view of a recently built house. The owners want to install a mechanical heat recovery system. Using the diagram, describe how a mechanical heat recovery system provides warm fresh air to the entire house and removes stale air.

one fan extrads Stale warm air from wet rooms and it takes it to be ventiliation applience to be exhausted outsite
menwhile another fan draws fresh filtered air from outside and ~~takes it to the~~ ~~ten~~ Supplies it through ceiling terminals in the habitable rooms of a home

MHRV

29. The diagram shows a heat exchanger located within a MHRV system. Complete the diagram of a heat exchanger and describe how it operates.

A heat exchanger consists of several corrigated metal/paper plates both airflows pass through these plates, but on different sides As the airflows are separated. the air to the cool fresh air

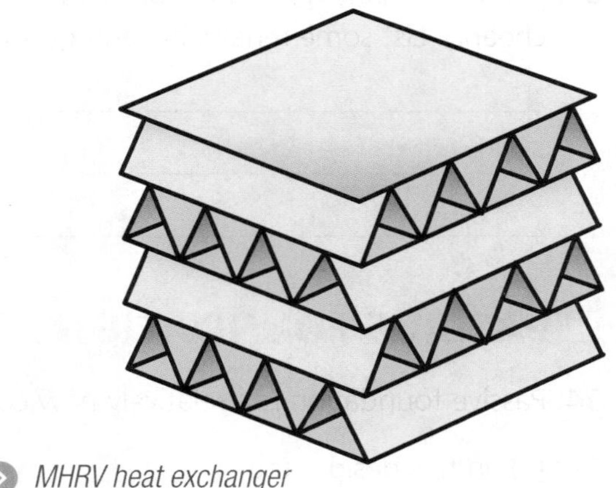

MHRV heat exchanger

30. (a) A heat exchanger consists of several ________ plates.

(b) Both airflows (________ and ________) pass through these plates, but on ________ sides.

(c) As the airflows are ________, the air cannot ________.

(d) The heat is ________ through the plates from the ________ warm air, to the cool ________ air.

31. The advantages of a MHRV system include:

(a) moisture reduction from kitchens, showers, etc.

(b) the removal of pollen.

(c) the removal of unpleasant odors.

(d) a reduction in energy requirements.

(e) a minimum of heatloss during the process.

32. List the advantages and disadvantages of a passive house.

Advantages	Disadvantages
it has low energy consumption it is economical to run provides constant comfort	·high lvl of workman ships ·Spectily training of worker ·high level detailing longer time to finish , mhrv require regular changing

☐ RENEWABLES

33. There are many different sources of renewable energy that can help to heat a passive house cleanly and cheaply. List some renewable energy sources commonly used in Ireland.

_______________ _______________

_______________ _______________

____

☐ PASSIVE FOUNDATION

34. Passive foundation is a relatively new concept in passive house design.

(a) In this design, the _______________ and _______________ leaf are totally _______________ so as to eliminate _______________.

(b) The internal leaf is supported on a _______________ foundation.

(c) The external leaf is supported on a _______________ foundation, which is formed using a mould made out of _______________.

(d) The entire floor is lined with layers of 100 mm thick insulation to _______________ the house.

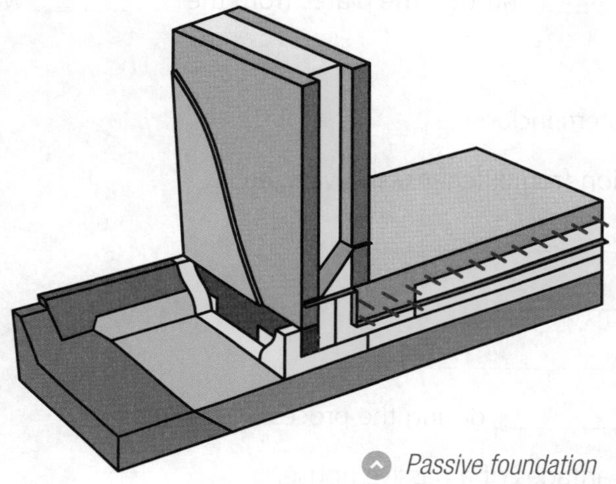

Passive foundation

35. Label the sectional view of a passive foundation. Include typical measurements where appropriate.

1. _______________
2. _______________
3. _______________
4. _______________
5. _______________
6. _______________
7. _______________

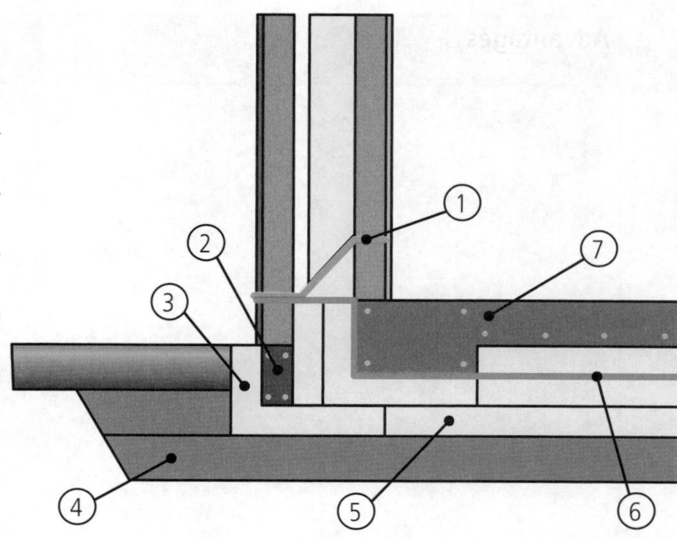

Sectional view of passive foundation

☐ PASSIVE HOUSE SECTIONAL DETAILS

36. The diagram shows a sectional view of a passive foundation and ground floor. Label the sectional view. Include appropriate measurements.

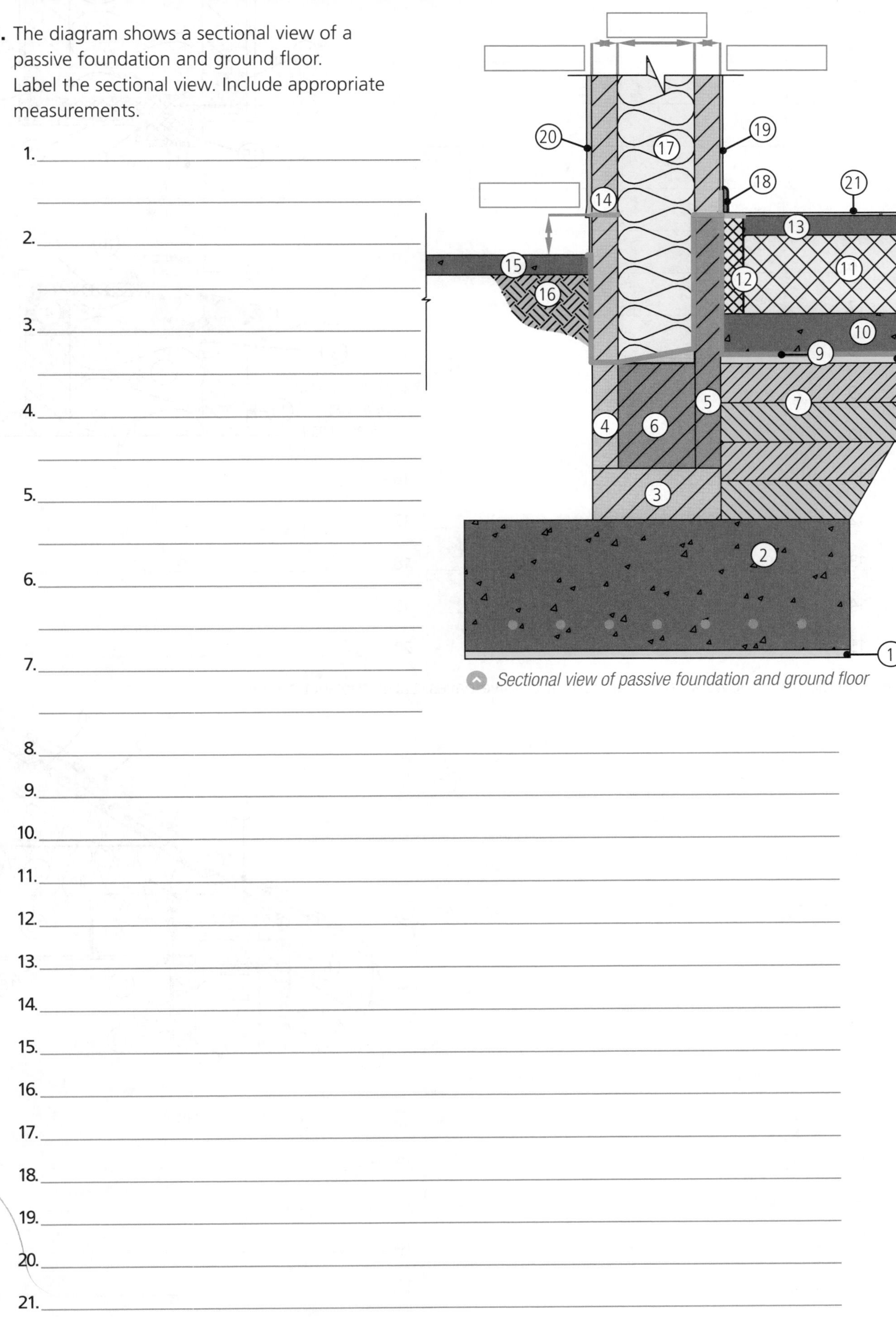

Sectional view of passive foundation and ground floor

1. ______________________________

2. ______________________________

3. ______________________________

4. ______________________________

5. ______________________________

6. ______________________________

7. ______________________________

8. ______________________________

9. ______________________________

10. ______________________________

11. ______________________________

12. ______________________________

13. ______________________________

14. ______________________________

15. ______________________________

16. ______________________________

17. ______________________________

18. ______________________________

19. ______________________________

20. ______________________________

21. ______________________________

37. The diagram shows a sectional view of a passive cill and lintel. Label the sectional view.

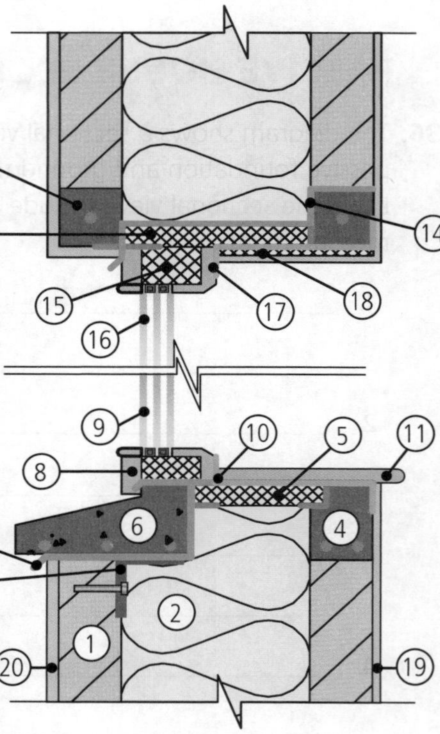

Sectional view of a passive cill and lintel

1. ______
2. ______
3. ______
4. ______
5. ______
6. ______
7. ______
8. ______
9. ______
10. ______
11. ______
12. ______
13. ______
14. ______
15. ______
16. ______
17. ______
18. ______
19. ______
20. ______

38. The diagram shows a sectional view of passive eaves. Label the sectional view.

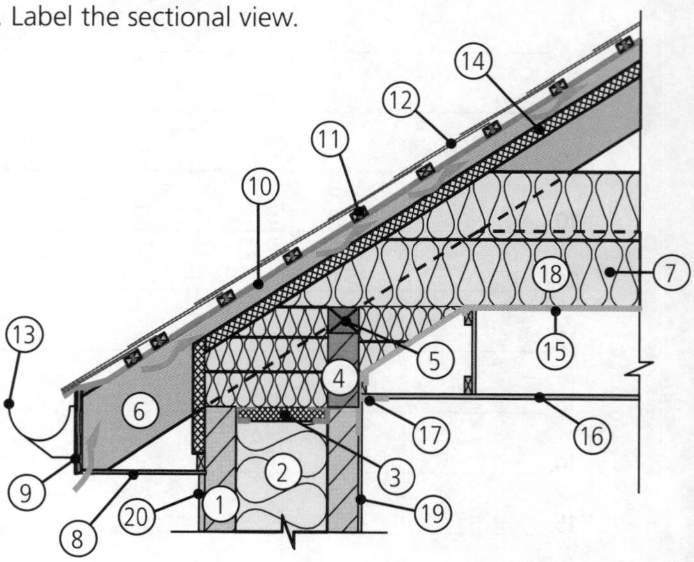

Sectional view of passive eaves

1. ______
2. ______
3. ______
4. ______
5. ______
6. ______
7. ______
8. ______
9. ______
10. ______
11. ______
12. ______
13. ______
14. ______
15. ______
16. ______
17. ______
18. ______
19. ______
20. ______

THEORY QUESTIONS

HIGHER LEVEL

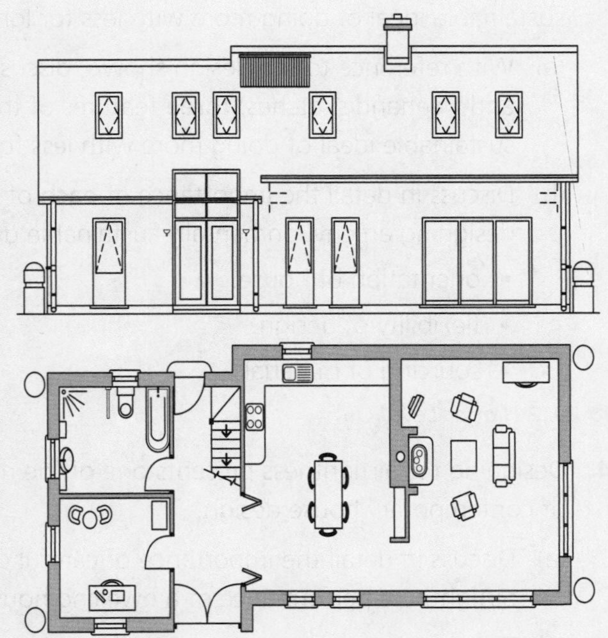

1. The elevation and ground floor plan of a house are shown. The house has three bedrooms and a bathroom in the attic space. The external wall is of timber frame construction with a rendered concrete block outer leaf. The house is designed to have low environmental impact and be suitable for first-time buyers.

(a) With reference to the design shown, discuss in detail, using notes and freehand sketches, **three** features of the design that contribute to the house having a low environmental impact.

(b) Discuss in detail the importance of each of the following when designing a house suitable for first-time buyers:

- modest in scale.
- easy to modify.
- proximity to services.

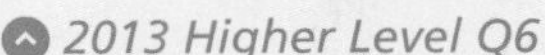
2013 Higher Level Q6

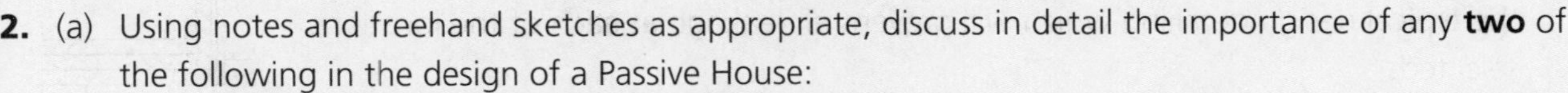

2. (a) Using notes and freehand sketches as appropriate, discuss in detail the importance of any **two** of the following in the design of a Passive House:

- building orientation.
- thermal mass.
- primary energy demand.

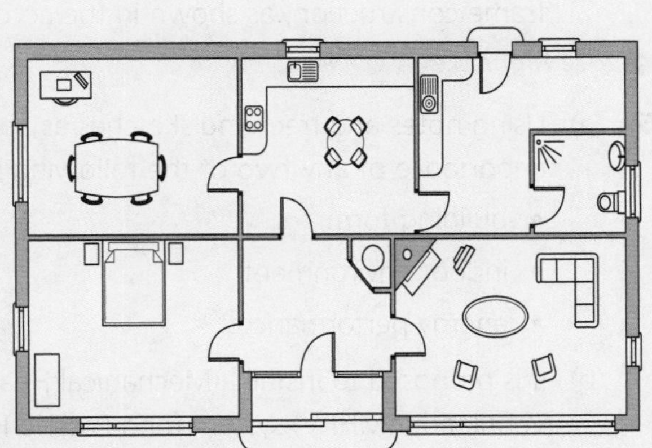

(b) It is proposed to install a Mechanical Heat Recovery with Ventilation (MHRV) system in a Passive House, as shown in the drawing.

Draw a single-line diagram of the given room layout and indicate a preferred location for the MHRV unit. Show a typical design layout for the ducting to the MHRV unit and indicate clearly the direction of airflow in all the ducts.

Describe how a Mechanical Heat Recovery with Ventilation (MHRV) system works.

Note: Show a plan of the room layout only, it is not necessary to show the furniture.

(c) Discuss in detail **two** design considerations that should be taken into account when deciding a preferred location for the MHRV unit in a Passive House.

2013 Higher Level Q10

22

3. The elevation and ground floor plan of a house are shown. The house has a study / office as shown and also has three bedrooms and a bathroom upstairs. The external wall is of timber frame construction with a concrete block outer leaf. The house is designed to have low environmental impact, reflecting the sustainable ideal of doing more with less for longer.

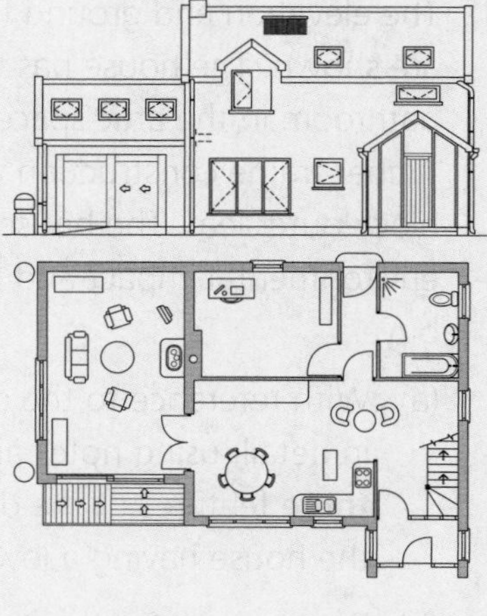

(a) With reference to the design shown, discuss in detail, using notes and freehand sketches, **three** features of the design that reflect the sustainable ideal of doing more with less for longer.

(b) Discuss in detail the importance of **each** of the following when designing an environmentally sustainable dwelling house:

- orientation of house.
- flexibility of design.
- sourcing of materials.

2012 Higher Level Q6

4. Designing for airtightness presents one of the most challenging aspects of contemporary house design.

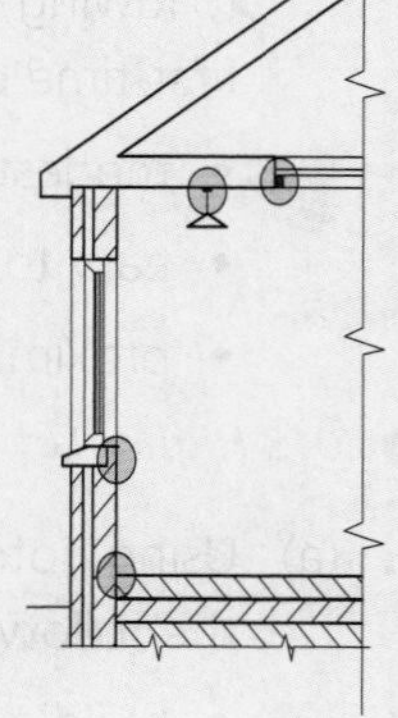

(a) Discuss in detail the importance of careful design detailing in improving the airtightness performance of a dwelling house.

(b) The drawing shows an outline section through a portion of a single-storey house of timber frame construction. The outer leaf is of rendered concrete block and the ground floor is an insulated solid concrete floor. Select any **three** locations from those circled on the sketch and show, using notes and freehand sketches, the typical design detailing which will prevent air leakage at each of the locations selected.

(c) Discuss the advantages of including a service cavity in an external wall of timber frame construction, as shown in the accompanying sketch.

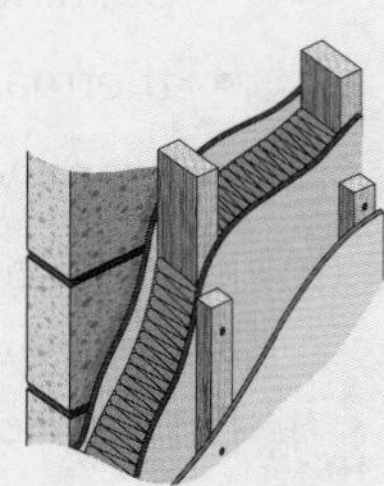

2012 Higher Level Q9

5. (a) Using notes and freehand sketches as appropriate, discuss in detail the importance of any **two** of the following in the design of a Passive House:

- building form.
- indoor environment.
- energy performance.

(b) It is proposed to install a Mechanical Heat Recovery with Ventilation (MHRV) system for a Passive House, as shown in the drawing. The location of the MHRV unit – M – in the utility room is shown. Draw a single-line diagram of the given plan and show a typical design layout for the ducting to such a unit. Indicate clearly the direction of airflow in all the ducts and describe how a Mechanical Heat Recovery with Ventilation (MHRV) system works.

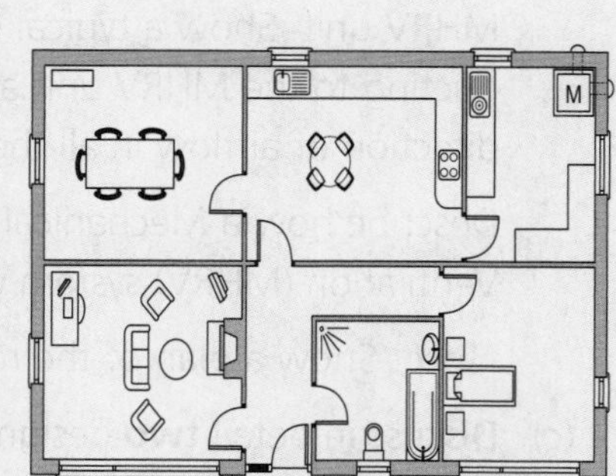

Note: While a plan of the room layout is required, it is not necessary to show the furniture.

2012 Higher Level Q10 (a) and (b)

NOTES

NOTES

NOTES

NOTES

NOTES

NOTES